D1759896

THE LIBRARY

UNIVERSITY OF
WINCHESTER

KA 0286532 7

Also by Len Platt

JOYCE AND THE ANGLO-IRISH (1998)

ARISTOCRACIES OF FICTION: The Idea of Aristocracy in Late Nineteenth- and Early Twentieth-Century Literature (2001)

MUSICAL THEATRE AND AMERICAN CULTURE (with Dave Walsh, 2003)

Musical Comedy on the West End Stage, 1890–1939

Len Platt

palgrave
macmillan

© Len Platt 2004

All rights reserved. No reproduction, copy or transmission of this publication may be made without written permission.

No paragraph of this publication may be reproduced, copied or transmitted save with written permission or in accordance with the provisions of the Copyright, Designs and Patents Act 1988, or under the terms of any licence permitting limited copying issued by the Copyright Licensing Agency, 90 Tottenham Court Road, London W1T 4LP.

Any person who does any unauthorized act in relation to this publication may be liable to criminal prosecution and civil claims for damages.

The author has asserted his right to be identified as the author of this work in accordance with the Copyright, Designs and Patents Act 1988.

First published 2004 by
PALGRAVE MACMILLAN
Houndmills, Basingstoke, Hampshire RG21 6XS and
175 Fifth Avenue, New York, N.Y. 10010
Companies and representatives throughout the world

PALGRAVE MACMILLAN is the global academic imprint of the Palgrave Macmillan division of St. Martin's Press, LLC and of Palgrave Macmillan Ltd. Macmillan® is a registered trademark in the United States, United Kingdom and other countries. Palgrave is a registered trademark in the European Union and other countries.

ISBN 1–4039–3225–5 hardback

This book is printed on paper suitable for recycling and made from fully managed and sustained forest sources.

A catalogue record for this book is available from the British Library.

Library of Congress Cataloging-in-Publication Data
Platt, Len.
      Musical comedy on the West End stage, 1890–1939 / Len Platt.
         p. cm.
      Includes bibliographical references (p.) and index.
      ISBN 1–4039–3225–5 (hardback)
         1. Musicals—Social aspects—England—London. 2. West End (London, England) I. Title.

ML3918.M87P55 2004
782.1'4'09421—dc22   2003066379

10 9 8 7 6 5 4 3 2 1
13 12 11 10 09 08 07 06 05 04

Printed and bound in Great Britain by
Antony Rowe Ltd, Chippenham and Eastbourne

KING ALFRED'S COLLEGE
WINCHESTER

02865327   782.81
           PLA

This book is dedicated to Nell Platt and Lizzie Rebbeck

Contents

List of Illustrations

The publishers and author wish to state that they have made every effort to contact the copyright holders of material reproduced in this text. If, however, any have been overlooked, the publishers will be pleased to make the necessary arrangements at the first opportunity.

Preface

The origins of this book can be traced very precisely to my cousin, Alan Rebbeck. That so much of this preface should be given over to an explanation of his part in things is an indication of his importance in this respect. Now in his mid-sixties, Alan has worked in the theatre all his life, in both America (he lived in New York for many years) and England where, in the 1960s, a highlight of his career was playing alongside John Mills in a very successful West End adaptation of J. B. Priestley's *The Good Companions*. This show marked the apex of a relatively brief but exciting trajectory. Thereafter, Alan worked a great deal in theatre, film and television, but the early promise of fame and fortune was never entirely fulfilled.

Alan has a particular fascination with early West End musical comedy, which goes back to his childhood. One of the first pieces of music he recalls noticing seriously was an old recording of the Edwardian musical comedy *The Arcadians*; he would have been about ten years old when he first heard it. This started a long relationship with a culture that in the 1950s was already well beyond the out-of-date. Under the pervasive influence of American styling and energy, West End musical comedy was virtually dead before my cousin was born. The only place where it continued to enjoy any kind of presence was in the world of suburban amateur, or 'pro-am', dramatics. Here a few of the old shows remained on the repertoires. Indeed, as a young aspiring actor, Alan had played in such productions at the Royal Artillery Theatre, Woolwich. He once appeared in *A Country Girl*, for instance, originally a vehicle for one of musical comedy's big stars, Evie Greene, and, in a production a few years later, for an even bigger star – Gertie Millar. He also appeared in *The Arcadians* and several productions of the First World War hit, *Chu Chin Chow*. This, then, was an intimate relationship, but with a culture that was, by my cousin's account, sadly neglected and well on the way to becoming forgotten outside a small circle of enthusiasts.

My introduction to musical comedy, just a few years ago, was by way of Alan's admiration for this material, significantly enabled by his large collection of theatre literature and memorabilia. Of particular interest here were the old Victorian and Edwardian playgoers' magazines, especially *The Play Pictorial*. Each edition of this gem, which continued to be published through the 1920s and 1930s, begins with perhaps ten pages of advertisements mostly aimed at women, confirming an essential musical comedy constituency that is often neglected. Commentators inside and out of music theatre history invariably situate musical comedy of this early period as a male culture, especially in its consumption, which is often understood in terms of the voyeuristic gaze. *The Play Pictorial* suggests otherwise. There *is* the occasional boy-racer advert for such commodities as a Peugeot car on sale new for £100 or Pirelli's tyres 'first in every race', but for the most part the implied subject of these magazines is female, indicating the very emphatic importance of women to the musical comedy fan base. Hence the many appeals to women's clothes fashion. *The Pictorial* promotes dresses, hairpieces, jewellery, shoes – everything imaginable connected with theatre-going style – and advises on the up-and-coming. An editorial begins by identifying 'the chief features of the autumn modes', which 'may be briefly described as everything that is inclined to give a graceful "line" to the figure'. Women's health and 'personal hygiene' are regularly targeted, as in an advertisement featuring a drawing of a young woman discreetly placing in the post box her order for 'Southalls' Towels...a boon to womankind'. Ladies' underwear is promoted with much less circumspection and produces some of the loudest copy, as in 'Sphere Suspender! The Suspender most loved of all ladies of all nations!' or 'Junoform! The Elastic Bust Reducer! Makes you measure two to four inches LESS the minute you put it on!'[1] Women were central on the stage of musical comedy, but they also clearly figured in the auditorium where they and their male partners both identified with this culture and apparently ogled it, although perhaps for different reasons.

The main section of the *Pictorial*, however, the real core of the magazine, is a plot summary of the featured musical comedy show, each edition being given over to a new West End hit, accompanied by photographic images. These give some sense of what the shows must have been like. They portray the actors and actresses posed at key narrative moments – dramatic, comic, romantic – and, most importantly, they capture this theatre's investment in the most up-to-date stage technology. Some of the lavish sets involved spectacular and technically demanding effects representing earthquakes, horserace meetings, department stores and the exoticized otherness of 'Japan' or 'India'. These images, and sounds – the thin, warbling voices and romantic melodies that are among the earliest phonographic reproductions of any kind of music – are the remnants of musical comedy most easily accessible now, although even these are proving harder to come by and more expensive as collectors create a market for such commodities. It needs to be stressed that for all its quaint strangeness, and it does seem very much of another age, this was a culture that was once hugely popular and thoroughly of the moment.

Despite my sense that here was something interesting and potentially significant, at the start of this project I must confess to having had no real feeling for musicals as musicals. Although my understanding of their significance has changed greatly during the course of working on this book, that first prejudice has not shifted substantially at all. Coming from the sixties generation which saw musicals as being utterly beyond the pale, there was a time when I could quite easily have dismissed the whole of music theatre as a puerile anti-culture. I would no longer admit to such extremes, of course; nevertheless, I have approached musical comedy as an academic and not as a music theatre enthusiast. My more usual territory is literature, particularly in its 'modern' and 'modernist' formations, and my critical position has been most shaped by cultural studies and cultural materialism. The latter is 'a theory of the specificities of material and literary production within historical materialism', which tries to demystify the hugely prestigious and romanticized category that has been 'literature' and to link its production to precise historical conditions. Essential here is the understanding that literary theory cannot be separated from cultural theory, even if it can, as Raymond Williams maintained, be distinguished within cultural theory;[2] the broad point being that from such critical perspectives the writing and reading of literature is always sociological, political and historical, as well as aesthetic and formalist.

I do feel obliged to emphasize quite strongly, if only by way of apology to my cousin, that all this puts the current study at some distance from the enthusiasts' version of musical comedy. Although Alan Rebbeck is certainly responsible for starting this book, and it benefited hugely from his extensive knowledge, this is not the book that he would have written or necessarily have wanted. In some ways I wish I could have written an account more sympathetic to his feeling for musical comedy and musical theatre generally, but that was never likely. I am only grateful that he has not expressed any dissatisfaction with the treatment meted out. On the contrary, he has, as usual, been generous and open-minded.

Apart from the interest stimulated by *The Play Pictorial* and early recordings, there was a further incentive for starting work on this subject – the discovery that although the play texts or 'books' for musical comedy in this period have never been published (this is true even of blockbusters like *The Arcadians* and *Floradora*), they do exist. They were required to be deposited for licensing purposes with the Lord Chamberlain's Office and are now kept in the manuscript room of the British Library. The prospect of working on such a large collection of unpublished and largely unknown materials proved attractive enough. The realization that these texts could be read as literature in the wider sense became decisive in making this possible and went very much against expectation. From the limited accounts in musical theatre history, most of it American, it seemed that the play texts of West End musical comedy of this period were not much more than a series of fragmented sketches and jokes cobbled together around some tuneful melodies and sedate dance routines. The clear suggestion was that these texts, like the whole shows in most accounts, were worthless ephemera. It was quite surprising then to discover in a show like *Floradora*, for instance, a fully developed play with a narrative completely bound up with contemporary society and culture. This text is, in fact, a complex formulation, highly suggestive of *fin de siècle* concerns, interests, prejudices and fantasies. Far from being simply escapist – although it is that – *Floradora* engages with fundamental issues about modernity. It is an Empire show, in its themes and in the important material sense that it once travelled the Empire over a number of years. It deals with the impact of Western power and commerce on what is tellingly constructed as more 'innocent' culture. Also, at the heart of this apparent trivia there is a treatment of the crucial issue of the nature of responsible power in modern 'mass' society and its relationship with the outgoing traditional authority of the landlord. At the same time, the show involves a fascinating response to the status of modern 'science' as phrenology. In this way it displays, at the end of the nineteenth century and in a popular tradition, a healthy questioning of the success of 'the Enlightenment project', while maintaining the essentially upbeat optimism that is characteristic of this culture. As might be expected of a modern commercial entertainment, this show also makes a substantial investment in glamour and spectacle, but it is important to stress that the interest of *Floradora* is not just visual. It works in more cerebral ways, containing an underlying critique of eugenics, for example, which helps to place the show politically, again in relation to contemporary science culture, and, more importantly, to confirm important distinctions in the English middle class. If the intelligentsia signed up to eugenics in significant force, it appears that a broader-based, more commercial middle class was perhaps more sceptical about the prospects of establishing social hygiene and 'national efficiency' through programmes of social engineering based on statistical analysis.

Floradora is no narratological exception. It is not a particularly 'good' or 'bad' script, nor is it among the musical comedies especially engaged with its time. It is, in fact, typical of a culture that was narrative by nature, and the stories it told, though romantic and escapist, were almost without exception self-consciously modern and thus had status as 'signs of the times'. Neither just reflective of society nor simply mediating, musical comedy was, as is all culture, constitutive. Part of the social fabric, it shows how, in a particular historical period and among the 'public' of that period, social life was materially conceived, understood and celebrated. The primary aim of this book is to recover that construction or, at least, to establish a partial recovery shaped and determined, no doubt, by a current sense of the important social and cultural terrain. Although this study does make some investment in outlining the development and fall of musical comedy in theatre history terms, it is not, then, a theatre history. First and foremost, it is a cultural studies approach to what is represented here as the text of late nineteenth- and early twentieth-century West End musical comedy.

* * *

Apart from my thanks to Alan Rebbeck, who was so important to the research, unstinting of his time and support and a real initiator, I would also want to thank the librarians and other workers in the manuscript room of the British Library and of the London Theatre Museum and Library. These were always helpful, knowledgeable and patient. Peter Bayliss, a former head of department at Goldsmiths College gave considerable support in his newer role as voluntary coordinator of a large University of the Third Age branch. Encouraging us to bring out our work in progress for public consumption, Peter and his team organized a number of lectures and study days where Alan, a pianist and singer, Mike Peake, and I talked and played our way through various versions of musical comedy. The engaged responses from this student body, some of whom had personal reminiscences of the culture, helped to formulate our ideas in quite important ways and contributed significantly to our appreciation of musical comedy and of its more intimate impact on individual lives.

There are many colleagues at Goldsmiths College who helped with this book. Nigel Fuller helped with the illustrations. James Souter read and commented on chapter 5. Helen Murphy, Linda France, Paru Raman and Martin Williams – none of whom is a particular fan of the musical – listened politely and contributed where possible, as did our undergraduate students on the BA in Social, Cultural and Creative

Processes. Special and particular thanks are due to another colleague, Dave Walsh. Dave is an expert on the whole range of musical theatre and an eminent sociologist. He read early versions of this study and made invaluable suggestions. He also generously made his, at that time unpublished, work on musical theatre available and allowed free use of it, especially that on the 'megamusical'. This reappears, in modified form, in chapter 6. All these friends and helpers suffered from the usual indiscretions and sheer selfishness of those who get caught up in ideas and writing about them, but none more so than my immediate family, especially Sally, who gets unreserved thanks.

1
Themes and Approaches

Musical comedy and the musical

Musical comedy is often understood as a phase in the development of musical theatre. It takes position after ballad opera, burlesque, vaudeville, the minstrel show and, in some accounts, operetta and revue as a stage in what many see as the 'maturation' of musical theatre. In this teleology the musical is formed by an aesthetic process that reaches a climax, if not an 'end', with the great 'book' musicals, or musical plays, in the tradition of *Porgy and Bess* (1935), *Oklahoma* (1942), *South Pacific* (1949) and *West Side Story* (1957). These are the shows characterized by their 'unprecedented integration of song and story' and also by their capacity to extend well beyond the signifying range of 'light' and comic musical theatre.[1] Very different from the hotchpotch assemblage of song, dance and sketches that typified the early musical stage, they are the master texts of musical theatre often recognized as the grand accomplishment of what the form had been promising since the earlier Golden Age of Gilbert and Sullivan and the Viennese operettas of Johann Strauss. Indeed, they have been seen as nothing less than confirmation of modernity's capacity to produce a genuinely 'serious' popular art form. Whatever doubts might be expressed about the versions of musical theatre that followed – the 'concept', 'rock' and 'mega' musicals sometimes presented as postmodern pastiches or hybrid versions of the 'real' thing – these great book musicals, although originally very much part of the culture industry and without exception huge commercial successes, are now rescued from the ephemeral and securely positioned as part of the canon. Often revived by national theatres and supported by subsidy, this one-time 'popular' culture is now routinely considered 'highbrow'. In some accounts it possesses a status to rival that

1

of opera and indeed is sometimes understood, quite misleadingly, as a species of opera.[2]

If musical comedy was a stage on the road to the fully-fledged musical, however, it was one that lasted for a very long time and included a large number of texts that many would identify as being key to musical theatre. In fact, for many years musical comedy was *the* predominant musical theatre, outpacing operetta for most of its history despite some retro moments, in the 1920s, for instance, when Romberg's *The Student Prince* (1924) and *The Desert Song* (1926) returned to the more prestigious and aristocratic of the styles. From the turn of the century onwards, musical comedy was established as a mature and hugely popular cultural form in Britain, Europe and America. Following a brief period of displacement by revue, it reached prominence in the 1920s as a defining culture of the 'jazz age'. The shows written by Jerome Kern, Guy Bolton and P. G. Wodehouse for the Princess Theatre – including *Very Good Eddie* (1915), *Oh Boy* (1917), *Leave it to Jane* (1917) and *Oh, Lady! Lady!* (1918) – were among the American forerunners of an extraordinarily productive decade for musical comedy, dominated by the work of Kern, the Gershwins, Rodgers and Hart, and Cole Porter. *Lady, Be Good!* (1924), *No, No Nanette* (1925), *A Connecticut Yankee* (1927), *Funny Face* (1927), *Paris* (1928), *Fifty Million Frenchmen* (1929) and *The New Yorkers* (1930) were just some of the big hits of the decade. Popular musical comedies of the 1930s included *Girl Crazy* (1931) and *Anything Goes* (1934). By this time often constructed as a variety of book musical, musical comedy resurfaced in even more complex forms with *Pal Joey* in 1940, followed by *On the Town* (1944), *Annie get Your Gun* (1946), *Finian's Rainbow* (1947) and *Kiss me Kate* (1948). The 1950s saw *The Music Man* (1957), *Gypsy* (1959) and *Guys and Dolls* (1950) – the last, with its high levels of music, dance and play text integration, exemplifying just how complex and sophisticated musical comedies had become. Behind the light and frothy surface of things a show like *Guys and Dolls* had aesthetic design and execution and became the subject of serious critical analysis. More than just 'fun' or 'entertainment', *Guys and Dolls* could be formulated as a complex art object. In this guise it achieved 'power and unity', derived in part 'from the rhythms associated with specific characters. The "guys" and "dolls", even when singing their so-called "fugues", display a conspicuous amount of syncopation and the half-note and quarter-note triplet rhythms work against the metrical grain.'[3] From this high point, musical comedy, for a variety of reasons, began to diminish significantly, although the 1950s did not see the end of the form. Even the 1960s, a decade which was iconoclastic in terms of popular culture, saw a continuation of the tradition with such highly successful musical comedies as *A Funny Thing Happened on the Way to the Forum* (1962), *Hello Dolly* (1964) and *Hair* (1967).

By any standards this was an important culture in its own right and not just in terms of the 'flowering' of the musical in its book form. More than a mere staging post in the development of the musical, musical comedy produced some of the great shows of the twentieth century and was crucial to the nature of the musical, particularly to the clarity of its definition as a cultural form distinct from other kinds of musical theatre – burlesque, variety and, in particular, the more highbrow forms, opera and operetta. It was musical comedy that took the biggest steps in making the play and dialogue central to the musical and it was through musical comedy that the play and its music and dance became not just open to vernacular traditions, but crucially dependent on them. Contemporary dialogue styles, modern and often urban themes, street dances and jazz music – all, to a very considerable extent, became assimilated to musical theatre via musical comedy. This process was clearly vital to the formation of the 'musical', both in technical and aesthetic terms and as culture, and conditioned it as a genuinely popular form. With its characteristic appeal to social cohesion and its focus on contemporaneity as pleasure, musical comedy was the essential musical theatre and fundamentally shaped the status of the musical as modern culture.

Musical comedy at the *fin de siècle*

This current study is concerned with an early and obscure part of musical comedy history: musical comedy on the West End stage between 1890 and 1939. From the perspective of over a century on, late Victorian and Edwardian musical comedy now looks quaint, small-scale and 'British' in a stereotypical way. In its heyday, however, it had a very different registration, one that resonated with important cultural concepts – especially with the idea of modernity in many of its key *fin de siècle* formations. This commonly accepted description of Europe at the 1890s is often conjured by certain key descriptors that include, as Rhonda Garelick and many others have shown, the industrialization of culture – 'the fascination with the public commercialized personality; the great rise of mass-produced entertainment; and a concomitant concern for the decay of high culture'.[4] Musical comedy involved all these elements of the *fin de siècle*. An important prototype 'mass' culture, it was one of the earliest 'star' vehicles. It utilized the most modern forms of technology, distribution and marketing available, and was intensely consumerist in its design, execution and general orientation. A cultural commodity of great significance, it was a market winner whose rise was concurrent with and responsive to rising standards of living and changed expectations about the quality of modern life. A new awareness of consumerism was essential here. For the 'first time in British (and perhaps human) history the sheer fact of scarcity receded from the cockpit of social organisation, as average per capita income rose from a slender margin of 25 per cent above subsistence in 1870 to a comfortable 150 per cent above subsistence in 1914'.[5] Musical comedy was not simply dependent on this important economic condition for its ticket sales; it also reproduced consumerism in a theatrical extravaganza that transformed the Edwardian stage into a fantastic celebration of fashion, shopping and general excess. It was for this reason that musical comedy had such intimate relations with the wider modern marketplace. The most eminent clothes designers of the day and the elite department stores of the West End collaborated closely with the musical comedy stage, in part because it was one of the first important platforms for product placement on a serious and increasingly spectacular scale.[6] *Our Miss Gibbs* (1909), the best known of a string of shows set in department stores, is highly suggestive here. Staged in the musical comedy version of Harrods, it opens with an astonishing display of fashionable women parading on the shop floor of 'Garrods', watched not only by the audience, but by the shop assistants strategically placed on the first floor balcony where they witness the condition to which presumably they aspire (Illustration 1). The opening chorus is an anthem to the wondrous variety of the modern consumerist age and its most potent emblem, the department store – the one-stop site that has the means to satisfy just about every want, including the desire of men and women for each other ('if a lady you should meet / It's better here than on the street'):

> Do you want a hair in curl or switches?
> Mattresses, ladies' riding breeches?
> Pianolas, petticoats,
> Or Quaker Oats?
> Or tennis nets,
> Or cigarettes,
> Enamel chains
> Or aeroplanes?
> Precious stones,
> Gramophones?
> Cauliflowers, paperweights,

Illustration 1 Musical comedy, modernity and the department store (*Our Miss Gibbs*)

> Or bromide plates?
> A telescope,
> A cake of soap?[7]

Musical comedy had a highly developed capacity for responding to and formulating the fashionable and the mainstream, its character in this respect being centrally shaped and determined by the maintenance of a delicate balancing act between exuberance and respectability. Although it presented as a risqué culture and sought alignments with versions of bohemian licence, it was more substantially a product of the commercialization of a cleaned-up West End stage.[8] A borderline culture positioned somewhere beyond, but never entirely outside, the 'Victorian', it was very much the 'latest thing' of the late 1890s and 1900s. At the same time, it was decisively reflexive of national, masculinist and bourgeois identities that had strong continuities with the past. In these respects and others musical comedy remained an insider culture, although with an instinct for adventure. This too was suggestive of the *fin de siècle*, albeit in a particularly restrained and British way.

Elements of the intelligentsia may have despised it and the Lord Chamberlain's Office been alarmed at its modern directness and frankness in the early days, but musical comedy was a moderate version of the carnivalesque 'low' culture that 'troubles the high'.[9] For all the stances taken against Victorian conventions and the demotic poses struck against 'high' art, particularly opera, musical comedy aspired to and cultivated the acceptance of the respectable classes and of those beyond. The practised taunting of authority operated in part in fools' day terms, as a stylized form of harmless dissent. It was also a marker of the engaging charm of musical comedy, part of a wider strategy that set out to court the high and the influential. Indeed, musical comedy became part of late Victorian and Edwardian social spectacle, the definitive glamour culture, in fact, of *fin de siècle* England, in terms of stage representation, which was, in its West End form, expensive and modern, and of the accompanying fan culture. From *An Artist's Model* (1895) onwards, opening nights at theatres like Daly's and the Gaiety became style events of the highest order. Royalty, both domestic and overseas, often attended – the Gaiety was Edward VII's favourite theatre – as did the rest of aristocratic society.[10] The Dukes of Cambridge, Newcastle and Westminster, the Earls of Dudley and Tweedmonk, Lord Victor Paget, Lord Drumlanrig, Lord Stavordale, Lord Granville, Lord Monsell, Lord Keyes, The Master of the Rolls and Lady Esher and the Rajah of Cooch Behar were among the many regular titled attendees. According to W. McQueen-Pope, historian of the Gaiety, 'Debrett was in the stalls and boxes' at the famous benefit given for Nellie Farren at the Gaiety in 1898.[11]

The extent of this prestigious patronage may have been exaggerated in traditional theatre history, precisely for the purpose of positioning musical comedy as a glamour culture, but it was not invented. Of course, there was a wider, more everyday constituency to musical comedy and it has been seriously neglected, but the high-style element in the audience was a real enough phenomenon and central to the cultural registration of musical comedy. It may also have been one reason why untitled luminaries from all walks of life were willing to be identified with these shows. Alfred de Rothschild was a great supporter of musical comedy and the likes of Max Beerbohm, Henry Irving and Oscar Wilde paid their respects at least. George Moore, the Irish novelist, was a friend of the musical comedy scriptwriter 'Owen Hall' (Jimmy Davis) and a regular at the 'bohemian' parties Davis held in Curzon Street. He recalled in later years the 'adorable game' that circulated around this theatre crowd.[12] Even the clergy, sometimes directly mocked by the text of musical comedy, could be tolerant. Father Bernard Vaughan, the London priest whose fiery 'cockney' sermons are alluded to in James

Joyce's *Ulysses*, was a family friend of Ellaline Terris and Seymour Hicks and attended some of their shows.[13]

Musical comedy sought consent and status. This was reflected in every aspect of the form and its institutionalization, from the policies banning drinking in the auditorium to the new imperatives placed on professionalism in performance. High standards of private and public behaviour were expected of its composers, writers and performers whatever their backgrounds, and their backgrounds were more varied than might be thought. Some 'artistes' came from the working classes, often transferring to musical comedy after music hall training. Ada Reeve, for instance, followed this route. Others, however, like Constance Collier, came from *déclassé* theatrical families. Others still had more conventionally bourgeois backgrounds. C. Hayden Coffin studied at University College to be a surgeon-dentist before becoming the essential romantic lead of musical comedy. Louis Bradfield, the son of a civil servant, also came to musical comedy from the middle classes. Other participants came from even more elevated backgrounds. Paul Rubens, for instance, the lyricist, composer and librettist, was from a well-off society family. The son of a stockbroker, he attended Winchester and Oxford. Lionel Monckton, one of the most celebrated composers of musical comedy, was the son of London's town clerk, Sir John Monckton and Lady Monckton. He was educated at Charterhouse and then Oxford. The composer Frank Osmond and the most prolific lyricist of the period 'Adrian Ross' (Arthur Ropes) were at Cambridge together. The latter was 'a one time-fellow of King's, author of a history of the Merovingian dynasty, and a serious poet'.[14] Ivan Caryll was Belgian-born and educated at the Paris Conservatory. Howard Talbot was American born and took medicine at King's before studying at the Royal College of Music under Hubert Parry.[15]

It was a further sign of musical comedy's drive for status and acceptability that middle- and lower-middle-class women came to the new theatre, as both audience and participants in production and performance. Following a trend general across British theatre, where managers voiced the opinion 'that it is from the drawing room, not from the factory, that our future actresses *must* come', middle-class women were recruited to musical comedy in an appropriation of drawing-room skills and what was assumed to be middle-class decorum.[16] Here as elsewhere, musical comedy played a crucial part in detaching musical theatre from its traditional stigmatizing.[17] Certainly, it was a culture that packaged women and sold sexuality, but it was characteristic of musical comedy's general conservatism and orderliness that this was done within the perimeters of the generally acceptable. If its eroticization of the stage

KING ALFRED'S COLLEGE
LIBRARY

was achieved partly as a product of changing times and sensibilities, as it undoubtedly was, it was also a question of meeting change with deliberate policy, ensuring that innovation was accompanied by restraint and 'good taste'. Thus the musical theatre stage became so cleaned up with musical comedy that by the late 1890s it could be thought positively prestigious for 'middle-class girls to enter the chorus', certainly of establishments like Daly's and the Gaiety.[18]

Musical comedy presented itself, and was largely accepted, as a respectable, mainstream culture. It may have developed from a much more heterogeneous and possibly demotic Victorian theatre – origins that have often been theorized in terms of power relations where the seedier side of Victorian theatre can appear quite subversive.[19] It is important, however, to distinguish musical comedy from this background. In its West End formulation, it was more organized, industrial and professional. Most importantly, it also made a self-conscious push for the middle ground of safe pleasure and this was the real sign of musical comedy's character and ambition. The flirtation with the high Establishment was important as a signifier of status, but it was the more sustained courtship developed with the theatre-going mainstream that determined the viability of musical comedy. Its core audience came from the middle and lower middle classes, a smaller social segment in 1900 than in modern Western Europe, both numerically and relatively, but a growing one, constituting as much as 20 per cent of the British population by the end of the period under discussion.[20] There was acute and growing segregation between the divisions of this broad middle class and at the borders of its articulations with the 'upper' and 'lower' ranks. At the same time there was, particularly in the metropolis, 'a slow but perceptible convergence in the outward appearance and manners of different social groups'. This had a gender dimension, as the historian Jose Harris points out: 'in the 1900s working people especially young women, looked more like their middle class equivalents then they had done a generation before'.[21] To what was, at the time, a unique degree, late Victorian and Edwardian society had to manage these complex and often contradictory modern dynamics. Anxieties about the defence of boundaries grew as the impulse to identify with the crowd at the centre reached new dimensions and proportions. Accurately reflecting and engaging with the taste and disposition of this fashionable, pluralist and, in some ways, quite volatile centre was the essential business of musical comedy.

If it did not constitute 'mass culture' as we now experience it, musical comedy could at least be understood as populist in ways that will be familiar. It was often discursively constructed as temporary modern fashion, for example, with all that entails. Many contemporary critics dismissed it as trivial or simply 'bad'. For the twenty-five years or so that musical comedy dominated London's West End, opposed cultural establishments ridiculed it, seeing in the 'new' entertainment yet more evidence of the West's inexorable decline. According to *The Era* in 1896, 'the musical play' was 'undergoing the usual penalty of general demand: it [was] degenerating in quality'.[22] Similarly, *The Times*, although admiring *The Shop Girl* (1894) for its energy, thought in eugenicist terms of this 'hybrid' entertainment that was neither 'comic opera' nor music hall.[23] Writing some fifty years later in a 'survey of light entertainment on the London stage', James Agate made the same point about musical comedy's contribution to cultural decline. Like so many before and since, he identified 'real' musical theatre in terms of operetta, declaring Gilbert and Sullivan to be 'the perfect marriage, after which comic opera rapidly degenerated into musical comedy'.[24] As with newspapers, literature, suburbs, retail stores and, indeed, the physical condition of the nation, the state of musical comedy was taken to illustrate nothing less than the decline of the civilized world. For many contemporaries it was a bastardized, impure kind of product, 'one of the most curious examples of composite dramatic architecture that we have seen for some time'.[25] All this disdain at what was seen as the cheapness of modern culture was a sure sign that musical comedy was making its mark with 'the public'.

Indeed, it raked in audiences and made huge fortunes. A largely forgotten show like *Chu Chin Chow* (1916) was performed a staggering 2,235 times in London's West End. In simple exposure terms, this entertainment would have had a much greater immediate impact than any number of texts that have since come to signify modernity itself. Sixteen years after its publication in 1887, there were just 16,000 copies of Nietzsche's *Beyond Good and Evil* in print in Europe.[26] Over its four-year run at Daly's *Chu Chin Chow*, a light piece of 'Wardour Street Orientalism', would have been seen by well over two million people.[27] It then went on tour, first to America then round the British Empire, including Australia. Finally, it returned to Britain and the provincial circuits, where it flourished for several decades.

In addition to blockbusters like *Chu Chin Chow* there were the thousands of local shows that never made it to the West End. Registered with the Lord Chamberlain's Office as playing in town and provincial city theatres all over the country from Herne Bay to Dundee, these were a good indication of the spread of musical comedy into an everyday, less glamorous, constituency.

The stars of musical comedy were much identified with this popularity. They became household names and an accompanying fan culture grew up around them. *The Stage Souvenir* (1904), *The London Stage Annual* (1903), *The Actor Illustrated* (1905) and *The Play Pictorial* (1896) were all devoted to modern musical theatre and its performers. On the back of the picture postcard boom, a large trade developed in cards carrying the photographic images of actors and actresses like Gabrielle Ray, C. Hayden Coffin, Gladys Cooper and Marie Studholme. The glossy sepia postcards sold at twopence each and hand-tinted versions at three-pence; Ellaline Terris, writing some years later, remembered being slightly alarmed at just how commodified her image became. 'One was confronted,' she wrote, 'by one's own features everywhere. It was almost like looking in Looking Glass Land and it was a little disconcerting.'[28] Other kinds of merchandising followed the shows rather than their stars. The success of *The Geisha* (1896), for example, 'started a Japanese craze in London; there were Geisha hats for women, Geisha ties for men and all kinds of goods sprang up in the middle of the night with the brand name of "Geisha"'.[29]

As the performers got older and the popularity of the genre declined, a significant reminiscence industry developed. By the late 1930s there were at least a dozen books published on the Gaiety theatre, the Mecca of West End musical comedy. Many musical comedy performers, producers and writers, like George Grossmith Jr, Seymour Hicks, Constance Collier, Ada Reeve, Arthur Roberts and Ellaline Terriss, produced auto-biographies. There were two biographies of the 'Guv'nor', George Edwardes, the Irish producer who, according to legend, did most to invent the idea of musical comedy, and many more personal recollections published about this figure, including one from the man who ran the stage door at the Gaiety for thirty years, James Jupp. Many of the songs of musical comedy survived as pub and parlour ballads. In these ways the shelf life of this culture was extended well beyond its Edwardian heyday.

Academics and enthusiasts

For reasons that will become clear, late Victorian and Edwardian musical comedy on the West End Stage has attracted very little scholarly atten-tion, certainly until quite recently.[30] For a culture that was once so popular and so much a product of the modern, West End musical comedy has been seriously neglected by historians of musical theatre and by cultural historians generally. A text like *Imperialism and Popular*

Culture (1986) is illustrative here.[31] It has material on virtually every conceivable aspect of *fin de siècle* popular culture, including music hall, comics and magazines, exhibitions, museums, popular fiction, and so on, but there is no reference at all to musical comedy, easily the most popular form of 'legitimate' (that is, licensed) theatre for a generation from the mid-1890s onwards.[32] Even more surprisingly, something like *Acts of Supremacy: the British Empire and the Stage, 1790–1930* (1991), while it deals with melodrama, pantomime and, again, music hall and colonial exhibitions, ignores musical comedy, despite the fact that these shows were taken all over the Empire and many dealt explicitly with Empire themes.[33]

This neglect is surprising for a number of reasons. Not only were the shows popular, they were, for all the reputation of being crude and formless, highly sophisticated in all sorts of ways. Production standards were continually being raised and new standards of professionalism were to characterize the development of musical comedy performance on the West End stage. For their day, and notwithstanding the notorious interpolations of comedy routines and songs, these shows had impressive levels of play/music integration. They had a libretto and a musical score. Dance was more stylized and less subject to innovation. Until post-1918, it rarely moved much beyond stage versions of social dances, refined balletic poses and showgirl walks. In other respects, however, West End musical comedy of this period constituted a development of the stage musical that should have been of much more interest, certainly to musicologists and historians of musical theatre.

Despite some brief periods of nostalgic reclamation, however, musical comedy has become a largely forgotten culture.[34] Little or nothing of what was once an important entertainment remains in contemporary memory. With the possible exception of *The Arcadians* (1909), the shows seem not to be generally recalled and the one-time phenomenon that was the Gaiety girl barely registers. While the names of music hall performers like Marie Lloyd, Dan Leno and Gus Elen still mean something, those of C. Hayden Coffin, Phyllis Dare and Edna May probably do not. Musical comedy songs that have managed to survive – 'If you Were the Only Girl', 'What do you Want to Make Those Eyes at Me For', 'Yip I Addy I Ay', to take just a few examples – are likely to have done so because they travelled first to the music halls and pubs. A song like 'The Honeysuckle and the Bee' will invariably be associated with the music hall rather than with the show in which it originated, *Bluebell in Fairyland* (1901).[35] It is symptomatic of this slippage that the mention of musical comedy, in most contexts, is likely to be misheard as a reference to music hall.

Certainly by comparison to music hall, musical comedy has faded badly, despite the fact that the historical record, while problematic for both, is superior for the latter in many respects. Publications like *The Era, The Stage* and *The Times* have listings of the production details and cast lists for all West End musical comedies and for a great many of the shows that stayed in the provinces. These sources also contain reviews, valuable for a number of reasons, not least because of what they can reveal about production styles. None of this exists in the same detail for music hall, even West End music hall. The music for these shows was published, as were the song lyrics, usually separately and as part of the 'book'. Some early music recordings also survive. These are often quite poor, partly because the technology used was crude, but also because the absence of audience tended to produce two-dimensional performances. Still, they give some indication of the characteristic singing styles of one-time stars like Gertie Millar. There is a great deal of photographic evidence, some of the best of which is housed in London's Theatre Museum and Library. This is of great help, both in reconstructing staging and costume and as evidence of the sophistication of the promotional machine that publicized shows and performers. Taken together these sources constitute a substantial body of material, although obviously not a complete record. The play texts, which have been essential for this current study – indeed, they are a major focus of what follows – are an important if problematic source in this respect. Quite apart from the fact there these were subject to endless revisions and interpolations, most were never printed commercially at all. The only virtually complete collection is housed in the manuscript department of the British Library, which keeps the copies that were subject to the scrutiny of the Lord Chamberlain's Office. However, at least it *is* possible to read versions of a virtually complete script of these shows. Nothing like that can be done for music hall, because it had no such script.[36]

The idea that these shows were sparkling ephemera, leaving nothing behind 'like bright exhalations in the evening', is a myth, generated largely by musical comedy enthusiasts.[37] The relative invisibility of West End musical comedy is a more interesting phenomenon and the result of a convergence of quite distinct cultural histories and interventions. In the first place the neglect has been a product of musical comedy's total eclipse by the American musical in all its twentieth-century Broadway and Hollywood glory. Whereas music hall has remained fixed as a historical culture, with no tradition to replace it other than the 'variety' that was later subsumed by television, West End musical theatre became outclassed by a superior New World tradition. Although with the Lloyd

Webber musical there has been, in more recent years, what might appear to be a West End revival, this has occurred in a new, 'globalized' context, which has little to do with the earlier form.[38]

The genuine authority of American culture in this respect has been helped by an official history of musical theatre that has substantially underplayed the West End contribution. Alan J. Lerner's 'celebration' of 'the musical theatre' is characteristic here, an account that begins traditionally enough with Mozart and proceeds to trace the development of the musical through European operetta (Offenbach, Gilbert and Sullivan, Strauss Jr, Lehár, and so on) to the modern American 'book musical'.[39] Along with the less prestigious native elements that went into producing the full-blown American musical – vaudeville, burlesque, minstrel shows, melodrama for instance[40] – the 120 or so major musical comedies composed in Britain and staged in London's West End between 1892 and 1920 are largely ignored in this historiography, as are their performers, directors and writers.[41] There are no index entries at all in Lerner's account for Lionel Monckton, Howard Talbot, Ivan Caryll or Paul Rubens. Similarly, performers and producers like Gertie Millar, George Grossmith Jr, The Dare sisters, Letty Lind, Kate Cutler, George Edwardes and Robert Courtneidge, one-time celebrated figures who helped define this characteristically modern culture, are completely cut out.

In *America's Musical Stage: Two Hundred Years of Musical Theatre*, Julian Mates pays much greater attention to the popular and multifarious origins of the American musical, but has a blind spot similar to Lerner's as far as musical comedy produced in London's West End at the turn of the last century is concerned. Mates is perfectly willingly to acknowledge earlier British contributions to the development of the American musical, through ballad opera in the eighteenth century, for instance. An extraordinary gap opens up, however, when it comes to Britain's later role:

> A sort of sidelight shines about now. In 1896 *The Geisha* was the first American production ever to be labelled 'a musical comedy'. The term was useful for a while, as was 'farce-comedy' or 'comic-opera'. However, from the 1920s on, when our musical stage took the whole world as its oyster, the term 'musical' seems best able to express what America's musical stage is up to.[42]

This allusion to *The Geisha*, here referred to as an American show, is the only reference to West End musical comedy in the whole of Mates' otherwise very detailed account and yet a flood of shows transferred from the West End to Broadway and off-Broadway venues in the late nineteenth and early twentieth centuries. Between 1894 and 1910 alone these included *A Gaiety Girl* (1894), *The Shop Girl* (1895), *An Artist's Model* (1895), *The Geisha* (1896), *Monte Carlo* (1896), *A Runaway Girl* (1898), *Little Miss Nobody* (1898), *A Greek Slave* (1899), *Floradora* (1900), *Kitty Grey* (1900), *The Messenger Boy* (1901), *The Toreador* (1901), *A Chinese Honeymoon* (1902), *San Toy* (1902), *The Silver Slipper* (1902), *The Cingalee* (1904), *The Medal and the Maid* (1904), *The School Girl* (1904), *The Duchess of Dantzic* (1905), *The Orchid* (1907), *The Earl and the Girl* (1905), *Sergeant Brue* (1905), *The Catch of the Season* (1905), *The Blue Moon* (1906), *The Spring Chicken* (1906), *The Little Cherub* (1906), *The Dairy Maids* (1907), *Miss Hook of Holland* (1907), *Havana* (1909), *The Belle of Brittany* (1910), *Our Miss Gibbs* (1910) and *The Arcadians* (1910).[43] It seems inconceivable that this positive invasion of the American musical scene should have had no effect on the development of the American musical, yet that is the suggestion in Mates' account. The obvious effect is the preservation of the musical as the 'American musical', with its roots firmly established in a demotic national culture. Any links that do remain with the Old World are partial, subject to much qualification and substantiate only the most glamorous of origin myths.

Versions of this kind of agenda are apparent in less obviously proselytizing accounts. Gerald Bordman's history of American musical comedy, for instance, is much more authoritative, certainly than Lerner's account, and generally reckoned to be reasonably balanced. It does, indeed, acknowledge the existence of West End musical comedy, identifying the period 1892–1902 as a continuation of what Bordman calls 'English hegemony' over the musical stage and recognizing that at least one important American producer, Charles Frohman, 'mounted only imported musicals for Broadway...England...[remaining] the source of the most chic musical entertainments.'[44] But for all this recognition, Bordman does not offer any challenge to the standard historiographical principles governing the usual accounts of the 'development of the American musical'. Indeed, he takes great pains to point out that the West End shows, although popular, were somehow not 'real' musical comedy at all. They were, he insists, at best tangential to the American and authentic product.

This distancing is achieved in three ways. First, the West End musical comedy is understood as fake, modish and ephemeral, without any tradition behind it – apparently musical comedy in Britain happened overnight, transforming burlesque, whereas American musical comedy matured and had 'evolved a little more slowly'.[45] Second, any connection between the West End musical comedy and quality is dismissed. In a telling uncertainty, Bordman describes the London shows as being 'one- or two-dimensional at best', certainly by comparison to the work of Edward Harrigan, the late nineteenth-century progenitor of musical comedy in America who, apparently, was unique in moving 'beyond cardboard characterisations'.[46] Finally, the difference of West musical comedy is asserted through a crude historiographical understanding which sees *fin de siècle* European culture as still aristocratic, and revolving around the upper classes: 'the British shows grew out of a strikingly different society and reflected that society's often unique attitudes and tastes. For example, the elegant hauteur so many West End musicals affected was alien to our more democratic notions.'[47] The implication here is that the chic of West End musical comedy was local and compromised by old-fashioned contaminants. In this way musical comedy is refused the true status of what Peter Bailey has usefully termed 'popular modernism'.[48]

None of these arguments stands up to much scrutiny. It certainly is not the case that West End musical comedy was a bolt from the blue with little past and less future. It would be possible to construct, from a history of ballad opera, operetta, circus, burlesque, melodrama, minstrel show, musical hall, and so on, a developmental historiography for the early West End musical every bit as rich and demotic as for the American counterpart – although this present study does not constitute such a history, the issue of the origins of West End musical comedy is discussed in a later chapter. In terms of the quality argument, as Bordman pursues it, musicals, from whatever period or culture, simply cannot be judged seriously on the base of sophistication of characterization. But even if they were, it is difficult to see why Harrigan's work should warrant the status that Bordman gives it in this respect and even more difficult to see how the whole West End musical comedy output fails by comparison to Harrigan on this score. As for the idea that West End musical comedy reflected and supported aristocratic culture and society, this is simply false. It may have projected versions of aristocratic identity, but musical comedy in both Britain and America, as is made clear throughout this study, was at all levels the product of a bourgeois and petit-bourgeois culture in ascendancy.

Bordman's account does not address the neglect of West End musical comedy that has characterized the American history of the musical. It simply acknowledges that there was a 'British' version of musical comedy and then robs it of any significance. Finally, he sees this period of late Victorian and Edwardian cultural history as an 'intermission' before the real 'genesis' that took place between 1914 and 1937. This later period is, according to Bordman, where the modern musical is 'born'. 'British' musical comedy, although not entirely ignored, *is* left out of the real celebration, relegated, again, to the status of an interruption of the 'great tradition' of musical theatre.[49]

British traditions have mounted little resistance to this marginalization, primarily because Britain has traditionally made much firmer distinctions between art and popular entertainment than has America. Whereas in America the musical has become an institution, a cultural tradition entwined with nation-building and the national identity, in Britain musicals have been more usually understood as light, insignificant entertainments.[50] In many contexts it would still be seen as downright embarrassing to include musical theatre, let alone musical comedy specifically, under the heading of 'national culture'. This is all very different from the situation in America, where the musical is routinely studied and theorized. Here it 'not only reflects the historical, social and cultural character of American society, but also voices that society's own sense of its life and values'.[51] It is possible to read into the development of the American musical a history that engages decisive themes. Republican independence from the *ancien régime* becomes embodied in America's general embracing of the demotic cultural form that stood in sharp relief against European opera. Frontier expansion is reconfigured in a show like *Oklahoma*. The struggle for self-definition, realized perhaps most crucially in the American Civil War, is romanticized in a string of musicals from *Show Boat* to *West Side Story*. America's twentieth-century emergence as the most powerful modern state in the world becomes normalized in, for example, *South Pacific*.[52] No parallel to this kind of cultural signification exists for the British counterpart. Nothing in the history of British musical theatre has ever been seen to carry so much weight, not even Gilbert and Sullivan.

Drama has been the most prestigious form of theatre in British culture. Musicals, by contrast, figure much lower down the scale of things. They are typically constructed as 'popular' or 'low'. At the same time they are not usually significantly associated with either folk or working-class culture. It is partly for this reason that musical comedy has not been subject to any serious attempts at reclamation. Unlike music hall, which has had a long, if contested, history as a culture of resistance, or black musical theatre, similarly linked to repressed and compromised cultural identities, musical comedy cannot be seen in that way.[53] It did take critical positions but it cannot be rescued as a marginalized 'people's history', displaced and contained from above. Not a people's culture in that sense, it was not particularly subject to surveillance either, outside the usual concerns of the Lord Chamberlain's Office and more general censorship laws. Far from being positioned on the edge of culture, musical comedy was self-consciously seeking the market centre. Very much a culture of the modernizing, urban bourgeoisie, it can easily be perceived as being tame, conservative and commercial. It could also be seen as being 'British' in a sense that appears to have little modern relevance.

The effects of such perceptions are apparent in the relative neglect of musical comedy by the academic world. Again, the comparison with music hall is illustrative. In the 1970s and 1980s eminent historians took up the issue of music hall's cultural status with some vigour.[54] Music hall became part of a critical debate. Through a specific focus on such issues as the social composition of the music hall audience and the impact of the commercialization of music hall, Gareth Stedman Jones and J. S. Bratton tried to formulate positions on wider questions about the nature of working-class culture and identity and what was usually understood as its demise in modernity. Seen as important cultural territory, music hall was fought over. This had the effect both of preserving musical hall in some sense and extending its viability in cultural terms. Musical comedy, however, was not touched on in any of these debates. Neither a 'sub-culture' nor important enough to be considered as part of an 'ideological apparatus', the implication has been that this is a culture that can now be consigned to the end-of-pier museum. It remains very much a 'specialized field', which could easily be dispensed with, from a wide range of positions on popular culture, as commercial pap. The engagements of critical theory and cultural studies, especially since the 1970s, may have provided theoretical frameworks for handling a cultural form like musical comedy more seriously, but the application has not, for the most part, been forthcoming. Like model railways, stamp collecting and sea-side postcards, musical comedy inhabits one of those rare zones where nothing has changed very much. Separated from controversy and living culture, it has been left, by and large, to the care of the enthusiast.

The enthusiasts themselves have done a great deal to preserve musical comedy, in particular kinds of ways. A huge amount of work has been done on cataloguing musical theatre generally and, thanks especially to the monumental efforts of Kurt Ganzl and J. P. Wearing, musical comedy has become well established as part of that culture's history. Ganzl's encyclopaedias and his two-volume directory of British musical theatre have become the key texts here. The latter in particular, with its year-by-year account of musical shows playing in both the West End and the provinces between 1868 and 1984, is quite exceptional in its detail;

all subsequent researchers in the field must be greatly indebted to it. In the process of maintaining the historical record, Ganzl is also able to restore some balance to American historiography, although the eagerness with which he approaches this task is sometimes a little unfortunate. The relish he takes in the fact that in 1902 the major shows were 'British' and that, in 1904, 'there were no less than ten musicals running in London theatres, nine of which were successes and all British' means that he misses the opportunity of discussing the more important issue of what it means to construct culture in such terms.[55] Ganzl, a New Zealander incidentally, clearly has his own axe to grind in this respect, which is why he sees the domination of the Edwardian West End by 'foreign' shows, American or otherwise, as a malaise that challenges the 'supremacy of the British musical comedy'.[56] Essentially though, Ganzl's work is an impressive example of cataloguing, 'objective' for the most part, with the usual raft of qualifications. His support of the British show and his somewhat conservative conception of what counts as 'legitimate' musical theatre do compromise his authority to some extent, but the more serious problem with his work derives from the more general difficulties associated with compiling lists and catalogues.

However valuable the important business of attempting to keep the record straight may be, it cannot be assumed that this kind of approach somehow stands in for critical understanding and wider analysis. A cultural form does not get repossessed, nor can it really be interpreted, from lists – it gets catalogued, and this does not mean that it gets understood. Indeed, there are some senses in which the archivist's approach hinders textual reading and limits interpretation, for one result of 'collating' musical theatre and forming it into lists of plays, performances, 'colourful' personalities and anecdotes is that theatrical history becomes separated out from the wider cultural and social scene. The processes of collecting and matching, and so on tend to preside, with the result that wider perspectives can become neglected or ignored altogether. It is perhaps a hard judgement, but there certainly is a sense in which the intervention of the enthusiast, for all its value, has confirmed musical comedy's place outside any continuing significance. Work such as Ganzl's testifies that musical comedy once thrived in Britain. It is less effective, however, at reading what the cultural significance of the genre in the broader sense might once have been. For this reason, the intervention of the enthusiast is often taken as a sure indicator of the desperately outmoded and decisively finished.

Musical comedy, then, has been caught between some very powerful traditions. Displaced by America's sheer energy and authority and subject to all the conventional British snobberies, it has had little chance to emerge with any kind of dignity, let alone prestige. At the same time, it has had no status as a culture of the marginalized. Left to the enthusiasts, it has been reinserted into the history of British musical theatre, but this preservation has had its limitations. If musical comedy has no wider cultural significance outside the theatre encyclopaedia, it remains much diminished.

Musical comedy as cultural intervention – the text of musical comedy

In fact, musical comedy does have a considerably wider registration. The central argument here is that musical comedy, whatever else it may be, is a fascinating expression of British society and culture at the *fin de siècle*, a shrewdly designed product using all the modern resources at its disposal to define and celebrate an essentially bourgeois vision of the good times rolling. Its engagement with wider society and culture goes way beyond the occasional allusion to a specific contemporary event or issue, although there are plenty of those in musical comedy. Indeed, musical comedy manages very much more sustained and complex positions established in relation to a whole range of issues that have emerged as being key to the period – issues around national identity, for example, gender, sexuality and class. These more fundamental engagements often appear not as momentary references, but more complex textual dispositions. They are expressed only in part through simple gestures. There are also more sustained and mediated techniques, frequently involving the signifying implications of narrative, which take on dimensions of allegory and participate in metonymic and metaphorical meanings, especially around the idea of modernity. This latter is the essential domain of the musical comedy story.

That is to say, musical comedies, like all cultural products, are constitutive and have an explicitly reflexive relationship with the societies from which they stem. They can be properly analysed in terms of what Geertz terms the 'thick description' of culture, where the organization, construction and meaning of cultural products becomes treated in terms of how they are lodged within, and lodge within themselves, the cultural and social structures of the society of which they are an expression.[57] Musicals generally have a special significance here. As well as reflecting the historical and cultural character of society, they often operate as strong expressions of society's own sense of its life and values. The narratives, lyrics and formal qualities of movement, rhythm and structure create a fantasy that is often escapist, but invariably more than 'just entertainment'.[58] Here the musical show becomes the site of a characteristically open, direct and unapologetic expression of the ideals, dreams, anxieties and frustrations of its audience. This means that, conventionally, musicals work to produce a utopian view of life. Musical comedy is no exception.[59] Although it is often more hard-edged and engaged than other forms of late Victorian and Edwardian theatre (burlesque and melodrama, for instance), its pleasures can often be found in its expression of qualities that audiences' real lives lack. In this way musical comedy becomes a powerful vehicle of popular collective expression, articulating the tensions, and reconciliation, of everyday relations between individuals and society.

It is important to emphasize that the combination of song, dance and drama that distinguishes musical theatre from other forms and genres is linked to both precise historical circumstances and specific ideological beliefs. Thus the current study seeks to offer a socio-cultural analysis of the musical as a phenomenon of popular culture emphatically linked to British society at the turn of the last century. It interprets the musical in terms of its relationships to such historically determined formulations as 'Britain', 'patriarchy' and, especially, 'modernity', tracing its development in relation to the development of national, gender and class identities and the challenges of the modern condition. It sees the musical as a vehicle for British myths, ideologies and dreams, one that gives voice to their collective expression as a popular articulation of society and its values. This study is a musicological or dramaturgical one, then, only inasmuch as music, dance and drama are the means through which this expression and articulation are structured and organized as musical theatre. Similarly, this study is not a theatrical history *per se*, although it does recover and address that history in some ways. The aims here are both to examine how a tradition of musical theatre was established out of live British popular culture and entertainment and to register the systematic spread of the musical across Britain and the wider world, by way of its commercialization, commodification and transportation. This study examines, then, how a large and varied mass audience was created and stimulated by the commercially effective, highly institutionalized and profitable character of a theatrical system, although for only a relatively short period of time. As a kind of sub-theme, this text associates the heyday of musical comedy with Britain's consolidation as a world power, and sees in its fall not just a displacement by new cultural technologies – although these were crucially important – but also the effects of the ownership and dissemination of a competing modernism which was to transform the musical into the 'American musical'.

The investigation is taken up through an examination of specific musicals and in particular of the play narrative of musical comedy, an emphasis requiring some introductory comment because it could be understood as highly problematic. It invites the obvious criticism of concentrating too much on a single element of the full theatrical experience. The musical show is a multiple thing, a matter of spectacle, song, dance, comic routines, costume and lighting. Alan Mates is not the first theatre historian to have observed that 'perhaps an aesthetic of the musical stage is needed, one that provides the possibility of evaluating a *total* work of art, or viewing each element as part of a whole rather than in isolation'.[60] Theorizing musical comedy too specifically in terms of narrative, it might be argued, would represent a distortion of how the genre worked, partly because it misses so much, but also because it puts strain on a single element that was typically too unsophisticated to support such weight. Narratives were, it has often been claimed, convenient pegs on which to hang the 'entertainment'. To analyse them seriously might seem to be investing them with very much more significance than they deserve.

More importantly, the suggestion that the musical comedy narrative *is* important, and even complex, implies a reading that is potentially at odds not just with conventional ideas about the multiformness of the musical theatre text and the alleged poor condition of the late Victorian and Edwardian specimens, but also with some extremely influential theorizations of modern popular culture. For someone like Daniel Bell, following the culture industry theorists, one crucial characteristic of modern culture is its movement away from complex narrative meaning and the subsequent reliance on the immediate sensual experience. This is often understood in terms of both aesthetic decline and the implications for social order and consent, with the state and corporate life expanding their influence in and through a 'culture industry' whose main function is as a soporific. Here astonishment, delight and amazement would become key to the cultural experience, displacing more traditional and cerebral engagements with, for instance, a spoken theatre text. Hearing and seeing would become more forcefully deployed than listening and 'reading'; extravagant design, spectacular costumes, again in theatre terms, would take over from more complex and literary textual effects. Sights and 'also sounds ... [would] become central in the production of meaning and identity', indeed the dominant social outlook of modernity in Bell's *The Cultural Contradictions of Capitalism* is considered to be 'visual', with the characteristic positioning being more outwardly disposed than inwardly regarding.[61]

Now musical comedy is in many ways highly suggestive of a modern culture that is visual; indeed, it may be one of the first cultures to exploit the visual spectacle in modern ways. However, that did not necessarily make it mindless fodder for the masses. Nor did it mean that words and scripts became redundant. The scripts were a crucial part of musical comedy and, again, much more sophisticated than has been previously thought. It could be argued that the invention of musical comedy as a form distinct from other kinds of musical theatre was largely a matter of developing narrative and a product of the work of script writers, people like Jimmy Davies, James T. Tanner, Seymour Hicks, Arthur Wimperis, Basil Hood and Paul Rubens, in Britain – and there were many other accomplished writers besides who tried their hand at musical comedy.[62] These included the playwright Mark Ambient (co-writer of *The Arcadians* and *The Light Blues*), J. M. Barrie (*Rosy Rapture*, 1915), P. G. Wodehouse (co-writer, among many other musical comedies, of the wartime hit *Kissing Time*, 1919) and Edgar Wallace (*Are you There?* 1913). The books produced by such figures helped to establish the genre's claim that the 'new' theatre was a modern product. Producing the contemporary voice, telling the modern story, was key to the marketing of musical comedy, to its self-identification in relation to other musical theatre forms and to its eventual character as it became established. Burlesque, usually understood as a forerunner of musical comedy, was fragmentary by comparison – a series of scenes, songs and routines not formed into story. Opera was sung story without any of the contemporaneity of dialogue or, indeed, any modern narrative styling at all. As in operetta or light opera, the stories of opera were conventionally 'historical' or mythic. They involved past times, high romance, fantasy and fairy tale. The status of opera as a 'higher' genre, with an 'official air', was partly determined by the fact that its narratives were located in some 'other' time.[63] By contrast musical comedy specifically implicated story and the story of modernity, thereby defining itself against the older, more conservative and 'higher' cultural counterparts. It was precisely its narratives of life in the fashionable department store, the seaside resort, the film studio and on the Stock Exchange floor that made musical comedy more contemporary, more engaged with the modern bourgeois world and more fun than operetta or opera. Musical comedy certainly considered itself to be entertainment, but it also told an important story about the condition of modernity. Placing the contemporaneous against figures and emblems representing tradition and conservatism, it consistently aligned itself with the forces of innovation at a time when many cultural forms – the novel, *fin de siècle* anthropology, sociology, philosophy and even science – were taking quite different positions. It was not 'analytical' in any rigorous sense, of course, but in constructing modernity through its stagecraft and, above all, its narratives, it was inevitably engaging in a debate of considerable importance. It did not always and consistently court controversy; far from it. In insisting on reproducing the now, however, and on staging engagements between the flagging past and what was perceived as the dynamic new, its story lines participated in that great enterprise of making the modern manifest. In this way musical comedy possessed what Bakhtin called the 'novelistic spirit', a spirit specifically defined by him in terms of an alignment made with innovation and much concerned with reproducing a sense of the cultural present.[64]

Although the following chapters make many references to a wide range of production and performance characteristics and to the theatrical history of both early and post-war West End musical comedy, the main emphasis here is on recapturing this 'novelistic spirit' and constructing it as product of late Victorian and Edwardian society and culture. Chapter 2 examines in more detail the modernity of musical comedy and what it reveals about the nature of 'popular' or 'conservative' modernism in three main ways. First, it examines musical comedy in terms of its self-identity as a new form quite distinct from burlesque, operetta and music hall. Second, musical comedy is constructed as a modern product in a more material sense – in terms of the conditions of its musical, lyrical and narrative composition; the technological requirements of its production and the economics of staging and distribution. Third, the modernity of musical comedy is understood in terms of the musical comedy script self-consciously engaged with the condition of modernity. It is here that the modern*ism* of musical comedy, its interpretation of reality as a new estate, becomes most explicit.

Chapter 3 focuses on musical comedy's treatment of other cultures as being crucial to its status as a modern culture. It examines the reproduction of continental Europe in West End shows, its stylized fantasies of 'Germany' in shows like *The Girls of Gottenberg* (1907); 'France' in *The Belle of Brittany* (1908); 'Denmark' in *Dear Little Denmark* (1909), and so on. The diminutive versions of European powers staged in such productions are understood partly as defensive responses to insecurities about Britain's world position in the Edwardian period. They are compared to the more anthropological representation of 'Oriental' cultures in shows like *The Geisha* (1896), *San Toy* (1899) and *The Blue Moon* (1904).

The instructional disposition displayed here is considered in terms of an ideological positioning in respect of ideas of nation and imperialism. Musical comedy, as a national and a global culture which toured the Empire and beyond, is analysed as one of the key cultural forms through which late Victorian and Edwardian society supported a popular politics of imperialism.

It has often been observed, and not just by Bordman, that West End musical comedy was obsessed with traditional aristocracy and landed society. Indeed, there was scarcely a single West End show that did not feature this traditional elite, an elite that was experiencing the most serious challenge to its authority precisely at the moment that it was being made the subject of an astonishing protective instinct, not just on the stage of musical theatre but in popular culture generally. The stage aristocrat, invariably married to figures representative of modernity – the shop girl, the secretary, the actress, and so on – is central to musical comedy and much more than a means of reproducing Cinderella-type rags-to-riches stories. Although it was important to bourgeois culture to reflect a world in which social mobility was not just possible but preordained in the right circumstances, it was also important to preserve in some form the old authority. The survival of aristocracy in musical comedy became a way of mediating between old and new versions of social order. Chapter 4 argues that the cultural representation of this elite is key to understanding the social polity of musical comedy, the central social and political stability that it attempted to maintain as its idealized version of order in the modern world.

As well as being typically implicated with ideas of aristocracy, musical comedy was also a characteristically feminized culture, in terms of investment in showgirl extravaganza and by virtue of narrative. The plots of musical comedy usually centred on female figures, as the titles of shows suggest. There was a cluster that involved 'belles' – *The Belle of Cairo* (1896), *The Belle of New York* (1908) and *The Belle of Mayfair* (1906) – 'Miss' shows – *Miss Hook of Holland* (1907) – and 'Princess' shows – *A Persian Princess* (1909) – for instance. Above all there were the 'girl' shows – *A Gaiety Girl* (1893), *The Shop Girl* (1894), *The Circus Girl* (1896), *A Runaway Girl* (1898), *A Country Girl* (1902), *The Girl from Kay's* (1902), *The Earl and the Girl* (1903), *The Schoolgirl* (1903), *The Girls of Gottenberg*, *The Quaker Girl* (1910), *The Girl in the Taxi* (1912), *The Sunshine Girl* (1912), *The Girl from Utah* (1913), *The Pearl Girl* (1913), *After the Girl* (1914), and so on. Thus a central tradition of musical comedy was produced, and finally spoofed in the 1914 revue entitled *The Girl from Dunnowhere* (1914). Chapter 5 understands this gender orientation partly in terms of a staging of femininity as spectacle, which defined standards of respectable voyeurism for the period. It also argues that musical comedy made a key association between the condition of modernity and the feminine. This association functioned in complex ways, with the essential signification securing modernity as a glamorous, but safe and largely secure, territory.

The final chapter discusses the decline of West End musical comedy, a process that began just before the First World War and accelerated in the 1920s and 1930s. A number of factors were responsible for this cultural shift. Essentially, however, the process is understood here as a product of American competition and a changing Britain. The rise of the musical as a characteristically American cultural product is explored as an echo of America's rise as *the* twentieth-century superpower and of Britain's consequent displacement. Thus the West End musical comedy declined in tandem with a wider decline, making its final appearance not as a living culture, but as a culture of the past nostalgically recreated by Noel Coward in such shows (and films) as *Bitter Sweet* (1929), *Cavalcade* (1931) and *Operette* (1938). In this way musical comedy became not only an important culture in terms of both theatre history and the wider history of the late Victorian and Edwardian eras, but also as a theatre which continued to be serviceable beyond. Here it figured as a ghostly reminder of what was typically represented as the innocent glory days when nothing less than the authentic British character flourished, free from the knowing cynicism of the 1930s, and, apparently, for the last time before the second apocalypse of the twentieth century.

2
Our Sickly Age's End – Musical Comedy and Modernity

West End musical comedy has often been understood as a quirky, trivial and, for all its celebrity, curiously local phenomenon. Partly as a matter of showbiz tradition, it has been represented in terms of an imagined sense of production where the stars and their performances become elevated, highly individualistic and crucially dependent on tribal intimacies with the West End 'in-crowd'. In this way the whole form and the culture that accompanied it become diminished, neatly contained as a colourful piece of theatre history that was never more than 'just entertainment', and where the central social relationship was between star and fan.

As social and cultural historians are beginning to demonstrate, this very partial view of musical comedy is misleading in virtually all respects.[1] Most obviously it obscures the sheer scale and contemporaneity of musical comedy, the fact that it was a crafted modern product that utilized advanced technologies in its construction, marketing and global distribution. Far from being parochial and small-scale, musical comedy operated on a newly professionalized stage in a West End that was being transformed in the 1890s. It was partly located in, and crucially associated with, the renewal of the eastern half of the West End. This important development involved the construction of Northumberland Avenue, Charing Cross Road and Shaftsbury Avenue, and the consequent marginalization of the slum district of Seven Dials, a piece of urban planning that 'facilitated the flow of middle-class suburbia to dozens of new theatres and music halls' and 'cemented the image of the West End as England's paramount entertainment centre'.[2] Musical comedy was the most successful theatre of this burgeoning late Victorian and Edwardian entertainment industry and key to the establishment of the West End as a modern retail and pleasure Mecca.

For success as popular culture, musical comedy needed to be fashionable and well positioned in terms of the wider contemporary perspectives. As observers often recognized, it was very much a twentieth-century product and highly suggestive of the modern age in all sorts of ways. *The Times* reviewed it in 1908 as 'a dramatic art which is one of the signs of our times'.[3] William Archer found it 'subtly and sensitively modern', understanding its significance as 'the real New Drama'.[4] For an age that was acutely aware of its own modernity, of its susceptibility to change, musical comedy seemed to resonate powerfully. If modernity was characterized by an accelerated pace of industrialization, urbanism and consumerism, musical comedy was all of these – industrial in its making, urban in its themes and in terms of its imagined audience constituency, and consumerist by virtue of its marketing strategies and its particular appeal to contemporary notions of consumer practice. In an age of rapidly developing political democratization, it made strong appeals to a 'mass' identity which it formulated as being young, canny, self-regarding (although generally dispensing buckets of goodwill to others) and, at its best and most efficient, female. For a fast, new times world, this was a vital, energetic culture which both utilized modern processes in its making and reproduced the modern world in its most compelling disguises – as an all-pervading spectacle, an all-accommodating pleasure and an all-encompassing harmony. In short, the modern world was the essential context and referent of musical comedy. It provided not just the material basis for its production, but also the complex subject position in which the text of musical comedy placed itself. It was with modernity, then, that musical comedy became so characteristically *fin de siècle* and it is for this reason that this chapter is devoted to an articulation of the modernizing and modernist dimensions of musical comedy. These were fundamental to its formal constitution and as the key determinants of its representational and signifying practices.

The development of musical comedy as a new form

The great age of musical comedy in Britain ran from the mid-1890s to just before the Great War when revue became the new, albeit temporary, ascendancy, challenging the supremacy that musical comedy had enjoyed for over twenty-five years. This culture was a product of both the end of Victoria's reign and the beginning of a new century. Embodying many of the essential and often contradictory characteristics of that watershed period, musical comedy was a *fin de siècle* affair, retreatist in some ways and certainly escaping into romance and fantasy.

At the same time, and in sharp contrast to many other cultures of the day, it embraced dynamic cultural change and technical innovation. It was a 'modern' culture in its characteristic attitudes towards the idea of the modern and in terms of its material and aesthetic construction. At a time of steeply rising disposable income, George Edwardes, usually attributed with having invented musical comedy on the West End stage, exploited the market for a high-class, progressive and innovative show that had strong, commercial production values. Thus musical comedy positioned a large, all-singing, all-dancing cast around stage settings that were ostentatiously imagined as modern spectacle. It performed to a sitting, comparatively restrained and markedly non-smoking clientele. The performance itself was a fully-fledged show rather than a variety bill, the musical comedy being a single scripted play. This also implied levels of audience compliance higher than the music hall format with its series of acts.

The embracing of modernity was apparent in the emergence of the new kind of show from its Victorian theatre background. Musical comedy was both a hybrid affair, suggestive here of modernity's capacity for assimilation, and a 'formula' that articulated with the standardizing, bureaucratizing dynamics of the modern.[5] It was also determinedly innovative. An entertainment designed to be fit for the modern world, it made a strong and highly successful appeal to notions of a mainstream fashionability. Although it borrowed many of its comic elements and musical ideas from more traditional music theatres, it took great pains to present itself as distinct, an advance on these forms that implied the growing sophistication and technical superiority of the modern world. Sometimes it went further, presenting itself as a complete fracture, a literally new form that owed nothing at all to tradition.

The fashionability discourse, and its 'progress' counterpart, characterized publicity and commentary on musical comedy, obscuring its links with older, declining forms. There were, for example, strong connections between music hall and musical comedy. Certainly in its early days, the success of musical comedy depended to some extent on the popularity of interpolated music hall routines and it was quite common for individual performers, attracted by the higher salaries, to make the transition from one to the other. Arthur Roberts, Ada Reeve and Connie Ediss were among the many performers who made the move from the halls to the theatre. Taking the reverse route was less common but certainly not unknown. In the later days of music hall, when it had become considerably modernized itself, and sanitized, it was quite possible for as aristocratic a theatrical couple as Ellaline Terris and Seymour Hicks, one-time romantic leads of the musical comedy stage, to perform music hall without too much sense of strangeness.[6] Similarly, individual songs sometimes migrated from music hall to musical comedy, and vice versa. Comic business was often imported from the music hall, particularly where a show was thought to be flagging. Indeed, it has been suggested by at least one old musical comedy performer that the assimilation of music hall humour produced the decisively English strain of musical comedy, as distinct from the American, French or German varieties.[7] In the authorized versions of musical comedy, however, these close inter-actions either disappeared altogether or featured as the exceptional travel that implied the distance more conventionally maintained between the two theatres and their distinct implied audiences. For all the increasingly common ground and mutuality, musical comedy was specifically designed *against* music hall, as a sophisticated alternative for contemporary audiences.

There was an even wider distance placed between musical comedy and operetta, or light opera, although, as with music hall, musical com-edy had strong, even familial, relations here. John Hollingshead, who took over the Gaiety in 1868 and ran it until 1885, was much in compe-tition with D'Oyly Carte and Gilbert and Sullivan. He regularly staged opera bouffe and operetta and brought 'the pick of Continental' com-posers to London, including Offenbach, Hervé, Lecocq and Jonas.[8] Similarly, before he became Hollingshead's partner at the Gaiety, George Edwardes was much involved in operetta. He had been D'Oyly Carte's right-hand man at the Savoy. Both the inventor of Gaiety burlesque and the 'Guv'nor' of musical comedy were thus steeped in light opera and it is hardly surprising that there were strong connections between the two forms – musical borrowings, exchanges of comic business, obvious in the migration of *japanoiserie*, for instance, and, again, the transference of personnel. For all these connections, however, musical comedy was marketed as being quite distinct from operetta. It was perceived as being less 'earnest', and, again, more concerned with contemporaneity.[9] While operetta was typically characterized by a turn for historical romanticism, musical comedy in England maintained its emphatic focus on modernity and presented itself as being self-consciously up-to-date. Its themes were modern and it dramatized these in a modern ver-nacular dialogue. It is worth emphasizing here that musical comedy was a play with music. It was not sung theatre, but a narrative interpolated with songs, much like the modern musical in this respect, and it demanded more natural styles of performance than light opera. One corollary to this relative informality was that less technique was demanded of the singers. What was produced was a much more vernacular performance. Many of the most popular performers of musical comedy could sing and entertain, but they were not generally thought of as classical musicians. This was crucial to the contemporary styling of musical comedy and to its status as popular culture.

Like most 'mass' culture, musical comedy made its most overt appeals to a clientele constructed as the fashionable and the contemporary, rather than to a middle class. But it was, in all sorts of ways, a bourgeois culture. It was popular among both the more traditional middle class who discovered a new enthusiasm for theatregoing in the late nineteenth century and with a 'broadly popular audience'.[10] This latter included the growing constituency of young men and women who worked at the boundaries of conventional class divisions in commerce and retailing. Far from conforming to stereotypes of responsible thrift, self-help and serious-minded Protestantism, this wide social grouping, in middle-class family mode as in its petty-bourgeois variety, was consumerist in the modern sense. Jose Harris points out that they were 'wholly unlike their French counterparts ... [They] sought money in order to spend it ... All contemporary observers agreed that the ethic of conspicuous consumption had soared to a crescendo by the 1900s.'[11] The main point about the overemphasized distinctions separating musical hall and operetta is that they functioned in relation to consumerism and the consumer classes in a number of important ways. First, they operated as an important marketing device helping to name and clarify the specific identity of musical comedy in a diverse entertainment environment that was becoming increasingly competitive. They also implicitly served to distinguish musical comedy from snobbish and 'aristocratic' culture on the one hand, and 'inferior' working-class entertainment on the other. However complex the real relations between these cultural forms might have been, this shorthand, in conjunction with a whole range of other signifiers, had the important function of confirming the musical comedy audience in its place and assuring it of its status as the clients of a new age of consumption.

The relationship with burlesque, however, was formulated in rather different ways, largely because burlesque's relationship with musical comedy was simply too strong to be ignored. The Gaiety theatre, first home of musical comedy, had also once been the home of burlesque. Its audiences, now gripped by new musical comedy, were very much linked to the audiences that had applauded burlesque. In its Gaiety form, burlesque reacted against operetta much as musical comedy did. Typically, it was a comic parody of 'high' culture interpolated with songs, dance routines and comic business. It involved mock poetics, much rhyming and word play. In the 'jolly' form, most favoured by the early generation of Gaiety theatre audiences, this kind of musical theatre was based on 'an old story or chapter of history' treated with humour and made 'grotesque'.[12] Something of an intervention positioned between Gilbert and Sullivan and music hall, just as musical comedy was, burlesque had to be recognized in some way as the progenitor it was. It was for this reason that, in most accounts, musical comedy appeared not as the modern replacement of burlesque, but as the improved version in a progressivist historiography that had obvious connections with other, and very much more prestigious, liberal versions of evolutionism.

Musical comedy knowingly exploited itself as a commercial and progressive commodity, especially in its marketing and promotion and the implied historiography that accompanied these. Here George Edwardes figured as the visionary, arriving to continue where John Hollingshead left off, breathing life into a fading popular tradition. On the basis of a string of burlesque successes between 1885 and 1890, including *Little Jack Sheppard, Faust up-to-Date, Carmen up-to-Date* and *Cinder-Ellen up too Late*, he was generally attributed with modernizing the form. Burlesque comedy became more 'spicy', its song and dance more contemporary with dialogue, moving away from the old mock rhythms and rhymes. Again, in the authorized version Edwardes was also credited with deploying new production standards, making staging even more spectacular and insisting on modern and glamorous costumes, for the Gaiety chorus as well as the lead actors. Indeed, the Gaiety girls became key figures in this progress history. Losing the old theatrical tights that had so scandalized Victorian sensibilities, they became subject to a thorough professionalizing programme. Receiving expert training in singing, elocution and fencing and, finally, being squeezed into the most expensive of modern fashions, they reappeared on the West End stage transformed into the high class and elegant. Refined, but with an edge, in this form they were to figure shortly as new century icons of the West End stage. Within a few years, they signified 'to London precisely what the Ziegfeld Girls of a later generation would be to Broadway'.[13] Under Edwardes, then, what Ganzl has called the 'new burlesque' *evolved* into a more contemporary kind of theatre.[14]

Whatever the simplifications of that history, it is easy to see its importance. These self-promoting versions of theatre history enabled musical comedy to be formulated simultaneously, and in a very short space of time, as both iconoclastic rebel and progressive heir. Musical comedy was both 'making it new' and developing the old traditions. Both dimensions were important to its visibility and status. They help to explain why musical comedy quickly became the most talked about and patronized musical theatre since Gilbert and Sullivan. By 1894 Edwardes had two great commercial successes on his hands, *A Gaiety Girl* and *The Shop Girl*. The former played a total of 413 performances on its first West End run. By 1894 the show was on tour playing to audiences in New York, Boston, Washington, Brooklyn, Pittsburgh, St Louis, Chicago, Milwaukee and San Francisco. With *In Town* (1892), a prototype musical comedy, and *The Shop Girl* it was taken to Australia where it played in Melbourne and Sidney. After touring for a number of years, it returned to London for a second shorter run at Daly's in 1899. *The Shop Girl* played 546 performances at the Gaiety, before a disappointing run in New York, which took exception to the play, some have said because of political tensions at the time between Britain and the US over Venezuela.[15] Whatever the reason, it was well received in South Africa and Australia, and there was a West End revival in 1920, which played a further 327 performances before closing in 1921. With these two shows what Ellaline Terris described in her memoirs as the 'Edwardian Age' was very much underway.[16]

By 1895, just two years after its first fully-fledged appearance, musical comedy was in the ascendancy. It had very little to fear from the Savoy entertainment, which by the end of the nineteenth century appeared tame, *passé* and distinctly Victorian:

> There's a class of play much patronized, it's frequently the rage
> And it's often unintentionally humorous,
> For of all those incongruities displayed upon the stage
> Those revealed in comic opera are most numerous
> All the stories are perplexing, and the book is often 'rot'
> But the artistes seldom speak it, since as frequently as not
> They are too intent on gagging to develop any plot
> It's always done that way in comic opera.[17]

Burlesque fared differently, but no better. With the rise of musical comedy it was necessarily pushed into absolute redundancy as the prototype form. The feel-good sensibility of musical comedy struck a strong chord with *fin de siècle* audiences and, by the early 1900s, it was, without question, the dominating theatre of the West End. Edwardes' success continued at the old Gaiety with *A Runaway Girl*, *The Messenger Boy* (1900) and *The Toreador* (1901), *Toreador* being the last show produced before the theatre was demolished for a road-widening scheme. But there were other producers now eager to take on musical comedy in what became a highly developed culture industry context. By 1920 musical comedy had appeared all over the West End, at Daly's, the Lyric, the Apollo, the Criterion, the Shaftesbury, the Prince of Wales, the Adelphi, the Vaudeville, Wyndham's, His Majesty's, Hicks's and the Aldwych. Managers such as Charles Wyndham, Frank Curzon, Tom B. Davis, Oscar Asche, Alfred Butt, Charles Frohman and Robert Courtneidge had spectacular successes with the form, producing some of the most popular shows of the period. The top three shows in terms of length of initial West End run – *A Chinese Honeymoon* (1901), *The Arcadians* and *Chu Chin Chow* – came not from Edwardes, but from Curzon, Courtneidge and Asche, respectively. For all this spread, musical comedy remained most closely identified with Edwardes in subsequent theatre history. He was generally acknowledged as the 'inventor' of musical comedy and the central participant in its progressive development.

Industrial entertainment – musical comedy as modern commodity

The development of musical comedy, at both the Gaiety and, even more so, at Edwardes' other London theatre, Daly's, can be characterized as modern in a number of other ways.[18] It was first a matter of increasing spectacle and extravagance in an age whose identity was being decisively characterized in precisely the same terms – as show, performance and spectacle. *An Artist's Model* produced at Daly's in 1896 was perhaps the first musical show to establish lavishness as a key marker. Its second act was a landmark in rising production standards, with the ballroom set alone costing a then incredible £2,500 to build. *The Geisha*, with its extraordinary staging of 'Japan', raised the stakes even higher. For some critics the spectacle element of this show was enough by itself to ensure success. The *Telegraph* critic claimed that *The Geisha* was 'worth seeing for its stage pictures alone'.[19] All West End musical comedies thereafter were expected to be progressively more spectacular, with the string of hits at Daly's – *San Toy, A Greek Slave* (1898), *A Country Girl, The Cingalee* (1904), *The Little Michus* (1905), *The Merry Widow* (1907) and *The Dollar Princess* (1909) – taking the lead. Often the rising stakes involved ever more extravagant costuming, a feature that has been well documented in musical theatre history. Ganzl's account of *The Pearl Girl* conveys a strong impression of the lengths gone to in the registration of glamour and high fashion:

> The green and sulphur hunting ensembles of the opening scene
> (Phillips & Son, 58 Regent Street) were highlighted by the white
> piqué riding habit worn by Joan Hay – the heart of a costume hailed
> by *Play Pictorial* as 'a masterpiece'. The mannequins of the 'Maison
> Palmyra' dripped with pearls from the house of Tecla over dresses
> from Martial Armand & Cie (of Place Vendôme and 125 Bond Street),
> while Marjorie Maxwell as the genuine Madame Alvarez featured a
> huge leopardskin muff and a crested hat in a black and white outfit
> from Maison Lewis of Regent Street [Illustration 2]. The outdoor
> scene at 'Hurlelagh' gave the cue for a perfect torrent of fashionable
> clothes: Cicely Courtneidge in white satin and gemstones; Iris Hooey
> in a lovely confection of white brocade and lace striped and tied in
> orange, a crossover skirt with an accordion-pleated tunic and sleeves,
> topped by white osprey feathers on a perky black hat and a huge
> string of pearls; Dorothea Temple in green satin and black lace orna-
> mented with jet; and all the men in polo gear specially made by
> Turnball and Asser of Jermyn Street. The costume credits ran on and
> on – Reville and Rossiter of Hanover Square, Davies, Jamieson &
> Wood of Maddox Street, Gamba for shoes, Clarkson for wigs, Salter
> and Sons of Aldershot for the polo sticks.[20]

Rappaport has theorized such fashion spectacles as 'sites of consumption' and partly in terms of late nineteenth- and early twenty-century
versions of consumer psychology. She sees contemporary dramatists,
critics and retailers as being united in their assumptions about women,
'or at least a feminized public', and the way it bought goods and was
entertained. It was commonly thought, and perhaps still is, that 'consumer desires' would be stimulated by 'women's visual pleasure' and
that such pleasure was very much triggered by the desire to possess. The
extravagant parade of clothes fashion on the stage, then, would both
attract 'a feminized public' and send it out shopping.[21]

No doubt this kind of crude thinking was common enough among
entrepreneurs from the worlds of fashion, retail and theatre, but it is
important to realize that the spectacle of musical comedy often went far
outside the realms of consumer desires. Theatrical costume might be
attractive and approximate to what could be bought in a West End store,
but equally it was often extreme, outlandish, exotic and thus beyond
even the wildest of retail dreams. Moreover, musical comedy spectacle
took many forms other than costume display. It included the staging of

Illustration 2 'Marjorie Maxwell as the genuine Madame Alvarez featured a huge leopard skin muff' (*The Pearl Girl*)

utopias, other cultures, horse racing, country estates, other planets and an earthquake at the end of act 2 in *The Mousmé* (1911), where Robert Courtneidge staged the destruction of Tokyo (Illustration 3). According to Ganzl, this single effect, in a show that almost ruined Courtneidge financially, was 'talked about by playgoers decades later'.[22] Clearly, this

Illustration 3   Mr Robert Courtneidge's staging of the destruction of Tokyo by earthquake (*The Mousmé*)

imperative to amaze involved something other than subliminal promotion and popular psychology about the 'female mind'.

Primarily the role of spectacle in musical comedy was to confirm its status as a modern culture and to celebrate modernity's astonishing capacity for reproduction and assimilation. In part, this was a matter of engaging with the modern in material ways. As well as being compelled to represent modernity, musical comedy was a physical *product* of the modern, one that utilized a wide range of contemporary skills and technologies. Not only disposed towards the modern in narrative terms, it was also modern both in terms of how it was made and organized and in its characteristic production values and styles. Modern technology was at the service of this imperative. *The Earl and the Girl*, for instance, contained a scene in which eight girls were lowered onto the stage on swings wreathed in garlands of electric light and swung out into the audience by chorus boys. It cost the then fabulous sum of £1,000 to stage this single effect. In another café scene from the same show, girls danced on a tabletop in shoes designed to make an electrical connection. This cost £1,200 to develop, but proved too unreliable to use. With 'the show itself' becoming 'the star', state-of-the-art technology characterized the development of musical comedy spectacle and underlined its teleological status as an advanced form.[23] Thus *Chu Chin Chow*, a show once thought to be superlative in its effects, was exalted in *The Times* precisely as a product of the modern. Using terminology more usually reserved for 'high' culture, the reviewer found in this curious pantomimic show 'fantastic, polyphonic, polychromatic Orientalism... everything is by turns and nothing long – a kaleidoscopic series of scenes now romantic, now realistic, now Futurist or Vorticist but always beautiful'.[24]

Musical comedy was a modern commodity, and proud of its status as such. It was analogous in its construction to the generality of classic modern systems of production. Whatever creativity can be associated with writing and composing these shows, musical comedy was not essentially individualist in terms of how it was made but, rather, the result of collective effort. There were teams of writers, lyricists and composers. Thus *The Times* review of 1908 sees *The Honourable Phil* as a 'broth' concocted by 'a good many cooks', with the implication that this has spoiled things.[25] Once the show was written, songs and scenes, from a variety of sources, would be interpolated, which meant that the number of people involved in the authorship of a single show could be multiplied. Labour was divided into specialist roles, even at this compositional stage, among workers who produced quickly and tried to keep abreast of popular taste and fashion. Originality and innovation certainly had great value under such a system but not exclusive value. It was also important to establish the typicality of the musical comedy show. Plots, comic business, dance routines, melodies, and so on very quickly became regularized. As early as 1899, a reviewer for the *Illustrated Sporting and Dramatic News* was complaining that it seemed 'difficult in any one musical comedy to get away from the musical comedies which have preceded it'.[26] A musical comedy could be seen as something bolted together from a number of standard constituent parts, like the product of an industrial conveyor belt. Success was a matter of striking the right balance between innovation and familiarity. If things went too far either way the result could be problematic, but the strongest critical spleen was reserved for the shows that had nothing new to offer. The critic of the *Illustrated London News*, for instance, writing in 1905, was one of many complaining about the predictability of the shows: 'the Gaiety, in piece after piece, offers a pert Cockney story which relates the eccentric doings of a group of Cook's tourists and winds up in some Continental-costume ball'.[27]

These conditions continued, only more so, once the show was in production. Quite apart from the obvious continuation of teamwork, shows on the road were subject to rigorous review systems. Tried out, or quality assured, often in the provinces, the shows were then adjusted, sometimes fundamentally, as the run went on. They may have dealt in fantasy, but it is not helpful to understand these shows in terms of the mystifying 'aura' sometimes attributed to high art. They were put together along Fordist lines in ways that often seemed to appropriate the spirit of modern capitalism. Musical comedy was unashamedly enterprising and was quite literally corporate in some respects. Expensive productions were routinely floated on the open share market just as a joint-stock company would be. By the mid-1890s the Gaiety was itself a joint-stock company, with Edwardes as managing director, Walter Pallant from the Stock exchange in the Chair and no less a figure than Alfred de Rothschild as principal shareholder.[28] Rothschild, incidentally, was also called on to negotiate new contracts with the fiery Marie Tempest, the darling of Daly's audience, a task that George Edwardes was apparently not keen to undertake himself. In all these ways, and others, musical comedy was an 'industrial' and commercially developed cultural form. 'Gay', 'charming' and 'pretty' were the terms in which it was often praised, suggesting a camp and traditionally feminized culture, but it is clear that musical comedy in the making was very much more hard-edged. Of course, these production characteristics were not the exclusive preserve of musical comedy. They accompanied the development of other cultural forms and would have been present in earlier musical theatre to one degree or another. In 'burlesque, music hall and lyric opera ... theatres became analogous to the industrialized factory, growing increasingly specialized in what they offered'.[29] But it is certain that with musical comedy there was acceleration in all departments. The shows were on a bigger scale, there were more of them, they were more professionalized and they made more money. In a real sense, they were global. *The Geisha* with its bizarre notions of racial otherness had phenomenal overseas success in France and America and the Empire, but also in more unexpected places – South America, Hungary, Italy, Spain, France, Latvia, Switzerland, Russia, Czechoslovakia and Scandinavia.

A further way in which it is possible to characterize the modernity of musical comedy is in terms of its capacity for assimilation, a product in some ways of the imperative to produce 'new' shows, but also part of a globalizing instinct and again, suggestive of the theatre's reproductive powers. This was reflected in part in the genre assimilation of musical comedy, so that there were musical comedy versions of pantomime (in *Chu Chin Chow*), of the Christmas fairy play (in *Bluebell in Fairyland*) and, above all, of operetta (in *The Merry Widow*, for example). The same kind of dynamic was also apparent in the extraordinary cultural/geographical appropriations of musical comedy. The London-based, shop girl locus was periodically returned to throughout the period, but musical comedy after 1895 most typically became a matter of 'doing' other cultures. The musical comedy treatment was applied to classical cultures, as in *A Greek Slave* or, more usually, to the foreign and exotic. *A Runaway Girl* was one of the first musical comedies to capitalize on exoticism, reproducing a wild Corsica in its first act and a seductive Venice in its second. Orientalism in musical comedy began with *The Geisha* and *The Belle of Cairo* and continued, with variations, through such shows as *San Toy, The Messenger Boy* (partly set in Egypt), *A Chinese Honeymoon, The Blue Moon, The Cingalee, The Mousmé* or *The Maids of Japan* and *Chu Chin Chow*. West End musical comedy also staged Holland, Denmark, the Hispanic Caribbean, France, Austria, Germany, America, Canada, Spain and, even, in *The Silver Slipper* (1901), the planet Venus. It might be thought that this enterprising and adventurous spirit marked a shift in musical comedy's orientation towards the modern, but in fact often only confirmed things in this respect. This handling of other cultures was a very specific treatment, which meant not only that 'doing Japan', for instance, involved wild stereotyping and the crudest of metonymical relations, but also that the meeting of the 'foreign' in Indian, Ceylon and Burma invariably involved more permutations on the familiar collision of modernity and tradition. Needless to say, it was very much the modern that was represented as the superior, advanced and progressive culture. The further implications of these stagings are discussed in a later chapter. For the moment, it needs to be stressed that for all the variety of musical comedy settings, there was a strong consistency in terms of treatment. In this way modernity remained at the forefront of many musical comedy narratives, irrespective of setting.

The success of musical comedy is often explained in musical theatre history not as a dynamic commercial intervention, but in terms of a personnel usually clustered around Edwardes, and it was the case that Edwardes did build a team of impressive talent. Lionel Monckton and Ivan Caryll, who first collaborated in *The Shop Girl*, became, along with Leslie Stuart and Howard Talbot, the most important musical theatre composers. The Gaiety script writing team included the prolific James T. Tanner as well as the gifted Jimmy Davies, author of *A Gaiety Girl*. A number of lyricists became firmly associated with Edwardes and the Gaiety, including Harry Greenbank, who died young in 1899 from consumption, his brother Percy, the ubiquitous Adrian Ross and Paul Rubens. In terms of cast, Edwardes had put together an initial Gaiety ensemble that set the standards for future enterprises: Seymour Hicks and Ellaline Terriss (romantic leads) were paired for the first time in *The Shop Girl*. George Grossmith Jr was established early on in his 'masher' roles. Ada Reeve provided the music hall charm and bite and 'Teddy' Payne became a favourite comedian. To cap it all there were the fabulous Gaiety girls, with an initial line-up that included Topsy Sinden and Violet Monckton and later featured Constance Collier and Fannie Ward. As Ganzl points out, the Gaiety girls had always been crowd-pullers, even in the burlesque days, but now they became something rather more 'as the gaze of fashionable London fixed itself on them'.[30] These figures were clearly vital to the success of musical comedy, but ultimately its astonishing popularity involved a whole range of factors besides the talents of its makers and performers. To put it simply, it was 'of its times', at least for the cultural centre that it was attempting to appeal to and, indeed, formulate. It was bright and breezy. Audiences could enjoy the frivolous and the faintly risqué without compromising their respectability. And they could invariably depend on the musical comedy standard, a standard so defined that it could be replicated in other theatres, around the country and on tour overseas. Above all, at a time when many intellectuals were seeing a West in decline, the collapse of the progressive dynamic once thought to be a universal of modern history, musical comedy demonstrated otherwise. Like department stores, modern travel, exploration, convenience foods, sporting achievement and a host of other manifestations of contemporary life, musical comedy showed that the intellectuals had got it badly wrong – that modernity, far from being in a state of decadent collapse, had lost none of its awesome power. The new theatre was very much more than 'just entertainment' in this respect. It showed how a modern, 'civilized' entertainment industry could establish its capacity to charm and amaze, deliver fun efficiently and at good value for money and reconcile all those things with making substantial profits. In these ways it represented the modern most completely and could legitimately claim status as a representative form of modern capitalism.

Musical comedy as modernism

The idea of a modernity characterized by industrialization, commercial sophistication and technological innovation is, of course, entirely familiar. Most would accept that whatever else the modern might be, it includes these processes. The theorization of the more subjective experience of modernity, 'the forms of consciousness' accompanying the development of the modern world, is much more problematic.

The effects of the rational reorganizing of the world on its subjects has been both culturally reproduced and systematically theorized in a huge variety of conflicting, competing and often internally contradictory ways. Modernity has been understood as animated/dull, multiform/uniform, individualist/conformist, radical/conservative, and so on. Thus, in an interesting account of the 'English subjects of modernity', Alan O'Shea, heavily influenced by Berman, finds convincing evidence of 'optimism' as a key response to 'the early twentieth century – the belief that the emancipatory elements of the "project" of modernity were achievable through both political and technological means'.[31] He cites electricity, for instance, as an advance understood not only in terms of industrial efficiency, but 'as transforming communications so radically as to remove all obstacles to human unity and even invested with magical healing powers'.[32] At the same time, however, O'Shea recognizes a contradictory counterpart to this version of the modern, operating at precisely the same historical time and largely in response to the same dynamics and conditions. Here a more fragmented Baudelairean view of things pervades, where the modern consciousness experiences life not as whole and purposeful but as fragmented, fleeting and contingent. Modernisms, as readings of the modern condition, are often subject to internal ambiguities in this way. They are also always formally constituted and in this respect never as close to real lived experience as they might claim.[33] Important modernisms of the late nineteenth and early twentieth centuries, for instance, understood the modern as a feminized and feminizing culture, which was interpreted in terms of *both* liberal progress and decadent regression. At the same time, there were highly masculinized versions of contemporaneity. These similarly were read as *both* forward-looking/progressive and retrospective/conservative. Whatever values might be attached to these modernisms, there is no way of knowing which, if any, approximate to a 'typical' modern experience, because there is no such single experience. All modernisms are necessarily interpretative and will both engage with and take position on and as ideology, often in complex and difficult ways.[34]

The starting point for understanding musical comedy as a modern*ism*, as opposed to a modern product, must be its most obvious and defining characteristic: its celebration of the modern as pleasure, excitement and vitality. Initially at least, the almost entirely unqualified nature of this quality must make musical comedy seem unusually uncomplicated as a modernism. An incredibly welcoming disposition is seen everywhere in musical comedy. The images it exploited were typically chosen because they were representative of new technologies and what was constructed as a new *Zeitgeist*. The telephone, the Kodak camera, the aeroplane, film, typewriters, the lift, revolving doors, department stores, motor cars – innovations such as these took on iconic status in this new theatre. The idea of technological change was frequently used to establish the keynote of things. *The Arcadians*, for instance, the quintessential Edwardian musical comedy, opens with an 'airship' descending into a Utopia previously untouched by modernity. It goes on to dramatize the relations between the timeless idyll and the new. Shows like *The Shop Girl*, *The Girl from Kays*, *The Girl Behind the Counter* (1906) and *Our Miss Gibbs* begin with what was once taken to be the busy glamour of the new department store, complete with '*lifts up and down*' to represent '*time-saving luxury*' as the stage directions of *Our Miss Gibbs* have it.[35] Similarly, *The Girl on the Film* (from *Filmzauber*) (1913) begins in the offices of a busy filmmaker and the opening routine celebrates the 'bright biograph picture screen' and 'cinemagic'.[36] Scene 2 of *The Schoolgirl* opens in a new Stock Exchange amid telephones, 'tickers' and typewriters. The opening song is a celebration of 'new times' culture:

> The art of stockbroking-de-luxe,
> With its air of refinement and polish,
> Is brought to a pitch
> Of modernity which
> Must needs old-fashioned methods abolish.[37]

Staging of this kind, often at the outset of a show, implied an embracing of modernity – of energy, excitement and inventiveness. Such an orientation towards the modern did not end with the opening scenario however. It was, as we have seen, sustained in costume design, and styles of speech became modernized in musical comedy. The working-class idiom of music hall and the camp proprieties of the mainstream, late Victorian stage were both displaced by a more relaxed style of speaking, intended to be suggestive of fashionable modern society.

Above all the text of musical comedy frequently allegorized the nature and impact of modernity in its narratives. The essential story of musical comedy involved placing old against new, tradition against innovation and exploiting the subsequent entanglement. In *Floradora* old landed aristocracy meets new money in a version of the dynamic that recurs in such shows as *The Shop Girl* and *The Merry Widow*. Sometimes the contrasting pattern was gendered, as in *A Gaiety Girl*, which places a group of traditional aristocratic woman against a group of modern musical comedy actresses. Sometimes it was both racialized and gendered.

The Geisha, for instance, positions 'native' girls from a 'primitive' culture against wealthy fashionable English women.

Technological wizardry was also implicated at this narratological level. In *The Girl from Up There* (1901), for example, the work of old-time magic is undone by the creative powers of Colonel Marcelus Whizzle, inventor of the hydraulic corkscrew, the self-washing shirt and 'a lightning machine'.[38] There were endless permutations to this basic set-up, but the outcome was invariably the same – a victory for modernity, or at least a reconciliation which strongly accommodated notions of progress and development. Significantly, the very 'first' West End musical comedy turned precisely on a narrative that exploited the modern/tradition dichotomy in very marked and obvious ways, although before seeing how it did so it might be helpful to comment on the theatre history issue controversy over which show *was* the 'first' musical comedy.

Theatre history has engaged in some debate over which of the early 1890s productions can lay legitimate claim to being the first 'authentic' West End musical comedy. Some aspects of this debate throw light on why and how the modern/tradition dynamic of musical comedy, and the dependency of this dynamic on narrative, is so important, because establishing the first invariably amounts to establishing the nature of the genre. It is, therefore, significant that of the three candidates for the status of first West End musical comedy – *In Town*, *A Gaiety Girl* and *The Shop Girl* – the claims of the first, produced by Edwardes, but at the Prince of Wales, are usually regarded as being least impressive because of failings in its narrative.[39] Here once more the connection between narrative and the modern status of musical comedy is confirmed. *In Town* was, in many ways, a decisive break with burlesque and an important intermediary on the road to the fully-fledged musical comedy product, but its story was wildly underdeveloped, providing not much more than a setting for Arthur Robert's comic routines. This was enough, in the view of most commentators, to undermine its claim to be the first musical comedy. It was, for all the modern fashions paraded on stage, a series of 'turns' dressed up as a plot, 'a variety entertainment in disguise', according to *The Era*.[40] The claims of the next two productions from Edwardes, however, *A Gaiety Girl* and *The Shop Girl*, are usually thought of as being very much more substantial and it is these that have had to compete most fiercely for the title of first 'real', and 'British', West End musical comedy. Some commentators have argued for the latter, finding in this show, again, the decisive break with tradition, 'the introduction of musical comedy … [and a] veering away from the operettas of Gilbert and Sullivan'.[41] Most, however, would place *A Gaiety Girl* as the serious innovator and usually again, the decisive factor has to do with narrative and modern styling.

Sidney Jones' score for the show has never been admired in terms of its originality. It was lively enough, but derivative as most musical comedies were in this respect. What has been thought new about *A Gaiety Girl*, however, is the levels of integration between Harry Greenbank's song lyrics and the play narrative and, above all, the coherency of the comedy script written by 'Owen Hall'. Certainly in its day, it was this play, with its relatively 'natural' dialogue and topical, risqué jokes, that woke up the critics, and the censors, to the idea that something new might be happening on the West End stage. *The Times* reported on 'a comic opera of a somewhat advanced type' where 'licence is pushed further than has ever before been attempted in our day'.[42] *The Era* had more difficulty in distinguishing precisely what this 'sometimes sentimental drama, sometimes comedy and sometimes downright variety show' really was, but recognized the dialogue as being 'brilliant enough and satirical enough for a comedy of modern life', as, indeed, it often was:[43]

> *Gladys Stourton*: I would love to go far away and fight the Zulus and Matabeles. I would love to fight for my country.
> *Harry Fitzwarren*: You mean you would love to fight for *their* country.[44]

A Gaiety Girl was an outspoken show, but more than that it was crucial to the definition of 'gaiety' as an idea. If at one time the word had simply designated a lively crowd roaring their approval of Nelly Farren's legs hugged in 'fleshings', 'gaiety', with Edwardes' new production values and Davis's intervention, now took on altered and fuller dimensions which had much wider cultural resonance. The old voyeurism was still there, but in a new designer style, and was accompanied by a politicized spirit, a *joie de vivre* expressed as a *fin de siècle* antidote to conservative values.

In Davis's groundbreaking play, the disposition for modernity came to life not just in periodic jokes made at the expense of the religious, legal and military establishment, but through the main plot dynamic of the piece, which became a staple of early musical comedy. This turned on a sustained confrontation between vibrant modernity and outmoded tradition, represented in *A Gaiety Girl* by a group of young actresses on the one hand, and a group of snobbish, female aristocrats on the other. They meet initially at a military barracks where the aristocrats, chaperoned by Lady Virginia Forest, are looking for husbands. The Gaiety chorus is comprised of 'bright young things' from town invited to lunch by Major Barclay. For Lady Virginia, however, these women are highly problematic – not just socially inferior and from a stigmatized profession, but also a positive impediment to her matchmaking ambitions. 'Actresses,' she says, 'stand terribly in the way of the best families.'[45] On first being introduced by her nephew, Charley, to Alma, the Gaiety girl he will fall for, Lady Virginia sinks despondently into a chair. Alma's spirited response shows no sign of embarrassment or deferment: 'Your aunt seems delighted with the introduction Charley. Are the upper classes always as cordial as that?'[46] As the play develops, the two groups of women move even further apart, with Alma being accused of stealing a diamond comb by the end of the first act. However, the play becomes increasingly insistent on interrogating this difference. It points out parallels between the women, which, without exception, elevate the status of the Gaiety girls. When they are accused of being 'fast', for example, because they appear in bathing suits, they respond with a song that turns the criticism back against their aristocratic counterparts: 'a fellow with money you rush at / In a way that an actress would blush at.'[47] The rest of the play articulates a curious reversal, where the Gaiety girls take on the dimensions of aristocratic grace, as they appear 'like young Duchesses going into a drawing room'.[48] At the same time, the traditional aristocrats learn that gaiety is irresistible. 'High spirits might be vulgar,' as one of them points out, 'but for all that we mean to indulge in them.'[49] By the end of the play a complete *volte-face* has been accomplished. Old tradition and conventional wisdom have been displaced. The tired elites not only know this; they also learn to embrace new ways. Among the last lines of the play are those which give Lady Virginia's blessing to her nephew's forthcoming marriage. 'I'm glad you are going to marry a Gaiety girl after all, Charley,' she tells her nephew. 'In a year or two, she will be all the rage of society.'[50]

In this way *A Gaiety Girl* positioned 'gaiety', and the actress, at the very centre of an imagined bourgeois-bohemia. Its entirely appropriate Gaiety girl/aristocrat metonym announced musical comedy as *the* contemporary musical theatre of the late Victorian stage. With considerable boldness, Davis had taken the word which designated the essential musical comedy theatrical space, and the troupe of singer-dancers who were to take London by storm, and from its associations concocted the first 'real' musical comedy show. 'Gaiety' with Davis became an idea, an attitude taken towards the modern. Max Beerbohm knew this when he recognized the new Gaiety theatre as 'a temple' serving the idea of gaiety, 'that special and peculiar sort of gaiety with which we have always associated [musical comedy]'.[51] Just as 'decadence' was a key signifying concept for some intellectual communities of the 1890s, so 'gaiety' was to become something of a rallying point, but for a very much more mainstream cultural identity. If decadence was the defiance of languid individualism against the 'levelling' of contemporary life, the kind of gaiety involved in Davis's formulation produced something like the opposite: a carnivalesque indulgence in *joie de modernité*.

All these elements were combined in Davis's play. It was superficially iconoclastic, enough to delay its licence until the very last moment, but its central impulse was more inclusive. It staged modernity as all-accommodating fun and sent out invitations to join in. Those that declined were, by definition, old-fashioned, or bluestocking, and certainly redundant. The next Edwardes hit, *The Shop Girl*, with its department store setting, was perhaps more immediately recognizable as 'modern' in some ways, but in its dialogue, costume and staging, it followed in the footsteps of *A Gaiety Girl*. For *The Times* the 'picturesque treatment' of modernity in the one was replicated in the other. 'The whole scene' of *The Shop Girl* was 'entirely modern, like that of *A Gaiety Girl*, which appears for the time to have set the fashion'. In this review *The Shop Girl* became an 'imitation' of *A Gaiety Girl*, albeit a triumphant one, 'for all concerned'.[52]

Here, then, the classic narrative form of musical comedy was set and, although it became subject to many revisions and permutations, the broad collision of modern and tradition remained a staple. In some shows – *High Jinks* (1916) and *Our Miss Gibbs*, for instance – the narratives were less heavily penetrated by the modern as an idea, but still there remained the sense of a culture that was at ease with the times – and this despite the periodic returns to high fantasy in plays like *Bluebell in Fairyland* and to the indulgence of a highly developed Edwardian taste for rural idylls in plays like *A Country Girl*. The rural shows for all their romanticized staging of the 'country' were careful to reconcile old England with the new and to avoid staging any ideas that could be taken to construct modernity as a threat to the rural and its traditions. There were many crossover images – modern film actresses on countryside location stepping out with farmers' lads, for instance (in *The Girl on the Film*), or country girls moving to the city to achieve success on the new musical stage (in *A Country Girl*). At the same time, there were shows where modernity subsumed rural life by reproducing it. *The Quaker Girl* takes a simple, nonconformist girl from rural England and removes her to Paris. Here her simple clothes become the great fashion of the day. The Quaker girl reality is replaced by the Quaker look reproduced as *haute couture*.

There were some challenges to this upbeat registration of modern life. In Paul Rubens' *Miss Hook of Holland*, the song 'Harwich to Hook' has a verse that reflects concerns about the future of 'our mad Aeroplanet':

> We live in a terrible whirl
> We can't seem to move fast enough
> And soon we shall be
> Saved from crossing the sea
> Whenever the water is rough.
> For what with new Tunnels and Tubes,
> We shall never see sunshine and showers,
> We shall travel in shoals
> Like rabbits or moles,
> Through this mad Aeroplanet of ours.[53]

But such dissent for the standard musical comedy position was usually expressed in very much engaged and highly qualified ways. *High Jinks*, for example, begins with the usual images of modernity – fast cars, telephones and a professional world, here imaged by the doctor's office, rushed off its feet – except that, in this instance, the vitality and enthusiasm so characteristic of modernity in musical comedy seem to have been displaced by dislocation and nervous energy. This is a speeded-up, dehumanized world, a Chaplinesque version of modern times, albeit located in the middle-class office as opposed to the working-class factory. The 'High Jinks' of the title is the name given to a perfume discovered in the Himalayas, central to the plot because this discovery is the soporific that will benefit mankind by calming metropolitan *angst*. In this way the neurosis of the new will be worked on by the wisdom of tradition, except that before it can do so there must be a reformulation in modern terms. 'High Jinks' becomes marketed and packaged as 'a big business undertaking'. But far from transforming things, 'High Jinks', as its brand name suggests, is itself transformed in yet another testimony to the assimilative powers of modernity. Here any sense of musical comedy testing contemporary life becomes qualified by the ease with which modernity adapts and is self-regulating.

Floradora works similarly. This show, set on an island in the Philippines where, again, a natural commodity is subjected to modern marketing and distribution, is clearly concerned about the exploitative effects of modern commerce on more 'innocent' cultures and about its destructive effects on tradition. But the point about the corrupting modern here is that it is identified as being an aberration from the authentic modernizing dynamic, specifically connected with a greed and deceit that is racialized as American. *Floradora* is neither critical of the modern in itself nor disassociated from the idea of modernity. It is rather a question of getting the modern right and there are obvious racial and class allegiances implicated in the process – the legitimized modern man in the show is, ironically enough, an aristocrat, Lord Abercoed. Signifying a more organic, sensitive and humanizing modern way, he has a British or, to be more precise, British/Celtic identity. Cyrus Gilfrain, the villain of the piece, is a usurping, rather than a true, modern. Associated with all kinds of modern fakery and trickery from phrenology to the theme-park making of traditional landed estates, he is American.

The essential instinct of *Floradora*, as with almost all these shows, was identification with or, at the very least, management of the modern. Retreat was not a serious option. In this context, the show that seemed to position itself against modernity became the oddity confirming the strength of the standard association, sometimes in explicit ways. *The Honourable Phil* is highly suggestive here. Set on the remote island holiday resort of 'St Angelo', this get-away-from-it-all production bans all modern clothes. From the very beginning, as we have seen, modern dress, the 'top hat and frock coat of contemporary life', had been one of the hallmarks of musical comedy.[54] It is highly suggestive of a challenge, then, when traditional costume *has* to be worn in this play. The modern visitor who tries to smuggle in modern dress is fined 10,000 francs for breaking a twelfth-century law passed precisely 'to maintain the simplicity and primitive charm of the island'.[55] But although modernity seems to be ousted in this show, it remains the crucial underlying concept, the norm that entirely determines the terms of what was no more than a temporary, fool's day relaxation. Far from being the exception, a play like *The Honourable Phil* only demonstrated again the astonishing authority of contemporaneity over the musical comedy stage. The show's sense of itself as a riposte, quite apart from being entirely light and playful in tone, was an obvious acknowledgement of the unstoppable nature of the modern.

Even the most out-of-the-way places were circumscribed, and often invaded by, the modern. The typical Seymour Hicks production, for instance, exploited the glamour of traditional aristocratic society, and with its explicit gestures towards light opera was sometimes taken to be transgressive of the developing traditions. But Hicks' shows, for all their aspirations, remained musical comedies. Part of their status in that respect was the maintenance of the modern as the irresistible dynamic.

The Beauty of Bath, for example, is a play that romanticizes the high society life of Sir Timothy and Lady Bun and their twelve stunning daughters. Its location, however, is not the provincial Georgian city where aristocrats traditionally socialize, but London, a city adored in this show for its modernity. It is in this shrine to the modern that the socialite heroine of the play falls not for a member of her own class, but for an actor on the fashionable stage, and then for the sailor who is his look-alike. This play glamorizes and romanticizes the old landed elites, but presents this culture as one that must be responsive to modernization. Similarly Hicks' *The Gay Gordons* (1907) opens in a highly traditional, rural highland setting, but this too becomes infiltrated, this time by rich Americans who buy up the local castle in the standard manner. The modern young democrat of the play, who hates aristocratic privilege, finds herself falling for a soldier who turns out to be no less than the heir to the Meltrose estates. Here, then, old and new aristocracies merge in yet another comfortable image of reconciliation between tradition and the new times.

In all these ways and more the idea of the modern penetrated the narrative of musical comedy. Its predilection for all things contemporary and dismissal of what was constructed as stuffy and old-fashioned must have been as familiar and expected a component of the overall effect as the comic routines, the waltzes, the rags-to-riches stories, the conventional love plot and the equally conventional marriage ending. Certainly, this disposition was escapist in most ways. It involved sentimentality, wild over-simplifications and grotesque distortions. But it was escapism of a particular kind, where the imperative was not to retreat in tradition or fantasy *per se*, but rather to engage with a sanitized version of the new. It was clearly a romanticizing rather than a realist culture, but again romantic in a particular way. It had nothing in common with the retrospection and 'organic' cultural orientation of more conventional highbrow romanticism of this period. There was little or nothing to link musical comedy with William Morris and the craft movement, pre-Raphaelitism or the Celtic Twilight. On the contrary, musical comedy appeared to have had few longings at all for the past and no serious worries about the present.

'Sham. Nothing but sham' – *The Arcadians* and the modern

The Arcadians, not only one of the most popular of Edwardian musical comedies but also one of the few to have survived in any substantial way, is particularly illustrative here. First produced by Robert

Courtneidge in 1909 at the Shaftsbury, it played for two years and three months, and was performed 809 times. It also had a run of 193 performances at the Liberty Theatre on Broadway, followed by an equally successful world tour, returning to the West End for a revival in 1915. For the next thirty years it was a staple of provincial touring companies. Thereafter, it became the property of amateur groups, and one of the few musical comedies to have survived into relatively recent times. It is often considered as the classic musical comedy of this period. Certainly, it is characteristic – in its music, its staging and costuming, its love of spectacle and in the extremely foregrounded take on modernity which shapes the whole narrative dynamic of this show.

At first sight it seems an unlikely candidate for an illustration of how musical comedy embraced modernity. In the first place it opens in a utopian pre-modern rurality (Arcadia), where the Arcadians live in harmony with nature and are forever young (Illustration 4). They are incapable of deceit and such 'barbaric' emotions as jealousy. They express love openly and freely (they 'do not know' marriage), but in an ethereal, spiritual way.[56] Second, modernity in this show, represented by Jim Smith and his 'airship', which crashes in Arcadia, is initially a threatening, corrupting and even destructive force. As a representative of the modern world, Smith immediately sets out to exploit the innocents of

Illustration 4   Arcadia – a pre-modern idyll (*The Arcadians*)

Arcadia as thoroughly as possible. He is a colonial adventurer of the most unreconstituted kind, keen to capitalize on the Arcadians' open nature and eagerness to please. This exploiting dynamic is quickly halted, however, as the Arcadians, who are clearly not as impressionable as Smith imagines, use mysterious natural magic to reform and revitalize Smith himself. By the end of Act 1, 'Simplicitas', as he is renamed, has been transformed. He is restored to youth and, it seems, morally cleansed. Delighted by this success and appalled by Simplicitas' tales of home, the Arcadians now devise a missionary plan to return with their convert to London where they propose to apply their healing on a larger scale. They will redeem the 'poor monsters' that live in 'cages of brick and stone' in 'a sunless land', breathing 'a stifling fog of never-ending smoke'.[57] Their aim is nothing less than the restoration of a whole modern city – that is, of modernity itself.

At this point *The Arcadians*, far from celebrating modernity, appears to be functioning in exactly the opposite way. It is a version of the fall of humanity as Jim Smith unknowingly implies on his arrival in Arcadia, a place that 'looks like the Garden of Eden' and which he immediately attempts to 'buy'. His first instinct is for profit-making. Somewhere, he thinks, 'there's money in this'.[58] *The Arcadians* seems to be constructing modernity as a familiar transgression, a chronic departure from the natural state of things. The subsequent acts, however, produce an astonishing complication of what starts out as a simple and familiar allegory. Although the value of the 'pure and simple life' is not decisively challenged, the modernity represented in Acts 2 and 3, with its colour and excitement, takes on a new vitality quite distinct from the sad, polluted prison visualized initially by the Arcadians and it is this that shifts the narrative equilibrium of the play.

In the original production, the race scene in Act 2, set in England, became the opportunity for the usual elaborate production of 'colour and avant-garde fashion'.[59] The staging of Arcadia, with its woods, valleys and streams, and Tyrolean costuming, is now displaced by a different kind of spectacle, one that images the vitality and excitement of modern life. These staging and costume signifiers are reinforced in further ways, by songs and dialogue which are in modern vernacular as opposed to the now curious archaisms of Arcadia, and so on. Modernity is not unproblematic in this play, but nor is it the dire wrong turning of history that Arcadia thinks it is. On the contrary, the modern is fast, bright and, above all, 'gay'. Also, and most interestingly in many respects, it displays a hugely impressive facility for cultural reproduction.

KING ALFRED'S COLLEGE
LIBRARY

During Act 2, it is discovered that Simplicitas is not as reformed as the Arcadians think. His Arcadian identity is not much more than a disguise. The modern man in him turning out to be not so easily obliterated, he has retained all his acquisitive and exploitative instincts and in Act 3 he decides there is still profit to be made from Arcadia. His plan is to market the whole idea of Arcadia in modern London with the aim of creating a 'new craze'. So he subjects Arcadia to every modern dynamic, reproducing it as a hotel/restaurant which becomes highly fashionable. This 'swagger' joint is energized as a theme-park simulacrum of the real thing, complete with waitresses dressed as Arcadians, a vegetarian menu and copied versions of the key Arcadian equivalent to institutions. Arcadia the restaurant has a copy of the 'real' Arcadia's 'Well of Truth' and an imitation of its 'Bower of Love' (Illustration 5). These do not, of course, work the natural magic that the authentic ones do, but no one seems to mind. They are 'miraculous' for all that and work their own, special kind of *reproductive* magic. The Arcadian restaurant also makes money, and lots of it. Its owner is not so much 'a goose with golden eggs' as 'a modern ram with a golden *fleece*', with the pun being on 'fleece'.[60] There is a strong postmodern feel to this whole transformation, largely because of the obvious and strangely out of time echoes of Baudrillard, albeit without his characteristic pose of fascinated disgust.[61] *The Arcadians* text clearly adores the pace and colour of modern life, and relishes the modern way of imitation and pastiche. By its end, the play resolves itself, as all these plays do, at the level of love interest. It does, however, have some difficulty in closing the complicated relationship that has been set up between Arcadia and modernity. The former retains some remnants of its utopian status, but equally modernity retains high status. Not only does the modern world resist transformation into a 'real' Arcadia, it quite clearly is right to do so as far as this text is concerned. The Arcadians return to Arcadia, their mission to England having failed. Chrysea, one of the Arcadian girls, confesses to some liking of London for all its 'wickedness', but Sombra takes the firmer, less compromising line. 'Nothing here is true,' she says. It's 'all sham. Nothing but sham'. People are not only untruthful, they 'cannot understand truth'.[62] For their part, the moderns continue on their decadent, immoral, but entirely compelling way with Simplicitas reverting to his 'Jim Smith' identity and Jack Meadows, the romantic lead, declaring himself to be 'sick and tired of Arcadianism ... You can have too much simplicity and naturalness', he maintains, thus striking the essential modern position.[63] For all its moral rectitude and despite its harmony with nature, Arcadia becomes here a deficient culture. It is, in the end,

Illustration 5 Arcadia reproduced in a London restaurant (*The Arcadians*)

bland. Far from being liberating, it turns out to be too circumscribed by its sanctimonious character and for this reason will be little missed by the modern.

Perhaps the most important point about *The Arcadians* is that, in common with so many shows of this period, it expressed a highly sophisticated consciousness of modernity and its processes. In this sense it was emblematic not just of musical comedy, but of the entire age. Jose Harris is not the first historian to have pointed out the newness of this sense of contemporaneity and its importance for understanding the *fin de siècle*. 'The consciousness of living in a new age,' she writes, 'a new material context, and a form of society totally different from anything that had occurred before was by the turn of the century so widespread as to constitute a genuine and distinctive element in the mental culture of the period.' *The Arcadians* not only staged this newness, but quite explicitly placed it in contrast with tradition, rurality, organicist society and a string of associated values – innocence, purity, authenticity – and still it was this new modernity, with all its fakery, cheapness and trickery, that came out on top.

Safe pleasure

From its highly romanticized and certainly sanitized perspective, musical comedy saw the awesome assimilative and reproductive power of the modern and staged it as the good and the gay. Perhaps more than any culture of its day, musical comedy was excited by modernity, this no doubt in part a product of its sense of itself as a rising modern commodity accelerating in popularity and, at the highest levels, enjoying huge material rewards.[64] In this respect this popular culture was quite at odds with more intellectual cultures of the day that had very much more authority and currency and which, in some cases, continue to have extremely high status. These highbrow responses were not, of course, all alike. There was, however, a marked consistency to intellectual cultures of this period, many of which seemed compelled to attack the modern condition as a kind of historiographical betrayal. Far from embracing modernity, a characteristic stance of the Edwardian intelligentsia involved nostalgia for the hierarchy that was felt to have collapsed into the monochrome sameness of 'mass' culture. An instinct for more traditional and even pre-capitalist values became characteristic of a *Zeitgeist* that understood 'mass man' and his habitat, the ubiquitous suburb, to be emblematic of the Enlightenment project gone rotten.

It is important to emphasize that this kind of anti-modernism, or, more precisely, insecurity about the forms modernity had been perceived to have taken, did not constitute *the* 'essential' Edwardian response, nor did it form anything like an official ideology.[65] Indeed, Edwardian social policy was thoroughly engaged rather than retreatist, the 'analysis and treatment of social problems [being] optimistic, progressive and ameliorative in tone'.[66] But in prestigious cultures of the day there was a distinct loss of confidence in 'progress', a cultural disposition that is easily illustrated. It shaped the astonishing power of Nietzsche's *Beyond Good and Evil* philosophy; motivated the mythopoetics of Eliot's *The Waste Land* (1922) and figured in the shadows of Bram Stoker's *Dracula* (1897), where modern culture became condemned to the terrible revenge of a diseased aristocrat. It coloured responses to New Woman identities, held to be ranged 'perversely with the forces of cultural anarchism and decay', and figured largely in the new 'science' of eugenics.[67] The entire *raison d'être* of the latter, of course, was to find a way of breeding out 'degeneration' in order to preserve a highly racialized construction of modernity. The following quote from *The Suburbans* by T. W. H. Crosland, however, is not illustrative of any of these extremes. It is characteristic rather of a more homely configuration. This is concern about 'degeneration' in a 'middling' Edwardian mode, much stimulated by a sense of rapidly declining 'national efficiency' and determined to restore modernity to the 'right track'. In 1904 Crosland wrote how,

> [in the suburbs] you will understand, as it were, intuitively and without further ado, the cheapness and out-of-jointness of the times; you will comprehend the why and wherefore and *raison d'être* of half-penny journalism ... you will perceive the whizzers, penny buses, gramophones, bamboo furniture, pleasant Sunday afternoons, Glory songs, modern language teas, golf, tennis, high school education, dubious fiction, shilling's worth of comic writing, picture postcards, miraculous hair-restorers, prize competitions, and all other sorts of twentieth century clap trap have got a market and a use, and black masses of supporters.[68]

Perspectives of this kind were so commonplace that it can easily be forgotten that they *are* just perspectives, and not the essential modern condition itself reflected in some unmediated way. This is where musical comedy becomes important for a wider understanding of the *fin de siècle*. It is the strongest reminder that there *was* a mainstream, or a number of mainstreams, and that these formulated modern times in ways that were often quite at odds with more intellectual cultures.

The dissent from degeneration historiography was at the centre of the difference separating musical comedy from its more prestigious cultural counterparts. Sometimes the opposition was made quite explicit. Leslie Stuart and Owen Hall's blockbuster *Floradora* (1899), for instance, specifically ridiculed the 'sham science' of phrenology, a 'science' that catalogued the traditional superiority of the West and purported to measure its contemporary decline into criminality and madness. *Floradora* also celebrated a dysgenic agenda; it contains a 'Celtic' landowner who is paired off cross-culturally and across class identities with a 'native' Philippine. There is no obvious concern in this show about the 'national efficiency', which was so much a feature of the Edwardian scene, or the purity of the race. For the most part, however, musical comedy's welcoming of the modern was a more general, fundamental matter. This culture did not talk directly to the likes of Eliot or Ezra Pound, both of whom despised modern mass culture, nor would one expect it to – although it did challenge what it saw as the distortion and pretension of modern art, expressing its preference for the pop-art exuberance of Adelphi posters over 'Beardsley and his female incongruities':

> Yet in Art – to be sure –
> As in literature
> Eccentricities certain to pay.
> For a dash and a dab
> Make a horse and a cab
> In the popular art of today.[69]

More importantly, everywhere it challenged the intellectual's insistence on the rottenness of things. Far from being overwhelmed with disgust at the West's cultural decline, musical comedy registered a uniformly upbeat tone. It positioned 'gaiety' precisely at the centre of its untroubled version of life and, on occasion, laughed at those who saw the *fin de siècle* in end-of-culture terms:

> Not for opera
> Cares a copper a
> Dame of fashion nowadays,
> Ibsen's rank arrays
> Mrs Tanqueray's
> Plot or passion, nothing pays....
> Though a Duse calls
> Yet the music halls
> Thronging thickly we attend
> Those at any rate
> Are degenerate
> Suit our sickly-age's end.[70]

Refuting dire predictions, musical comedy had no truck with disasters and fears about the immanence of apocalypse that so dominated other contemporary cultures. In this sense it handled ideas of the modern in ways that might seem unexpected and certainly out of step with many current perceptions of the period.

The 'profound transformation in the culture of the popular classes' was clearly *not* visualized by musical comedy as a collapse of civilization, but rather as a vital surge of *élan* that could be assimilated in largely unproblematic ways. It would be absurd, however, to understand musical comedy as unequivocal in its acceptance of the modern and entirely unrestrained in its welcoming of the modern condition, even though it appears to operate exactly in these ways. What it welcomed, of course, was its own *version* of the modern, a version that set obvious limits, not least to vitality and exuberance. West End musical comedy played at bohemianism, for example, but that did not make it the real Montmartre to take just one point of reference that would have circumscribed musical comedy's version of 'gaiety', albeit in quite invisible ways. Indeed, by comparison with its Paris counterpart, the London West End stage was a tame, controlled and confined environment. Meeting the imperative to produce *controlled* fun was precisely one sense in which musical comedy fulfilled itself as rationalist entertainment, securing a relatively compliant audience, establishing itself perhaps as a halfway house to the 'conservative modernism' that has been identified as characteristic of popular literary culture in Britain in the 1930s.[71] For all its energy and apparent hedonism, it was a safe staging of a world that from many perspectives *was* increasingly deracinated, individualistic and dangerous. Indeed, this was part of the argument of intellectuals who excoriated musical comedy and its like as frivolous, empty and trite. In their view, and it is a view that continues to carry weight, manufactured gaiety was precisely no more than frontage, a safety curtain perhaps, behind which the darker realties of Edwardian society and culture lay not redeemed or even addressed but festering.

As many writers have shown, the idea of *fin de siècle* often turned on a centrally defining dualism. The celebration of bright lights city life constituted one element of its central dynamic; the other was a 'deep-seated anxiety about the nature of human identity' in part generated 'by scientific discourses, biological and sociomedical, which served to dismantle conventional notions of the "human". ... Evolutionism, criminal anthropology, degeneration theory, sexology, pre-Freudian psychology – all articulated new models of the human as abhuman.'[72] The following chapters examine the darker and perhaps deeper side of musical comedy narratology in more detail, the sense in which 'gaiety' not only set out to displace and counter *fin de siècle angst*, but in which it may have functioned in more subliminal ways to suppress. It is worth concluding this chapter, which has been partly concerned with articulating a case for rereading musical comedy, with the observation that the centralizing of modernity as fun and excitement, far from being trivial, is symptomatic of one of the great historical transformations of the last two hundred years. Musical comedy was part of the much wider process by which the idea of modernity, of urban, industrial and commercial life, became newly imagined, not as an alien contamination of British culture, dismantling tradition and custom in its inexorable march, but as the 'natural' state of everyday existence. This surely is the great shift that Stuart Hall referred to in his 1981 essay 'Notes on Deconstructing the Popular', as

> the profound transformation in the culture of the popular classes which occurs between the 1880s and the 1920s ... The more we look at it, the more convinced we became that somewhere in this period lies the matrix of factors and problems from which *our* history – and our particular dilemmas – arise. Everything changes – not just a shift in the relations of forces but a reconstitution of the terrain of the struggle itself.[73]

From being the nineteenth-century culture of a powerful 'other' elite, imposing itself on the 'traditional' British way of life, this watershed period saw the modern transformed into the future as 'our' world. No longer an anti-culture, in mainstream urban culture the innovative became the new, unassailable reality, the universal dynamic that somehow now could be constructed as 'belonging' to everybody. Musical comedy with its astonishing facility to 'charm' and 'amaze' was very much part of that deeply ideological orientation. It helped secure modernity for posterity by rendering it the pleasure dome and the condition of the civilized.

3
Chin Chin Chinaman – Doing Other Cultures

Musical comedy's identification with modernity involved at the same time a strongly asserted linkage between the modern and a British identity. With modernity normalized as the universal condition to which all aspired, it was also the case that British culture, in this cultural form as in many others, figured as the omphalos of modernizing forces – *the* centre of invention, democracy, liberalism and rationalism. Above all, and especially in this popular cultural form, Britain was the focal point of a palpable vitality, staged as nothing less than the modern spirit and, equally importantly, of a social inclusiveness that appeared to welcome everyone to the modern estate. Here was continuity with 'Victorian' order and efficiency, but also a break with its sobriety and its hierarchical control. On the musical comedy stage, Britain represented both the authority and the freedom of something constructed at the *fin de siècle* as the new modern. In its technical style, scale and wizardry as much as its narratological preferences, musical comedy evoked the virtues of a modernity explicitly staged as pervasive and yet decisively racialized as British, and British West End at that.

This chapter is concerned with the considerable ironies involved in this contradiction between a modernism that was somehow both universal and yet fiercely local, inclusive and yet determinedly exclusive. For all its embracing of what in other contexts were problematic 'innovations' and even outsiderly positions and identities, musical comedy effectively excluded from its version of the modern almost all cultures apart from the British and a hybrid that might be termed 'British-American'. The tensions inherent in this irony were reproduced everywhere in musical comedy, in story lines, songs, jokes, staging, and so on, but perhaps most tellingly in what may be called the 'darker tones' of its text. Indeed, its typically 'gay' and confident character should be understood as the obverse of a more fundamental insecurity and nowhere was it more brooding than in its representation of 'other' cultures.

The nature of musical comedy's staging of race was crucially a result of immediate historical contexts, as this chapter shows. Its jovial normalizing and naturalizing strategies, although related to much older sociohistorical conditions of modernity and sociodiscursive formations, responded to particular historical circumstances.[1] Although the Empire was formally expanding at this time, accompanied by a much rejuvenated jingoism, the period was famously characterized by insecurities about Britishness and these in turn were much shaped by concerns about the viability of Empire. If musical comedy was less obviously bothered by the social hygiene and moral guardianship issues that often shaped responses to a perceived decline in 'national efficiency' in other bourgeois cultural forms, it was, nevertheless, a deeply patriotic culture. Highly sensitive to competition from national cultures that were modernizing elsewhere in the world and profoundly loyal to the essential 'British' qualities, musical comedy was instrumental to a politics of race that belonged very much to the late Victorian and Edwardian periods.

The Continental

Since the earliest days of musical comedy, non-British shows had been tried on the West End stage, without any great success. *The Belle of New York*, which began a long run at the Shaftsbury in 1898, was one of the few exceptions. The American shows that followed – *A Mystical Miss* and *An American Beauty*, both in 1900 – failed to capitalize on its popularity. Of the French shows, *La Poupée* (1897), more comic opera than musical comedy, had been the most successful, until *Veronique* started a long run at the Apollo in 1904. With these few exceptions, the first decade of West End musical comedy was essentially a local affair. This authority, however, was not to last. In one version of musical comedy history, the domination of the West End stage by British musical theatre began to be compromised very quickly – from 1905 in fact, the year George Edwardes began to invest seriously in bringing 'foreign' shows to the West End.[2] This development has been seen as the precursor to an 'influx' of Viennese waltzes and of new-style American shows. 1905 thus becomes a watershed year, marking for some the end of the glory days and representing the writing on the wall for Edwardian musical comedy generally.

The reason for Edwardes' shift into the overseas script market in 1905 is not entirely clear. The success of *Veronique* may have been a consideration.

In addition, two local efforts had nose-dived in 1905. The first, *The Officers' Mess*, was a show intended for the provinces but performed eight times at Terry's so that it could be billed as coming 'direct from the West End'. As a planned failure, its very short run was understandable and predictable. The *Miss Wingrove* fiasco, a Frank Curzon production, was much more serious. This effort involved established writers and composers, and a star cast, and was staged by an experienced and successful producer. Its failure was not expected, perhaps particularly when *The Times* could find it 'quite amusing' and foresaw the show settling down 'for a long run'.[3] It should have worked. It lasted, however, just eleven performances over nine days. With this collapse there were dark murmurings about the future of musical comedy. According to Ganzl, Edwardes shared these concerns and may have felt that his writing teams were running out of ideas. There was also the fact that Edwardes had recently been involved in two legal disputes over the authorship of shows. Buying established shows from the Continent would make further litigation less likely.[4]

Whatever the case, 1905 did not see the end of musical comedy; many of its biggest hits were yet to come, including *The Merry Widow*, *The Quaker Girl*, *Chu Chin Chow*, *The Maid of the Mountains* (1917), *Yes Uncle* (1917) and *The Boy* (1917). Nor did the buying of shows from the Continent necessarily de-Anglicize the West End musical comedy scene to any significant degree. Most of these 'foreign' shows were barely distinguishable from British productions once they had been through the process of adaptation for West End audiences. Before they appeared on the London stage, non-British shows, including American ones, often underwent extensive rewrites of both script and music. Translated in more ways than one, these revamped shows, far from constituting a foreign invasion, could quite reasonably be taken as examples of Anglicization at work. With new songs and scenes interpolated, usually all-British casts and the comic scenes rewritten for British tastes, by the time shows like *The Girl in the Train* (1910, from *Die Geschiedene Frau*) and *The Girl in the Taxi* (from *Die Keusche Suzanne*) reached London audiences they would have been utterly transformed. Under these circumstances it became difficult to determine the extent to which a show like *The Spring Chicken* (1905), based on the successful French farce *Le Coquin de Printemps*, remained 'foreign'. Certainly, that play in its London version, with music by Caryll and Monckton and a new book by George Grossmith Jr, seemed thoroughly Anglicized. A show like *The Merry Widow*, which played 778 performances at Daly's, retained much more of the original music, but its script was rewritten by Basil Hood and there were native and localized interpolations, the most famous being George Graves' comic routine featuring 'Hetty the Hen'. It was the British stars, Lily Elsie and Joseph Coyne, who performed this tale of European high society, and they did so in a West End production. Temporarily, musical comedy was no longer set in the Oxford Street store and the London shop girl identity was dropped, but this was no evidence of Ganzl's 'influx'.

The de-Anglicization of musical comedy was more apparent than real. 'Europe' had become popular in show terms, but this was a Europe subject to the West End musical comedy treatment. It was in part the fashionability, rather than any decline in local output, that produced not only the borrowing of plots and music, but also a crop of West End musical comedies set in Europe. Here the production was faked from start to finish in shows that produced cartoon-like versions of France, Germany, the Netherlands, and so on. From about 1907 the West End saw a string of shows that looked Continental in this highly theatricalized way and these may have contributed to the sense that British musical comedy was struggling. However, shows like *The Girls of Gottenberg*, *Miss Hook of Holland*, *The Gay Gordons*, *My Mimosa Maid* (1907) (set on the French Riviera), *The Honourable Phil* (set on a Breton island) and *The Belle of Brittany* were written and composed in England by the usual teams. All these were produced in either 1907 or 1908 (see appendix 1). As the clustered dating suggests, this was part of a fashion for 'foreign' looks, a new fad for a theatre that remained in more substantial respects determinedly West End and entirely musical comedy.

These stagings of continental cultures, then, were only approximate. The representation of 'France' or 'Germany' was a matter of arranging stereotypes in a picturesque way. The Netherlands, for example, in the Paul Rubens' show, is denoted by a canal, bicycles, clogs, excessive politeness and, especially, cheese. The show opens with a cheese market, has cheese carriers, cheese barges and contains references to just about every Dutch variety of cheese imaginable. It includes a song entitled 'A Little Bit of Cheese', which shows how the average day in the life of the Dutch is made up of intervals between cheese-eating ('Every Dutchman when he awakes / A little piece of cheese he takes').[5] *The Girls of Gottenberg* reflects 'Germany' similarly in a comic and two-dimensional manner. Opening in a military barracks, it depicts a militaristic Germany and develops a plot around competition between the Red Hussars and the Blue Hussars. Thereafter the play moves, predictably enough, to a German university where the girls are 'fair', 'strong' and intellectual.[6] The final scene is set in a beer hall. *The Times*, in a typically double-edged review, found the reproduction real enough, suggesting that the scene painters, 'Messrs Joseph and Phil Harker ... [had] studied modern German lithographs (the cheap kind; made for schools) to some advantage'.[7]

Denmark, in *Dear Little Denmark* (1909), is similarly 'done' by clocks, rustic villages, burgomasters and a fairy tale-like narrative which focuses on a chime of bells that protects the Dukes of Falsternone from illness, as long as it rings properly. Hicks' *The Gay Gordons* is not Continental, but it works in exactly the same way, managing to cluster an extraordinary number of 'Scottish' signifiers in the first few minutes of the show. It opens, in play time, on the Glorious Twelfth. A *'picturesque cottage'* stands on the moor with *'the heather at its best and the gorse in full bloom. Four peasant girls [lie] on a hillside'*. Highlanders enter *'carrying game'*.[8] At this point Janet McCleod, who lives in this remote place, appears and informs her family that they are about to be evicted because the whole of the Meltrose estates are 'to become Crown lands'.[9]

As these stereotyping tendencies show, musical comedy played to the nationalistic and patriotic sensibilities of its audiences. Even talk of dispossession at the hands of the Crown in *The Gay Gordons*, for example, somehow manages to avoid any sense of disloyalty because, as Janet points out, 'the King! Poor dear!' is not responsible. 'He has to work just as hard as we do for a living.'[10] Given this kind of disposition, one might have expected these other culture plays to provide the opportunity for plenty of jokes at the expense of the foreigner. Indeed, the whole reduction of the Netherlands, for instance, to cheese and bicycles could be understood as an extended joke at the expense of the Dutch and confirmation of their otherness. However, there are a number of qualifications and distinctions to be made here. The extent, degree and nature of racism displayed in these shows varied greatly, depending on both the cultures that were being portrayed and the contexts in which they were being staged. Shows where the narrative revolved around the British abroad, for instance, tended to be much more extreme in their portrayal of racial otherness than shows that were trying to 'do' Europe. *The Messenger Boy*, for example, was a play that involved the English, German and French in a race to Egypt. Here the representation of Europe and the Middle East was particularly evangelical, in part reflecting its contemporaneity with the Boer War and other colonial designs. The French are represented by a pretentious little man who cannot control his passions and the Germans by an utter idiot. Complete with comic names, one suggestive of stupidity and the other of femininity, Professor Phunckwitz and Count Marie de Lafleur become the absurd foreigners rendered speechless in the predictable way.

Phunk: I vill talk to Hooker, don't it?
Lafleur: Je suis français. Can I not talk?
Phunk: Yah! You talk but vat is in him – mit your English is broken so.
Lafleur: Oui – I break all e English I can. Revenge!
Phunck: I vas spoke the English like a nature – ain't it?[11]

It goes without saying that the hero and heroine of this play, as well as the 'good' colonial authority, are all English.

The Seymour Hicks and Harry Nichols play *A Runaway Girl* was even stronger in its racism. This show, for all its songs and gaiety, has a serious undertone. It is a warning to young English girls that there are dangers in following their romantic instincts abroad. Alice, the runaway of the title, is attracted to the life of a band of itinerant Corsican gypsies. But these romantic songsters turn out to be false. It soon becomes clear that they are dark, mysterious and dangerous. By the end of the play, the English runaway, so initially enamoured of the exotic other, learns to be afraid and returns to 'her own kind'. This hackneyed plot becomes the excuse for an attack on the foreign that becomes wide in its scope. In the middle of Act 1, there is a comic duet between couriers working for Cook's tours. This consists of the singers comparing notes on their experiences of 'national types'. The Scots, Turks and Swiss are all treated to stereotyping in song, as are, again, the Dutch:

> Though I don't know much
> Of the customs of the Dutch
> I believe that they make cheeses and their country's flat
> Little cats with dogs
> Little boys on clogs
> And the men are always smoking and their 'frows' are fat.[12]

This kind of self-contained diversion, a comic skit exploiting familiar and, certainly in this case, feeble jokes about strange foreigners was a staple of musical comedy. There was less of it, however, in the shows that set out to register a romantic representation of, for example, 'dear little Denmark'. The diminution in these shows was of a different order. First, because here the central conceit was that *all* the characters were Dutch or French or German. Thus the 'foreign' had to become a wider category that could embrace all the musical comedy types – the romantic lovers, the heroes and heroines, as well as the comic idiots. At the same time the staging of the Continent in these plays had to carry all the prettification of the standard musical comedy. The Highlands in summer, 'Brittany in daffodil time', the French Riviera in spring, Maxims, at any time, and so on – these were stage concepts constructed as romantic spectacle. The 'France', 'Germany' and 'Holland' depicted in these shows were no more 'authentic' than the West End displayed in a show like *Our Miss Gibbs*, but nor were they just excuses for xenophobia. They were sentimentalized versions – picturesque to the point of nausea – that exploited the original musical comedy configuration. They were also shows where the idea of modernity was least pressing. The locations that were most immune to modernity, at least to the collective mind of musical comedy, tended to be positioned just across the water on mainland Europe. Forever 'medieval', permanently rural and always feudal, musical comedy Europe was often rendered conservatively in this way, a charming place for sure, but also distinctly backward. At a time when the problem of the Britain's isolation in the world was exercising the government, and the country understood by contemporaries to be falling behind its competitors, in terms of both its hard industrial productivity and the well-being of its citizens, this comforting fiction no doubt served a purpose.[13] While the prime minister, Arthur Balfour, was seeking alliances with France and Japan, and trying to rescue an educational provision that was 'chaotic', 'ineffectual' and 'utterly behind the age ... not merely behind our American cousins but behind the German, the Frenchman and the Italian', life at the Gaiety and Daly's worked in different ways as a prop to Britain's declining position in the world.[14]

Antics Japanesy – Wardour Street Orientalism

The musical comedy reproduction of even more exotic cultures was similar in many respects, characterized by romanticism and comic reductionism. But there were also some substantial differences here, not least in the way that musical comedy perceived its own efforts. With the stage reproduction of France, the imperative was to make things pretty and picturesque. There was a much greater emphasis on getting things 'right' when it came to staging India, Japan, China, Ceylon or Burma. The approximations of 'doing' Europe became replaced by a combination of 'triumphalism' and 'an intellectual quasi-scientific discourse'. A hierarchical ethnology was constructed and combined with 'the perennial attractions of the pseudo-educational spectacle'.[15] This more anthropological approach, standard in end-of-century Orientalism, was typified in the 'Japanning' of *The Geisha*, and in the journalistic appreciation that accompanied the extraordinary staging of that show.

The creation of Japan for this show was entrusted in part to Arthur Diosy, founder and vice-chairman of the Japan Society and an eminent figure.[16] It also involved the choreographer Willie Warde, who studied Japanese dance at the Japanese exhibition village in London in order to produce dances 'executed on the Japanese lines, but just sufficiently Anglicized for those who want amusement rather than instruction'.[17] Authentic Japanese instrumentation was interpolated into the score and the clothes for this show were 'all worked by hand' and 'exported from Japan'. An image of 'mighty Fujiyama' dominated the first act backdrop and a teahouse exterior complete with chrysanthemum gardens and carp ponds was constructed for the opening set. With this the producers aimed, and succeeded according to many reviewers, in 'capturing' 'the spirit of Japan', albeit a Japan transposed by 'a *couleur-de-rose* air'. Those in the anthropological know were able to point out that not all the details were strictly correct. As one reviewer explained, the Japanese do not, in fact, marry in teahouses.[18] But this kind of 'licence' was taken to be permissible for the sake of an entertainment that effected 'a vision of Japan, very delightful and most alluring'.[19]

For all these claims of authenticity, however, a show like *The Geisha* was every bit as theatrically contrived as a *Miss Hook of Holland*. *The Geisha* was, of course, a highly romanticized version of things. In principle, it hardly differed from the kind of approach that produced Rubens' Netherlands or Denmark. The only real distinction, apart from the claims of authenticity, was that a play like *The Geisha* was mediated in different ways and more deeply so. The ambition to 'capture' *any* other cultures could be powerfully suggestive of national and modernizing ideologies, but this was especially the case where the subject was non-European and 'Oriental'. Reproducing the Oriental was particularly implicated with issues of British identity and British status in the world. Theatrical reproduction took on obvious parallels with colonial appropriation. The 'marvels' of modern staging became emblematic of the modernizing dynamic that was so frequently used as justification for Empire. For all these reasons, the staging of India and China implied an ideological space that was related to the staging of, say, France or Scotland, but at the same time distinct in terms of the imperative to reproduce the 'likeness'.

The trouble to which producers went in order to stage other cultures, especially non-Western cultures, was not, then, suggestive of the desire to know. Rather, it was startling confirmation of the dissembling and reproductive power of the modernized Western world. Just as an Edenic Utopia was 'magically' achieved in *The Arcadians*, so shows like

Illustration 6 'Wardour Street Orientalism' (*The Mousmé*)

The Geisha performed the trick of image manufacture. What was being celebrated in these pastiches was not the 'real' Burma, Ceylon, Japan, China, Cuba, and so on, but the metropolitan culture that could apparently reproduce the world's diversity so splendidly. It was the transforming power of the modern British stage that was applauded, as opposed to the prototype behind the alleged inspiration. The facsimile made the real impression, which is why so much review space was devoted to what were significantly termed 'stage pictures' (Illustration 6). The copy was marvelled at as copy. Thus the actress 'Miss Mary Collete' performing in *The Geisha* attracted special attention because she gave, the reviewer claimed, 'the most perfect imitation of a Jap girl'. She might have 'popped out of a teahouse at Miyanoshita or Atami'. Nothing like this kind of response ever greeted reproductions of France or Germany where, presumably, the mimicry was supposed to be transparent. Making manifest the truth behind the old primitive fear of the photograph that steals the soul, the actress in *The Geisha*, however, had done something greater, apparently becoming 'the Jap to the very life'.[20] 'Wardour Street Orientalism', as a censor in the Lord Chamberlain's Office put it, may have involved some degree of research and claimed educational value but, like very much more legitimate antiquarian and anthropological responses to other cultures, this was mostly work of appropriation, dedicated to the greater glory of the Western metropolis with its extraordinary powers of assimilation.[21]

This theatrical reproduction of other cultures imaged the general hegemony of modernity over the world. It also reproduced the imperial power of Britain specifically. There were many plays in which spectacle reproduced not just the 'charm' of other worlds, but also the amazing ritual of Empire. Here the ideological complicity of musical comedy became entirely explicit, with London theatres operating in precisely the way that colonial pavilions worked in the same period.[22] As Eric Hobsbawm has put it, 'the idea of superiority to, and domination over, a world of dark skins in remote places was genuinely popular, and thus benefited the politics of imperialism'. He goes on to show how colonial exhibits were a 'hit' because they

> touched a public nerve. British jubilees, royal funerals and corona-tions were all the more impressive because, like Ancient Roman triumphs, they displayed submissive maharajahs in jewelled robes – freely loyal rather than captive. Military parades were all the more colourful because they contained turbaned Sikhs, moustached Rajputs, smiling and implacable Gurkahs, Spahis and tall black Senegalese: the world of what was considered barbarism at the service of civilization.[23]

Musical comedy worked exactly in this way, especially in the many 'Oriental' shows that were perhaps the most popular and most fre-quently revisited of all musical comedy genre types.

The Messenger Boy will, again, serve as illustration here. This Edwardes production has Empire at its heart. It opens in London with a charity bazaar and an Adrian Ross lyric that advises young Britons to go East, following 'British legions to the newly rescued regions'. Here ambitions for wealth and fame can be satisfied, as can missionary instincts to 'aid the Oriental on the moral side and mental'. There is the assurance that the 'fuzzy-wuzzy' will be 'enraptured' by English attempts at 'instruction'.[24] The purpose of this charitable event, then, which has an 'Egyptian stall' and 'an Indian annex', is both to invigorate colonial service and materially sustain the less fortunate, or, as the opening chorus puts it: 'To feed the blacks with perfect stacks, / Of dainties never nigger ate.'[25] After this initial celebration of the British world mission, the show develops into a pantomime farce, with the usual love interest, set mostly in Egypt, (given what follows in Act 2, scene 2, it may not be coincidental that Egypt at that time was one of Britain's most recent and volatile 'dependencies'). The Sudanese crises of 1882, 1884–85 and 1896–98 and the Emin pasha relief expedition of 1887–89 produced some of the most spectacular bouts of popular excitement and agitation in a period punctuated by such moments.

By the end of Act 1, the show has developed into a travel adventure in the Jules Verne style; indeed, *The Messenger Boy* has its own 'Phineas Pott'. Act 1, scene 1 ends with a hurried consultation of timetables printed in 'Bradshaw's Guide', then the play moves to Brindisi, 'portside'. Act 2 opens with all the 'cosmopolitan' colour of a Cairo street market. Scene 2 of this Act, the last of the show and by far the most spectacular, begins in the much more formal surroundings of Lord Punchestown's imperial palace. The opening chorus is a hymn to Queen and Empire:

> Let the trumpets and the drums,
> As they blare and roll and rattle,
> Greet the Governor that comes
> Not to war and not to battle.
> For the tyranny is ended
> As a vision that has been
> And the land shall yet be splendid
> For the Queen!
> For the Queen!
> Round the world blow her banners,
> Night and morning hear her bugle call,
> And the royal road shall run between;
> Here is to Her Majesty, God bless her,
> To the Queen.

At this point, a 'chief' of the region emerges to pay homage and bear witness to the benevolent humanitarianism of a progressive Empire:

> Where my tribe once had its village
> By the Nile
> Lay the desert void of tillage
> Mile on Mile
> Now the water wheels are heard
> And the fields again are green;
> At the bidding and the word
> Of the Queen.[26]

This is only one Empire staging of many. It indicates just how fundamentally musical comedy was implicated in the widespread appropriation of other cultures, commandeering them to the cause of a triumphant modernity in ways that clearly benefited 'the politics of imperialism'. For the most part, musical comedy operated a one-way traffic in terms of culture. It might have appeared to be cross-cultural, but this was both an illusion and superficial. At its height, musical comedy offered fantasy versions of a fantasy world in which an essentially British theatre talked to the British public, at home and abroad. It did so in codes that often laughed at British manners, institutions and customs, and yet everywhere confirmed the superiority of the British. Cultural parallels – and these plays were obsessed with such parallels – involved the usual sorry stereotyping of the other. Hand in hand with the prettification of foreign parts described above, there was a studied ridicule of the Oriental.

As with representations of the French or Germans, mocking the Oriental was a standard piece of musical comedy business, but again the resonance deepened with the inevitable colonizing framework. Orientals were typically depicted as proud, boastful and licentious.[27] Above all, they were consistently exposed to ridicule for their ingratiating attempts at imitating benign colonial protectors. The 'comic mainstay' of *The Cingalee*, for instance, is a character called Chambhuddy Ram, played originally by a blacked-up Huntley Wright. Like the musical theatre itself, Chambhuddy is an imitator, a native aspirant who 'copies' everything English. In his case, however, the reproduction is an absurd failure. He is laughed at for his language errors, such gaffs as 'you have got the wrong purse by the sow's ear', and for his ridiculous appropriation of Western dress.[28] The butt of just about every piece of comic business in the show, his first appearance '*dressed in what he considers the height of English fashion*' sets the tone. '*He carries every possible accessory such as key, chain etc. and an elaborate umbrella*'[29] (Illustration 7). This was part of the double bind that imagined other culture as primitivist and reactionary and yet laughed at its attempt to modernize and be like the West. In the following song, such contradictions are exposed through lines that leave it open as to whether China is being laughed at for 'copying' or not copying. What is certain though is the funniness of the Chinaman:

> I used to think the Chinaman was twenty times as fine a man
> As any born of European nations;
> Our manners were superior to anything exterior
> And had been so for many generations!
> But now there's not a doubt of it

Illustration 7   Mr Huntley Palmer as Chambhuddy Ram (*The Cingalee*)

That China will be out of it
Unless we can effect a vast improvement –
We'll copy the variety of Western high society
And I will be the leader of the movement.

So we'll imitate the style
Of the blessed British Isles

> Though the reason isn't easy to divine –
> Ah!
> But they do it in the West
> So of course it must be best
> And I mean to introduce it into China![30]

In the same vein there were the familiar assumptions about the nature of foreign power and authority. *San Toy* exposes a Japanese political power that is arbitrary, corrupt and brutal. *The Geisha* finds the idea of a 'civilized Japan' a contradiction in terms. Japanese culture authorizes 'outrages' that 'we wouldn't allow in England'.[31] This show thereafter becomes significantly devoted to the exposure of 'Oriental injustice'. Chinese sculpture is mocked, again in *San Toy*, where Dudley (an English maid) is appalled by 'these hideous figures they put up all over the place'.[32] Chinese tea drinking styles were laughed at, as was Chinese tea ('Pooh! What is it flavoured with?').[33] In *The Cingalee* the idea of chewing betel produces a similarly disgusted response, and so on.[34]

The corollary to all this ridicule of the racial other was the affirmation of the English character. In a contrast that included all the usual moral, ethical and physical dimensions, images of 'the chaff and trickery of Japanese officials and artful John Chinaman' were played off against those of 'the gallant naval English officers with countesses in yachts'.[35] English men were portrayed as strong, broad-shouldered, courageous and loyal; the Oriental was sly, small and cowardly. A parallel contrast, and equally emphatic, separated the female roles. Thus again in *The Geisha* 'the merry little pattering and laughing Japs [were] well contrasted with some splendid examples of womanhood [i.e. English womanhood] headed by Maud Hobson and Miss Hetty Hamer'.[36] Other critics commented on 'the piquant contrast' between the 'rustic little Japanese' and the 'imposingly handsome' presence of English women, power-dressed in 'extreme modes of the moment'.[37] The eugenic implication was entirely transparent: 'As a fine contrast to these bowing and scraping little dollies, these playthings of women, came the commanding presence, the assertive dignity of the Anglo-Saxon represented by Maud Hobson, Miss Blanche Massey, and Miss Hetty Hamer.'[38]

This kind of representation is what might be expected of British popular culture of this period, a period often characterized by its patriotism, jingoism and racism.[39] Musical comedy coincided with an age of imperialism, when 'one quarter of the globe's land surface was distributed or redistributed as colonies amongst a half-dozen states'.[40] It was also an age marked by serious assaults on national pride and typified by powerful anxieties about Britain's place in the world. The imperial retreat imaged during William Gladstone's fourth ministry (1892–94) was a real and dreadful possibility to contemporaries who had lived through the Ashanti campaign of the 1870s; the Russo-Turkish War of 1878; the Afghanistan and Zulu disasters of 1879; and were later to experience the Boer War. The series of colonial conferences (1887, 1894, 1902, 1907 and 1911), set up to protect the future of Empire against the decolonizing momentum of the white dominions, was further evidence, if any were needed, of the insecurities that so often manifested in gung-ho patriotism. Thus the late Victorian and Edwardian political spectrum was crucially determined by positions on race, national identity and the issue of 'national efficiency'. Many of its heroes, Joseph Chamberlain, Cecil Rhodes and Rudyard Kipling, were products of the 'Great Game', and all political parties and groupings, from the Tories to the Fabians, found themselves arguing new and often radicalized positions on ideas around race and Empire.

The cultural effects of all this on popular literature, song, exhibitions, theatre, the press, and so on can hardly be overstated. It produced 'new traditions of Christian militarism, militarist athleticism in the public schools, and a recreated and perverted "medieval" chivalry'. Such formulations, often constructed in terms of an 'Anglo-Saxon' identity, 'contributed readily to the national rituals and political processes that were part of the British imperial cult'.[41] In such a context it is hardly surprising that the registration of other cultures in musical comedy not only indicated narrow-minded and insular ways of perceiving the world outside of Britain, but also served as a justification for imperialism. The general dimensions of the characterization signified, above all, a culture with a long tradition of colonial expansionism, although, at the same time, a culture growing deeply uncertain about its world role and having to come to terms with the early signs of the end of Empire.

Nor was the extent to which ideas of race and racial superiority penetrated into the central narrative fabric of these plays particularly surprising. Whereas some musical comedies alluded to the issues in off-hand jokes and stylized performances, others were much more centrally engaged with race and ethnicity. Compelled to revisit the site of the colonial transaction, to re-enact the plantation relationship and otherwise to repeat the encounter between Britain and the racial other, some of these shows were narratologically obsessed with race. They demonstrated that the representation of the other was very much more than 'mere' stereotyping for the sake of a guaranteed laugh. Indeed, in these often quite complex metaphors, one can see just how important the idea of the racial other was to the construction of the British sense of self. This is presumably why the territory was subject to such a thorough going over.

'Give me my little girl at Karikar!' – metaphors of empire

The most obvious way in which the British/native configuration was handled in these shows was by treatments of the 'sugary romantic theme where a foolish young English officer or planter made strictly honourable love to a sun-burnt damsel of the Far East'.[42] This was an especially compelling narrative set-up for musical comedy. Elaborate allegories were concocted around the story of what happened when the British officer met the native girl and these were not always as naive or 'sugary' as the contemporary critics claimed. On the contrary, they exposed contradictions and insecurities that were highly suggestive of deep currents in British society.

At first sight there might seem to be a surprising degree of 'laxity' or even liberation in the ways in which these plays appeared to handle the idea of the interracial. The story of romantic encounters between European (usually English) men and 'native' women, even where the status of the latter was softened by making them mixed race and aristocratic, was standard. The reverse situation, European women establishing liaisons with Oriental men, was also sometimes played out – in *The Geisha*, *The Blue Moon* and *The Cingalee*, for instance – although here the women involved were usually European rather than English. French was the favoured national identity for female characters who 'crossed over' in this way, a designation that said a good deal about English attitudes to a perceived French morality.[43] This somewhat surprising licence, however, had very little to do with any liberalizing agenda. The whole business of romance and even marriage between young English gentlemen and exotic Geisha girls, or 'Cingalee' princesses, operated in highly romanticized, fantastic and fetishistic contexts. Exchanges between East and West, colonizers and colonized, white and black, were made safe by the conventions of musical theatre (it was important to know, one imagines, that the 'real' Geisha girl, O Mimosa San, was not Japanese at all but Marie Tempest in Japanese clothes, made up to look Japanese, and that Nanoya in *The Cingalee* was 'really' Sybil Arundale). These were romantic interventions that *allowed* the symbolic breaking of conventions; they did not *advocate* such transgressions in the real world. Indeed, they offered very clear examples of how 'the stage ... offered a framed and bracketed space in which licence, violence and irresponsibility, physicality and other enjoyable but anti-social acts or sensations could be savoured and then rejected or denied'.[44]

Within these secure boundaries, it was possible to allude to some dangerous and controversial issues, white Europe's sexual attraction to the orientalized racial other, for instance. In *San Toy*, racial otherness is specifically part of the reason why the Englishman Bobbie desires San Toy. He wants her, as she herself knows, precisely because she is 'so deeferent'.[45] A similar eroticization of the other is apparent in *The Blue Moon*, where Jack Ormsby lustily declares that 'Evelyn's a jolly good sort, but for a real natural womanly beauty give me my little girl at Karikar! Such a mouth, Bob! Such a mouth, Major!'[46] The contrast here between sturdy English reliability and Oriental sexuality and willingness to perform could hardly be more striking.

In some ways, then, these shows enacted what has often been seen as the characteristically ambiguous position of modern Western culture to the marginalized world – a strange and uneasy mix of admiration and scorn, attraction and disgust, fascination and indifference. It should be emphasized, however, that such ambiguities were relatively subtle in these shows. What could not be missed, because they were so obvious and emphatic, were the allegorical levels of these romantic narratives that confirmed again and again both the rightness, and insecurity, of Britain's world position. Far from adopting liberalizing positions, these narratives utilized romantic love and sexual attraction between races as metaphors for representing the winning position of white authority in the modern world. They demonstrated very clearly how colonial discourse issued 'a demand both for order and disorder, producing a disruptive other in order to assert the superiority of the colonizer'.[47]

Thus at the centre of these highly politicized narratives was the dangerous other, an indigenous competitor for the hand of the 'native' girl who threatened harmonious resolution. The ensuring struggle had very clear racial and imperialist dimensions, where the issue was not simply whether the 'right' man would get the girl, but whether the 'right' race would prevail. San Toy, for instance, chooses the blonde-haired, blue-eyed Englishman, Bobbie, over her countryman, the vile Fo Hop. The latter is appalled to discover that San Toy should prefer 'the uncivilized Englishman to a Chinese student'. San Toy, for her part, responds to Fo Hop's suggestion that she must be sick of the invader by asserting that she has *not* had enough of foreign (i.e. modern) ways, 'very much not enough!'[48] With this, she becomes complicit in an Empire dynamic, one of the 'gratefully oppressed',[49] for Bobbie will always be her 'master'.[50] Not only has the best man won, so has the correct disposition of the racial other towards the modernizing colonial power.

The Cingalee repeats this narrative pattern, with Harry Verekker, an English aristocrat, falling for Nanoya, the mixed-race girl described as his 'little black and tan thing'.[51] Here too, a different claim on Nanoya, from Boobhamba, is rejected, as are further indigenous claims. Boobhamba presents himself as Nanoya's authentic husband and the rightful owner of both the tea plantation in which the show is set and of a fabulous jewel, 'the great, black, Pearl'. All these native entitlements, however, are magisterially dismissed by the play. Boobhamba ends up apparently compensated for his losses by the interest of an English 'governess' of large and impressive charms, Peggy Sabine, a women who likes ''er dark complexions'.[52]

The Blue Moon, again, repeats the essential pattern, including the ingredient that confers mixed-race status on the 'native' girl. Chandra (or Blue Moon) is the daughter of a Burmese nobleman and an English aristocrat. She was 'stolen' from her home by a shadowy tribesman figure in an event that sounds very much like the Indian Mutiny, when 'those dreadful creatures came down from the hills' and 'massacred everybody'.[53] Her recovery by the militaristic figure of 'Lieutenant Jack Ormsby' becomes metonymic of the 'normalization' of English/Asiatic relations.[54]

These texts, then, for all their frothy surface, carried very powerful and highly gendered messages about social control, racial superiority and the civilizing mission of Empire. If some exploited sexuality as a metaphor for colonial rule, others took a safer eugenicist line, insisting that races could play at 'mixing' but no more, producing meanings that simply did not avail themselves of any potential misreading. *The Geisha*, for example, permits only 'flirtation' between British naval officers and the local girls, allowing Golden Harp to go no further than an expression of interest in English sailors who are 'so white and clean'.[55] As shown above, the play works hard to separate the English and the Japanese. Lady Constance highlights the essential physical difference between English and Japanese women, asserting that the Geishas are deformed, 'undersized creatures'.[56] The play's plot ensures that serious relationships promote racial purity and are eugenically sound. Although the madcap figure, Molly, threatens to subvert things by posing as a Geisha and getting herself sold to a Japanese nobleman, it is quite transparent that nothing will come of this diversion. The idea that this delightful English girl will *really* end up in the 'harem' of a Japanese noble is never likely to materialize. In the dénouement Molly is restored to her English lover,

Fairfax, and O Mimosa San is restored to her Japanese soldier, Katana. It turns out that 'foreigners are all very well to flirt with, but for marriage' a 'countryman' is necessary.[57] Or as Dudley, the English maid in *San Toy*, puts it in response to the advances of a Chinese man:

> It's just like your cheek
> To venture to speak
> To *me* of your fond adoration
> You happen to be
> A heathen Chinee
> While *I* am a Briton by nation.[58]

There were ambiguities in the ways that musical comedy represented other cultures, but these should not be allowed to obscure the underlying consistency. For the most part, the characteristic production styles, representational modes and narrative signifiers were all of a piece. They functioned across a dynamic that assimilated, appropriated and diminished the racial other, while at the same time elevating ideas of the British identity and the universality of modern progressivism. Throughout, the reproduction of the foreigner and of English encounters with the emblematic East imaged the superiority of the West in general and Britain in particular. The only significant exception to these conservative positions was perhaps in the criticism sometimes levelled at the administration of Empire. For all the idyllic versions of plantation life,[59] concrete images of the 'domestic ideology which the British empire claimed to propagate across the world',[60] it was quite usual to find representations of the colonial system in operation that exposed something of its inefficiency and even, on occasion, its corruption.[61] *The Blue Moon*, for example, opens with a hill station setting where the whites are lazing in the sun, singing about their indolence:

> Our fair complexions soon get brown
> Beneath the sun that blazes down
> Upon this hill side station
> We find it rather warm for work
> The only thing we do not shirk
> Is cheerful conversation.

The 'coolie' chorus replies as follows:

> Every sahib keeps
> Plenty lots of coolie ooly

All the time he sleeps
Working hard at Punkah
Other jobs like these
We perform them duly-ooly.[62]

If this kind of light satirical edge was an exception to the rule, however, it was a very partial one. For the real target of these sallies into social criticism was usually not the Empire, racism or ideas of racial superiority at all, but that familiar theme of musical comedy, the absurdities of the British class system and the inefficiencies of those in authority.[63] Far from undermining imperialism, musical comedy made a serious contribution to its authorization. It participated in celebrating what was widely taken to be the key indicator of the unstoppable march of modernization – its sheer dominion over the world. Not just contemporary with this great age of imperialism, musical comedy was a constituent part of the legitimization of a huge territorial carve-up. Successful shows of this period constituted some of modernity's most elaborate reproductions of the exotic other. These were precisely illustrative of the reproductive power of the modern and its capacity for assimilating difference and they travelled all over the Empire and the wider world. Just what the impact of the shows abroad may have been cannot be known with any accuracy. It is not unreasonable, however, to imagine significant cultural effects in this respect.

Granville Bantock and F. G. Aflalo tell an interesting story that is of relevance here. Writing about their experiences on the Gaiety Company tour of 1894, in the very early days of musical comedy, they explain how they docked at Honolulu in Hawaii to be welcomed by a 'native' band. Conducted by a Professor Berger, the band played 'an admirable selection from *A Gaiety Girl* followed by "Auld Lang Syne" and the National Anthem. Where', the authors comment, 'is civilization going to stay its hand?'[64]

The foreign at home

It need hardly be said that musical comedy's complicity with Empire and patriotism placed it in the mainstream of society. There was nothing marginal about its attitude to other cultures or its staging of British strength, verve and general moral rectitude. Like its embracing of the modern, the musical comedy treatment of the foreign was key to its status as 'one of the signs of our times'. In a period when Fabian progressives could defend 'Imperial federations' as a necessary prelude to the

'Federation of the World', and when Joseph Chamberlain could attempt the mobilization of pan-Saxon trade unionism, there would have seemed nothing extreme about shows like *The Blue Moon* and *The Cingalee*.[65] It is more likely that their self-proclaimed status as entertaining anthropological instruction would have been widely taken at face value.

Similarly, it is easy to imagine how the 'coon' or 'piccaninny' songs of musical comedy would have been normalized in theatrical 'tradition', to the point where they barely registered cultural significance of any wider kind. These songs, leftovers from the minstrel show tradition, were usually interpolated quite randomly, without any reference to the plot, characterization or cultural setting of a piece. They involved not white actors playing 'coons' (American or Caribbean Africans in this context), but white *characters* in disguise. Removed from even the pretence of authentic identity, the 'coon' or 'piccaninny' was constructed as nothing more than a standard 'act', a role in reserve so to speak, that could be called on at any time. Act 2 of *A Runaway Girl*, for example, involves a scene where two white characters suddenly appear dressed up as 'piccaninnies' for a ball in Venice. In this disguise they dance and sing as piccaninnies do:

> When de twilight's falling an' de stars a-peepin out,
> When de night begins, when de night begins!
> Is de time our Mammy says de Bogey-man's about,
> And de gobble-ins, and de gobble-ins.

As painful as such representations are, in their day the 'coon' interpolations would have been no more controversial than the figure Chambhuddy Ram, who was meant to stand in for Anglicized Ceylon.

Indeed, the mainstreaming of musical comedy meant that serious, sustained controversy was to be avoided. It was critical that the culture be engaged and contemporary, but just as important that it constructed a consensus identity for itself. The fantasy of inclusivity, however obvious its boundaries may now be, was key to the cultural viability of musical comedy. This may be the reason why it avoided contributing to the Jewish 'issue', debated so hotly elsewhere in Edwardian culture. In particular, it avoided reference to the 'new wave' of migrants – the Ashkenazi Jews, victims of Russian pogroms who had been leaving Eastern Europe in quite large numbers since the 1880s. These migrations met with considerable anti-Semitism in a wide range of social, cultural and political guises. Musical comedy, however, was surprisingly restrained in this respect.

It seems highly unlikely that the musical comedy establishment would have been concerned at offending Ashkenazi Jewry *per se*. These new inhabitants of the East End were impoverished and formed discreet communities which maintained their own cultural traditions. They hardly constituted a viable audience for West End musical comedy. More traditional Jewry, however, often connected with musical comedy at the highest levels, would have been a different matter. Quite apart from the importance of Jewish writers, producers and performers to the West End stage, and of financiers like Rothschild, many of the key American impresarios were Jewish – Cohan, Hammerstein I, Ziegfeld and the Schuberts – as were many if its leading stars – Brice, Cantor, Durante, Jolson and Tucker – and many of its most important composers and lyricists – Arlen and Berlin, and later the Gershwins, Hammerstein II, Kern and Rodgers, for instance. With this kind of hugely influential constituency operating so centrally on Broadway,[66] it is perhaps not surprising that the anti-Semitism so characteristic of the British novel at this time became largely expunged from the scripts of musical comedy.[67]

Perhaps even more importantly, although there was a strong anti-Semitic culture in Edwardian England, specific anti-Semitic movements and a political discourse that produced an 'Aliens' Act of Parliament in 1905 to limit immigration, anti-Semitism did not represent a consensus position.[68] Rather, there were deep divisions, with anti-Semitism meeting resistance from some elements of liberalism, labour politics, religious nonconformity, and so on. Such controversy undoubtedly goes some way towards explaining musical comedy's relative retreat from this issue. Where it did implicate Jewry it tended to focus on well-established Anglicized or American Jewish identities; its role in this respect was suggestive of the kind of inclusivity it expounded elsewhere. It applauded those who had integrated and were rising in social status.

The obvious illustration here would be *The Girl from Kays*, a popular Edwardes show staged at the Apollo, which capitalized yet again on the currency of the shop girl identity. The heroine in the show, Winnie Harborough, who works in the millinery department of Kays' department store, holds ambitions for marriage to nobility. Finally, however, she settles for an American businessman about town, Max 'Piggy' Hoggenheimer. This millionaire, apparently based on Rothschild, was played by Willie Edouin in stock comic mode, not as a Jewish stereotype but as the bored, rich 'Johnny' who is reeled into matrimony. Indeed, Hoggenheimer's Jewish identity is signified by his name only. In other respects he is positioned as another kind of stereotype altogether, the wealthy, modern, somewhat idiotic young man with time on his hands.

Winnie's pragmatic attitude is also highly suggestive of integrative agendas. For all his idiocy, Max is regarded as an important contact and an excellent prospect. Whereas Winnie recognizes the status of traditional aristocracy, she also understands that the kind of money Max possesses opens doors. In one of her solo songs she tells how, 'Its very nice to be / A dame of high degree, / With blood and reputation beautifully blue', but 'Folks with cash can get / Inside the smartest set, / And that is what I shall proceed to do.'[69] Winnie realizes that social mobility in new times society has changed. Just as she can be elevated to money, so money can be elevated to power and status. and she determines to see 'Piggy' ennobled in due course as 'Lord Hoggenheimer of Park Lane'. (Rothschild himself had a house there.)[70]

This kind of representation was insensitive in some respects, but it was decidedly tame by comparison to the endless characterizations in fiction of 'alien', 'contaminative' Jews, dirtying the streets of London. These appeared across the spectrum of novel writing, from Oscar Wilde's *The Picture of Dorian Gray* (1891) with its 'fat Jew' theatre manager, a 'hideous ... monster' sporting 'greasy ringlets, and an enormous diamond glazed in the centre of a soiled shirt',[71] to H. G. Wells's *Tono Bungay* (1909) and his depiction of a London 'in decay, parasitically occupied ... by alien, unsympathetic and irresponsible elements'.[72] Such sentiments were absent from musical comedy. Where it registered at all, the Jewish identity was not just safe, but integrated into a notion of a British community. In this respect, it was both related to and resembled the musical comedy representation of the more generic 'American in Britain'.

This figure appeared in a great number of shows – *Floradora, The Shop Girl, The Earl and the Girl, The Gay Gordons*, to name a few – always emblematic of modernity and reflecting what is still constructed as Britain's 'special', but highly ambiguous, relationship with the New World. Thus 'America' featured as the returning figurative son/daughter who is monied and prepared to put his/her income at the service of the old country. There was a worried version of this intervention, however, as in *Floradora*, where America threatens to 'swamp' the slower, more stylish and more genuinely progressive modern that is constructed as England. More usually though the American visitor figured as a rescuer. He or she became implicated in marriage, sometimes into modern classes, but in the most typical scenario playing out love scenes with the old and declining English landed aristocracy. In this way, the American foreign, far from being mocked or diminished, enjoyed a particular privilege. In musical comedy, as in other cultures of the period, the American figured as a protector who would maintain the position of both the old aristocracy and the traditional Britain represented by that elite. As an emblem of the modern he/she combined with tradition to image what musical comedy presented as the harmony of a new and inclusive social polity.

4
Aristocracy and the Cultural Politics of Modernity

According to at least one historian of the musical, British musical comedy of this period was an aristocratic culture, tied to aristocratic values and for that reason quite distinct from the authentic musical, which was a demotic and essentially 'republican' form developed in opposition to the 'high' culture, specifically opera, of the old European landed elite.[1] The evidence for this claim was not to be found in the singing styles, dance routines or staging of British musicals. In these crucial respects, American, British and European musicals of this period were different but not entirely divergent, as the frequent adaptation of the same musical to all three cultures would suggest. It was not until the First World War and the assimilation into the musical of black American music and dance as 'jazz' that the formalities of the musical began to reconstitute the entire form as the 'American musical' with real authority. The reason why West End musical comedy could *seem* aristocratic was solely because of what was perceived as its narrative obsession with representing aristocracy and its apparent devotion to reproducing aristocratic glamour.

In fact, this quality, far from denoting the continued influence of aristocracy over British life, showed again the extent to which musical comedy was a 'respectable' and contemporary culture, produced by and responding to the needs of the new and developing middle classes. The impulse was not simply to reproduce aristocratic life in an act of deference but, more interestingly, to articulate the complexities and contradictions of the relationships between Britain's new social order and its old landed elites. This had a fundamental importance in Edwardian England, not because England remained an aristocracy, but precisely because this was the period that saw what contemporaries took to be a most dramatic decline in the status of that class. The idea of aristocracy in England, then, was only partly a matter of rethinking relationships towards tradition, although it clearly was that to some degree. More fundamentally, aristocracy was linked to change, in particular to the changing roles and responsibilities of the middle classes; to their confident assertion of authority over modernity, but also to the insecurities of their concerns about social cohesion and consent in an age of 'mass' society and democratization. The status held by aristocracy in musical comedy was a crucial marker not of an old-fashioned commitment to a dead culture, but precisely of the new form's contemporary relevance. It was in its representation of aristocracy that musical comedy got as close as it would do to the overtly political, because here it invoked the precise and immediate context of power and rule in contemporary society. This cultural version of aristocracy took on such of-the-moment meanings because it was happening precisely at the time when Britain's traditional ruling elite was falling into arguably the most damaging phase of its history. Indeed, the widespread impression was of a landed aristocracy in its death throes and with this something essential about 'England' was thought to be vanishing forever.

The aegis of real power – aristocracy in Edwardian England

The British aristocracy has frequently been theorized as a class under long-term threat. Some have put the origins of its decline in the English Civil War, and even earlier. More recent research, however, has examined the issue of aristocracy from a completely opposite angle, accounting for its survival into, and beyond, the early twentieth century. David Cannadine has shown how, whatever pressures it faced, the English aristocracy remained one of the most powerful in the world for most of the nineteenth century, more wealthy and exclusive than the titled classes of Belgium, France, Spain, Italy or Russia. The high proportion of land owned or controlled by this elite, even as late as 1870, was almost certainly without contemporary parallel. The results of Lord Derby's inquiry into land ownership, published as the *Return of the Owners of Land* in 1876, established that almost 75 per cent of Britain was owned by fewer than 5,000 people. Twenty-five per cent of England and Wales was controlled by a mere 710 landowners and, even more remarkably, just 12 men possessed more than four million acres, or some 17 per cent, of the total land area owned. At the slightly broader top end of landed privilege were 250 territorial magnates, each owning more than 30,000 acres and receiving an income in excess of £30,000 a year. The landed aristocracy was an elite economic group containing most of the richest people in the country and, indeed, a significant number of world-class fortunes. The patricians of this class, the Buccleuchs, Derbys, Devonshires and Bedfords, exercised enormous local and national influence. They were, as Cannadine puts it, 'truly the lords of the earth'.[2] With a virtual monopoly over highly esteemed titles, the 580 peers and 856 baronets of Victorian England formed *the* cultured, leisured and patrician class. They were quite simply unrivalled for sheer glamour, distinct from the new money of industry and nineteenth-century commerce in this as in most other respects.

By the end of the First World War this extraordinary privilege was under sustained assault. All landed estates had been hit in the late nineteenth century by the 'Great Depression'. Bad harvests, competition from the newly emerging super-states of agriculture and subsequent falling prices had a serious effect on landed incomes. Severely pressed tenants, faced with high rents and collapsing profits, blamed landlordism for the crisis and argued that the proprietors, protected by the law, were not bearing an equitable proportion of hardship. The result, in some parts of Britain, was agrarian politicization and social disorder on a scale not seen since the end of the Napoleonic Wars. Far more worrying for the landed classes than these radical positions, however, was a broad consensus, across the political spectrum, insisting that the state make more inroads into curbing the privileges of the great landlords. By the late 1880s the unthinkable situation had arisen where the landlord establishment could no longer rely on the support of the Conservative Party. The reason for this decisive separation of interest was in part the long-term shifts in urbanization and democratization that were pushing landlordism towards the cultural periphery; but there was also a more direct political context here. In 1884, the Third Reform Bill, extending the franchise to agricultural labourers, became law. This was a further blow to the power of the landed elite, finally shifting the balance of power in the Commons in what many saw, perhaps prematurely, as a complete removal of aristocratic authority. For the first time, the majority of the electorate were working class, which is why some historians understand this legislation in dramatic terms as 'the dawning of mass democracy', bringing 'into being a new sort of popular power which could, if it wished, make the possession of title, money and even land quite irrelevant'.[3] From this time on the House of Lords declared open war on the Commons, throwing out a whole series of legislative bills in the 1890s in an assertion of authority that was bound to provoke a strong response from the Executive. A retiring Gladstone remarked that the situation which had the Lords defying 'a deliberative assembly, elected by the votes of more than six million people', could 'not continue' indefinitely.[4]

Musical comedy was produced during the decisive period of what contemporaries perceived as a breakdown of the landed system. The first decade of the twentieth century staged a further and most bitterly fought political engagement between the old patricians and the representatives of the newly enfranchised masses. At the culmination were two pieces of legislation which marked the end of real political power based on land: the People's Budget of 1909, containing three new land taxes, and the abolition of the Lords' veto, which followed in 1911. Lloyd George, whose detestation of landlordism was highly significant in these events, planned a further, though largely unnecessary, 'Land Campaign' and would certainly have carried the programme through were it not for the outbreak of war.

This extraordinary development, described by Cannadine as 'one of the most profound economic and psychological changes of the period', made aristocracy a hugely potent and complex emblem.[5] However much the precise extent of its 'survival' in the inter-war years may be debated, the cultural impact of the perceived fall can hardly be doubted.[6] In part it illustrated the irresistible dynamic of modern liberalism. In this configuration aristocracy often featured, even in conservative contemporary culture, as a degenerating force declining in power and significance. Marie Corelli's *The Sorrows of Satan* (1895) is a classic example of this kind of take on aristocracy. An extremely popular work, which had a greater initial sale than any previous English novel, it has traditional nobility at it centre. Virtually all society is corrupt in this deeply moralistic tale, but it is 'swagger society' that leads the way. Aristocracy becomes anathematized here, as a greedy, corrupt class, dedicated to personal wealth, power and more venal sins – gluttony, for instance. 'One never realizes the extent to which human gourmandism can go,' remarks the narrator, 'till one knows a few peers, bishops and cabinet ministers, and watches those dignitaries feed *ad libitum*.' There is similar excess in sexual appetites – in the London of 'today ... my Lord Tom-Noddy ... has one wife and several concubines' – and almost all activities come down, in the end, to money. Lord Elton is symptomatic in this respect. A far cry from the straight-limbed, broad-chested aristocrats of a different tradition, this 'rickety little Duke' waits for his wife to die so that he can enrich his now 'thin blue blood' with the fortunes of a young American heiress. He is equally pecuniary in regards of his daughter. She is to be 'sold off', like the family estates, to the highest bidder.[7] It is important to emphasize, however, that Corelli's book, for all the venom of its assault on contemporary aristocracy, is not a political attack on the idea of aristocracy at all. On the contrary, the monster here is not tradition and privilege, but degeneration itself. Corelli's true target is not what the old English ruling class is, but what it has apparently allowed itself to become in the modern world. Like so much culture of this period, this novel constructs a modernity in which true value, absolute morality and real distinction are vanishing and it is in this context that old aristocracy took on the dimensions of a Derridean *hauntology*, a lost paradigm of quality that the vulgar, mechanistic world of mass production and consumption could only imitate in painful parody. Aristocracy, in short, became the high-status absence against which the modern was characteristically measured.

The origins of these powerful insecurities about aristocratic decline were complex, but essentially they were political in nature and thus often expressed in terms of concerns about the governance of modern Britain. Whatever doubts might be held about landed society elite, it could be perceived to have ruled with style and authority, and for an impressively long period. It had presided over the rise of Britain as a nation state and its formation of an Empire of unparalleled power and influence. Above all, it seemed to many to represent an absolute distinction that was intimately connected with Britain's standing in the world. The following is a description of Sir Robert Vermuyden, a character in *Chippinge* (1906), Stanley J. Weyman's historical romance suggestively set at the time of the 1832 Reform Act. It is highly illustrative of the kind of *angst* with which middle-class Edwardian culture sometimes faced the possibility of the final decline and fall of the long-standing national elite:

> It is easy to smile now. Easy to say that this was but an English gentleman, bound like others by the law, and Vaughan's own kinsman. But few would have smiled then. He, through whose hands passed a quarter of the patronage of a county; who dammed or turned the stream of promotion; who had made many there and could unmake them; whose mere hint could have consigned, a few years back, the troublesome to the press-gang; who belonged almost as definitely, almost as exclusively to a caste, as do white men in the India of to-day; who seldom showed himself to the vulgar save in his coach and four, or riding with belted grooms behind him – about such a one in '31 there was, if no divinity, at least the aegis of real power, that habit which unquestioned authority confers, that port of Jove to which men bow.[8]

Although this period is classically constructed as the era of late capitalism, it was in some ways the old aristocracy that seemed to contemporaries the social class of the moment, rather than labour or the bourgeoisie. Edwardian culture, especially in the forms that had popular appeal, was nothing less than fixated on the idea of aristocracy. What is observed in this obsession is not a passive charting of the fall of that elite, but the complex and often contradictory ways in which popular culture and respectable society attempted to visualize the emerging polity of a Britain without its traditional figure of authority.

Dilettantes and decadents – aristocracy in early musical comedy

The importance of the traditional aristocrat to musical comedy culture is suggested by the number of shows that referred to the aristocracy in their title: *The Earl and the Girl*, *The Duchess of Dantzic* (1903), *Lady Madcap* (1904), and so on. But these were by no means the only shows that focused centrally on the old landed elites. Indeed, no more than a handful of the West End shows listed in appendices 1 and 2 did *not* involve aristocracy and usually at some key narrative level. The corollary was that the country estate and the plantation overseas became important locations. *The Pearl Girl*, for instance, opens with 'a charming scene in Derbyshire' with the local gentry hunting otters on the Duke of Trent's estates,[9] although it was by no means the case that stage aristocracy was confined in any way to the expected settings. Whether the play text called for a shop floor, a racing track, the circus, a Japanese teashop, an island or a mountain in Canada, the aristocracy was present in numbers. To the first musical comedies, as to the last, old privilege seemed to be indispensable. Along with the embracing of the modern, there was an apparently overwhelmingly urge to provide space, often central space, for tradition in this respect.

In its early days, however, musical comedy was neither overprotective nor especially glamorizing in its representation of aristocracies. As one would expect of a culture so well disposed to modern mass society, musical comedy, again in contrast to the popular literature of the period, saw traditional aristocracy as fair game for criticism. It was perceived as an outgoing hegemony and the prototype musical comedy, *A Gaiety Girl*, took the opportunity of its departure to celebrate cultural change. While this show represented aristocracy as a class that must adapt or be forced into redundancy, others went further, visualizing an aristocracy that seemed incapable of salvation. In *The Shop Girl*, the traditional aristocrat was imaged as corrupt and beyond redemption. H. J. W. Dam's portrayal of Lady Appleby goes so far as to have her stealing money from the proceeds of charity to feather her own nest, sending, by way of compensation, illuminated religious texts and songs to the poor, whose need for edification, she claims, must outweigh any vulgar bodily need. She is mean-spirited and desperate, despising social aspirants and yet fawning over new money. In the same play, aristocracy is also characterized by its dissipation and irresponsibility. Septimus Hooley, the proprietor of 'The Royal Stores', makes a point of employing foundlings because he finds them 'at home with the aristocracy', presumably by virtue of their blood connections. *The Girl Behind the Counter* adopted a similarly strong antagonism towards aristocracy, representing it as degenerate and outmoded. General Sir Wilkie Willoughby figures as a lecher, and his son, Viscount Gushington, is an Edwardian version of the fop. He appears in the last act in fancy dress as Charles II carrying his 'little doggy'. 'It's not generally known,' he points out, 'but our family descended from the Stuarts, in fact we've descended so far we've nearly got to the bottom.' 'Gussie', a member of 'The Dilettante Club', although innocent enough, is entirely superficial, an 'appearance' who, in his pairing off with Millie Mostyn, the shop girl of the show's title, becomes fortunately combined with 'brains'.[10] There is in this resolution something of the aristocrat-saving agenda so common in Edwardian culture, but it is muted by the rather more challenging idea that it is from itself that aristocracy needs saving; and even then there are serious questions over whether the effort of intervening is really worth making.

New money, however, represented in *The Shop Girl* by the ideologically named 'John Brown', often came off much better. It was typically imagined as manly and hygienic, as in *The Girl Behind the Counter* in which Charlie Chetwyn, specifically contrasted to 'Gussie', is a 'real man', literally a gold digger who made his fortune in Africa, 'the land where', apparently, 'the best man wins'.[11] And new money was not only manlier; it was also as good as old money in terms of its influence. Thus Winnie Harborough, the heroine in *The Girl from Kays*, who holds ambitions for marriage into the nobility, finally settles for the American man about town on the grounds that all money, whatever its origins, can buy power and position. The suggestion, in this play and many others, is of a modernity in which social hierarchy, although a feature of modern life, is not as fixed as formerly. There was more social mobility and if the old aristocrats were to be replaced, the new incumbents were constructed as being no worse than those departing. The fortune-teller's song in *The Shop Girl* about 'the year/That's utterly fin-de-siècle' has

KING ALFRED'S COLLEGE
LIBRARY

precisely these sentiments, albeit in a more explicitly politicized form:

> The House of Lords in the course of years
> Will never be abolished.
> But Labour leaders will sit as peers,
> Excessively prim and polished.[12]

As might be expected of a modern bourgeois culture, early musical comedy was relatively sanguine about the prospect of the decline of traditional British aristocracy. It operated with a considerable degree of carelessness at the historical end of 'feudalism', at a time when landed aristocracy was entering the final phase of its decline in Britain.[13] *The Silver Slipper*, another 'Owen Hall' text, performs at the extremes of this easiness, constructing aristocracy as an old, retired and emasculated identity. Sir Victor Shallamar is 'too faded and weak and white to be a real man'.[14] Indifferent to the fate of his family and his only heir, a granddaughter, he devotes himself to a science that is ridiculed (astronomy) and to the pursuit of a young woman (a Venusian, actually) who despises him. By Act 2 he has become a complete embarrassment and is being advised to 'go home with nursey'.[15] Similarly in *The Sunshine Girl*, Lord Bicester is the aristocrat given a final chance to re-establish aristocratic rule. A noble of antiquity, whose 'ancestors came over with the Gold Broom', he has fallen on hard times.[16] But his college friend gives him the opportunity to find a place in the modern industrial world by having him impersonate the head of a model industrial enterprise, 'Soaptown'. In this role, Bicester proves a complete failure. He has no idea how to address his 'children, I mean my subjects; that is my employees', and even less how to run a business.[17] He delegates to a figure even more incompetent than he is and is recognized by the workers as 'nowt but a bloomin' fashion plate' and 'a real dud'.[18] Act 2 of *The Sunshine Girl* is concerned with the displacement of this traditional authority by the legitimate and benign 'manufacturer', who finally establishes a cooperative, with all his co-workers as 'shareholders'. It opens, tellingly enough, with a ball sequence that reverses the traditional function of spectacle in 'opera seria'. The glitz and glamour which once served to sustain aristocratic and monarchical rule is now framed by a discourse that runs in the opposite direction:[19]

> We are ladies of the County,
> Of the County, if you please.
> By our graciousness and bounty

> We betray our pedigrees –
> British County – haughty County,
> Cliquey County Pedigrees
>
> We are British County Magnates,
> County Magnates, and J.P.s.
> Thanks to us the County stagnates –
> County stagnates by degrees.
> Rather stodgy, Farmer Hodgey –
> Getting podgy by degrees.[20]

These shows also refuted the common insistence of Edwardian literature that new money was a foreign, and often Jewish, invasion. Musical comedy voiced strong approval for the 'counter jumper' who travelled the social ladder and loudly celebrated the end of deference. Shows like *A Gaiety Girl*, *The Girl Behind the Counter* and *The Girls from Kays* applauded the shop girl or the musical theatre artiste who stood up to the disdain of the old aristocracy. In *The Girls from Kays*, for instance, there is a song where a group of shop workers describe their outings with the 'nobs':

> An Earl with a yacht sometimes takes us onboard,
> But you must not conclude we are shady!
> And walking on shore down at Cowes with my lord,
> We all stumble – plump into my lady!
> She looks us up, thus – and she looks us down, so!
> While the Earl tries to stammer and stutter,
> The Countess is not the sort we care to know
> And so, being good girls, we just cut her.[21]

This is not to say that aristocratic identity was uniformly ridiculed in these shows. Even in some of the early plays, such as *Floradora*, *The Orchid*, *The Cingalee* and *The Blue Moon*, aristocracy was formulated in highly romantic terms as the best of British manhood and womanhood, particularly where colonial and race agendas were being played out. But the heroizing inclination was much compromised by qualifications, particularly when this musical theatre was new, most ambitious and prepared to go to some extremes to make its mark. Here the modernizing instinct of musical comedy was too strong to accommodate anything more than a very partial rescue of tradition. The more consistent heroes and heroines of this culture were not 'penniless and broken down' aristocrats, but the men, and especially women, who represented new money, new ambition and new resistance to deference.[22] An enlivened, class-busting dynamic, closely aligned to the centralizing idea of 'gaiety', was at the narratological centre of the new musical comedy. In this sense musical comedy aligned itself with bourgeois democratizing forces. Just as it was identified with new technology, so musical comedy was, in some ways, the culture of a perceived new society.

It would be absurd, though, to describe the representation of aristocracy in particular and social class generally in musical comedy as 'radical'. This was a romanticizing and escapist culture. It saw class relations in simple terms, ignoring the dynamics of social control, misrepresenting the realities of social cohesion and, most of all, constructing bourgeois Piccadilly as a metonym for modern life itself. There was quite simply no place for the slums and rookeries of Edwardian England in the staging of 'gaiety', or for factories and docks or steel works, or for any analysis of new authority in the modern world. But from its own, highly stylized perspective, early musical comedy did take positions that defined and embraced a new order. There was a liberating sentiment to musical comedy in this sense, which, however tame and distortive it now seems, was sufficiently strong at the time to attract the attention of the Lord Chamberlain's Office on more than one occasion.[23] Musical comedy visualized an end to the rigidities of what it constructed as old-fashioned stratification, ridiculing pomposity and officiousness and refusing to show deference on the basis of title. Above all, however, it applauded the wit of the sharp-minded opportunist of 'lowly birth', consolidating around this figure a new take on an old myth that the 'system' was there to be played. One implication of all this for aristocracy was that, while it might be able to survive modernity, it could not expect to withstand the force of change without making adjustments. Starting with *A Gaiety Girl*, the scenario where a moderate aristocracy learns to make its peace and come to terms with modernity became a staple of musical comedy.

Return to the feudal?

Many cultures of the Edwardian period were deeply suspicious about modernity and highly protective about ideas of aristocratic distinction, which is partly why traditional aristocracy, although diminishing in reality, was given an astonishing new lease of life in cultural terms in this period. Late Victorian and Edwardian literature is again illustrative here. In novels like *Portrait of a Lady* (1881), *King Solomon's Mines* (1885),

The Sorrows of Satan (1895), *Lady Rose's Daughter* (1903), *Sir Nigel* (1906), *Tono-Bungay* (1908), *The Good Soldier* (1915) and countless others, writers routinely mythologized the fall of the aristocracy as the collapse of civilization itself and typically tested aspiring forms of aristocracy against the imagined and much revised standards of the old. The new lords of commerce, industry and what Wyndham Lewis called 'bourgeois-bohemia' were generally found to be decisively wanting, and this produced a very marked nostalgia for the traditional order, even among avant-garde writers.[24] The redundant aristocrat of nineteenth-century literature became reconfigured as the symbol of lost quality, glamour and, above all, lost order. In literature of this period, popular and highbrow, aristocracy was typically identified with national and racial qualities of the highest order; just as estate life was identified with community and the modern city often aligned with amorphous chaos.[25]

Musical comedy did not share this heightened sense of immanent cultural collapse. It is the case that many shows, especially in the Seymour Hicks and Robert Courtneidge school of production, capitalized on the glamour and style of traditional aristocracy and in this sense could be said to have functioned as a romantic preservation of national myths about the old British elite. Shows like *The Beauty of Bath*, *The Catch of the Season* (1904) and *The Pearl Girl* were in many ways theatrical versions of society magazines; they delivered spectacle through elaborate stagings of estate balls and debutante parties complete with lavish costuming, elegant dance routines and, in some cases, narrative frameworks that positioned aristocracy at the secure centre of things. But few shows actively lamented aristocratic decline. *Floradora*, a play that pitted the new 'European Emporium' against traditional landlordism, and saw to it that the latter was restored, was something of an exception. Its sense of modernity as a degenerative force that placed old estates 'in the hands of strangers' degrading the walls of stately homes 'with placards like the coffee room of a Margate Hotel', was far from being the standard musical comedy representation.[26]

For the most part, musical comedy disengaged itself from the *fin de siècle* obsession with cultural degeneration and thus had no context for representing aristocracy as an emblem of civilization's fall. It was, however, a reconciliatory culture and, crucially, its conception of modernity insisted on notions of inclusivity. The modern was typically constructed as everybody's world and establishing rapprochement with the past was vital to musical comedy's maintenance of that status. This is why the marriage of the modern shop girl to the old culture aristocrat was so standard a narrative feature of these shows. In part it imaged a more flexible society, but also reconciled contemporaneity with its past and thus helped confirm the modern in its status as the authentic new order. Show after show – *Our Miss Gibbs, The Shop Girl, The Blue Moon, The Earl and the Girl, Floradora, The Girl from Kays, Betty* (1915), and so on – reached closure with this kind of pairing off, often accompanied by motifs of aristocratic return and purgation. *Our Miss Gibbs*, one of the defining shows of the tradition, concerns a country girl, Mary Gibbs, who has come to London to work at Garrod's. This obvious representative of modern youth and independence is being courted by a man she believes is a banker but who turns out to be a peer. Once Mary discovers the ruse, she feels not only that she cannot trust him, but that she has 'lost her respect for the upper classes' generally.[27] The rest of show concerns Lord Eynsford's attempt to restore himself and, by implication his class, to the good opinion of Mary and the modern world she represents.

Some shows specifically articulated the re-entry of aristocracy in terms of a return to the estate. In response to a perceived *over*-modernization, often understood in terms of the American effect, shows like *Floradora, The Gay Gordons* and *The Earl and the Girl* found traditional nobility and restored its status. The latter, for example, opens with an American leasing the suggestively named Stole Hall, although 'Crew Boodle' is ambitious for actual ownership and the title of 'Marquis of Stole'. All that stands in his way is the direct heir, 'young Wargrave', the absent adventurer who for most of the play figures as an evocative and elusive absence. Much in demand to be seen, interviewed and courted, he is, of course, eventually restored to his rightful estates – and the modern girl of the show's title.

Aristocrat-saving plots, where modern forces became directly responsible for rescuing aristocracy, were very common in musical comedy. This was often imaged by marriage into middle-class money. As Lady Barbara Cripps puts it in *An Artist's Model*, marriage is to be encouraged, because 'in the first place it is ordained by scripture and in the second it is rendered necessary by agricultural depression'.[28] Baron Papouche in *The Spring Chicken* marries a mercantile widow for her money. In other shows the saving of aristocracy involves the intervention not of capital, but of good sense and natural intelligence, and sometimes it required all three. In *A Country Girl*, Geoffrey Challinor, yet another returning landlord, whose father 'the old Squire' ruined himself, requires the good offices of his wily man servant, the support of the traditional villagers who remain loyal to 'the young Squire' and, finally, the love of Majorie Joy. She is especially over-determined in terms of her aristocrat-saving credentials: originally 'a country girl', she represents solid good sense; as a singer who has migrated to the city and made her fortune, she has the additional qualifications of being connected to both modernity and money. *The Merry Widow*, one of the most popular shows of the period, had a heroine constructed from a similar convergence. Count Danilo, a traditional aristocrat, is rescued from a decadent, hedonistic life by Anna, who started life as a peasant, but begins the play as the rich widow of a banker.

In this way musical comedy developed a marked ambiguity towards aristocracy. Often within the same show, aristocracy was decadent and effete, and yet somehow necessary to the maintenance of equilibrium, invariably imaged by marriage across the extremes of the social order. Thus in the most standard musical comedy, 'ordinary' modern women marry into the landed society, but this typical plot responds to much more than the simple fantasy of the rags-to-riches story.[29] Quite apart from the reversal that had aristocrats in need of new money, more was at stake in the successful outcome of these plots than good fortune. These marriages were highly suggestive of responses to wider issues of change and continuity. They represented, on the one hand, musical comedy's attempt to reconcile a lively, vibrant modernity with a more conservative instinct for tradition. At the same time, they imaged a new age polity where modernity and traditional authority embraced. Here was the suggestion of both confident assimilation and insecurities about the maintenance of rule and authority in contemporaneity. There were times when the ambiguities of this position, somewhere between democratizing innovation and custom, reached truly bizarre proportions.

Mixing with the nobs – Nelly Neil and the Countess of Rokeby

In 1907 Charles Frohman staged a musical comedy at the Aldwych entitled *Nelly Neil*. This show, with music by Ivan Caryll and book by C. M. S. McLellan, was intended as a star vehicle for Edna May, who had never quite repeated her earlier success in *The Belle of New York*. With a relatively short run of 107 performances, *Nelly Neil* was not a great commercial success, but it was notable in its own way. An astonishing treatment of radical political ideologies, it was the first and only attempt to give the musical comedy makeover to socialism/communitarianism and anarchism.[30]

The result was hardly orthodox, except in a musical comedy sense. Signing up to socialism in this context became not a matter of conviction to any principles, but of being smitten by the beautiful and 'plucky' Nelly. The show did, however, strike an immediately politicized and controversial note in its opening, which has a group of lords attempting to find their offspring who they fear have got in with 'bad company'. The play opens, then, with insecurities about a seemingly lost genera- tion of aristocracy, but it follows up with immediate assurance. These future lords and ladies, far from sinking into degeneracy, have adapted to the modern world in a most remarkable way. Now constituted as Nelly's 'followers', the sons and daughters of old aristocracy have transformed themselves into 'jolly' socialists and shopworkers. Former debutantes have rejected 'ostentation' and 'vanity' and now assist Nelly in her flower-selling business. In their opening chorus, they assault 'the degenerate British aristocracy' that produced them.[31] As the first act develops, further groups and institutions fall victim to Nelly's charms – the 'Stock Exchange', for instance, followed shortly and most signifi- cantly by the older peers themselves. At the end of Act 1, this band of unlikely socialists are led off to enjoy a 'simple life' at 'Simplicity Farm', where Nelly performs as 'a marvel of dainty simplicity'.[32]

It is important to the play text to emphasize the two-way nature of this strange alignment between socialism and aristocracy. Significantly, Nelly takes her followers to task for abandoning their elegant clothes and dressing up as workers. Being a socialist or a communitarian in this play involves a kind of Pied Piper submission to Nelly's vitality, but very little self-sacrifice otherwise. It might be a 'noble idea' to 'renounce all finery', but as Nelly herself puts it, 'we must never allow our noble ideas to interfere with our good looks. The only hope for us socialists is to be as artistic as aristocrats. Remember, I want to dazzle ... before I finish.'[33] With this camp version of the political, Nelly's 'way' becomes both glamorous and progressive. It is, in short, thoroughly assimilated to the musical comedy version of modernity. Upbeat and fun, socialism is pre- sented as a new thing for a new age:

> Try this way
> Come this way
> You'll find it leads to the swing,
> It leads you out
> From gloom and doubt
> To the house of cheerful things,
> Try *my* way
> Come *my* way
> When you find your own way's wrong
> The world moves fast
> Now don't be last
> You're missing the train – come along![34]

Nelly is figuratively and literally a true heir to the Gaiety girl tradition. Her disappointed mother, a former Gaiety girl herself, tries to restore Nelly to what she regards as a fit and proper place on the stage, but she need hardly bother. In all respects but the superficial, Nelly's role as an activist is no different from that of the standard musical comedy heroine. Her role is to sing and dance her way thorough a pantomime version of politics and reach a spectacular and harmonious closure, in this case a musical comedy millenarianist fantasy. The dastardly anarchists, led by the beautiful but dangerous Princess Rassolova, are defeated. Their plans to bomb Ricketts's bank leaving Nelly to take the blame are foiled. A striking *tableau* evoking the virtues of the 'simple' and 'natural' life and a new international order becomes the stirring opener to the final act. Inclusive of the French 'and the Americans, the Germans, the Russians and the rest', a homely gathering of nations stands in for social redemption.[35] Finally, temporarily forgetting her commitment to labour and a life on the land, Nelly agrees to marry Billy Ricketts, man about town and heir to the banking millions. Far from involving any clash between capital and labour, *Nelly Neil* ends up, in standard musical comedy style, outside a church – with an extra ironic edge because the flower shop girl marrying into money is a 'socialist'.

The Stage reviewer was distinctly puzzled by *Nelly Neil*. He found the political meaning of the show difficult to pin down, wondering whether McLellan 'intended to contrast the ideal Socialism in its most simple and visionary form with the warped Socialism of unreasoning and bloody anarchy'.[36] Apart from the curious muddling of socialism and anarchism, this was to take the idea on which the show was based much too seriously. The espousal of alternative politics certainly reflected Edwardian concerns about life without aristocracy, but it was also used in a gimmicky way here, by a culture whose viability was decisively linked to innovation. The politics of *Nelly Neil*, like the 'Japanning' of *The Geisha*, was partly a response to market imperatives, to the importance of finding a new package for what was by the turn of the century a standard commodity. As with the group of plays, including *The Quaker Girl* and *The Girl from Utah*, where the 'twist' involved religious nonconformity, *Nelly Neil* turned to 'social issues' for its 'unique selling-point', becoming in the process something like a pantomime pastiche of the Ibsenite/Shavian 'social' drama, although the show did not explicitly construct itself in such a way. *Nelly Neil* was not so much a political show as an application of musical comedy to an imagined 'political' domain.

As with all musical comedy treatments, this involved a great deal of romanticism, the usual diminution of subject and the standard cavalier innocence about potentially complex engagements with culture and society. The essential dynamic was, again, the appropriative one that would render potentially difficult, controversial issues – social inequality for instance – safe. Thus socialism is neither seriously espoused nor savagely mocked in *Nelly Neil*, but rather sweetened until it becomes not much more than a new role-play for the modern generation. Anarchism, likewise, is not engaged but shrunk to a stage evil. The commune retreat of the 'Nelly Neil Original Order of Socialist Thinkers' is not a serious attempt to understand or parody radical dissent, but rather an opportunity for entirely standard lovemaking scenes. Despite the change in packaging, *Nelly Neil* sees no deviation from the stock-in-trade production of 'stage pictures' and spectacle, and, for all its ostensibly politicized content, no significant change to the social world that had been typically imagined by musical comedy from its earliest days. Society here, as throughout the genre, is celebrated as a happy, modern, colourful play space. If social inequality is perceived at all, it is staged as picaresque difference and subject to all kinds of moderating influences. Transgression is usually a case of misunderstanding and mistaken identity. If there are such things as corruption and iniquity, these are controlled, circumnavigated and subject to the workings of a universal justice guaranteeing that whatever else might have to be endured, the right boy/man will always end up with the right girl/woman. These are the real terms of the polity imagined by *Nelly Neil* and it was within such controlled boundaries that musical comedy generally functioned.

Central to this polity was the highly significant response taken to aristocracy. *Nelly Neil* projects a safe and finally inclusive world. The concerns of nobility strike a keynote in the play's opening chorus. For its duration, the show remains protective, determined to nourish the condition of aristocracy in the modern world. Indeed, it is possible to read the whole show as an aristocrat-saving piece in the vein of, say, Mrs Humphry Ward's novel *Lady Rose's Daughter* (1903) or Robert Hitchens' *The Woman with the Fan* (1904) or even Baroness Orczy's *The Scarlet Pimpernel* (1905). Although McLellan's show does not rescue aristocracy from physical danger, it does seek to protect it from a dangerous commitment to out-of-date ideas and institutions. Above all, at a time when landed aristocracy in the real world was suffering what many took to be its demise, *Nelly Neil* finds a new, enlivened space for aristocracy to function in and not just in Nelly's wake. Although Nelly takes centre stage in this show, behind her stands the Countess of Rokeby as the owner of the estate where all the 'pretty young women' of England will learn 'the economic law of socialism'. They will be sent out to marry and in this way the whole of England will be 'converted'.[37] This is the strategy behind Nelly Neil's evangelicalism and the strong suggestion is that Nelly's enlightened friend from across the tracks is behind it all the time. In shows like *Nelly Neil* aristocracy was more than just on display. Certainly some shows did continue to celebrate the glamour and wealth of landed society as if nothing had happened to the status of the old elite, but most, like *Nelly Neil*, constructed aristocracy in very different and more complex ways. Redundant and displaced; lost and found; dispossessed and returned to fortune – aristocracy was dynamic in a narrative sense and often ambiguously positioned within the same show. On the one hand, it signified an abstract and simplified idea of riches and wealth obtainable with the right attitude and a few necessary qualifications:

> If you sigh in your ambition
> For the dignified position
> Of a countess – or it may be something bigger
> By my final magic touches
> You can emulate a Duchess
> And win half the British Peerage
> By your figure.[38]

More fundamentally, the figure of aristocracy plugged musical comedy into dialogue with the standard historiography of the modern age that positioned the values of landed society at the antithesis of a progressive dynamic powered by democracy, industrialization and the application of new technologies. It is for this reason that the collapse of aristocracy, its removal from political, economic and cultural power, became so strong an image of the final ascendancy of mass culture and society over traditional order, authority and distinction. At the same time, the idea of aristocracy became bound up with insecurities about the new age, and Britain's role in it. It was one of the hallmarks of musical comedy's engagement with modernity that it should attempt to sing and dance those insecurities away.

Musical comedy aristocracy and the First World War: *Theodore and Co.* and *Betty*

The First World War was a watershed period for musical theatre. It marked the end of the glory days of British musical comedy, but determined an ending that would be on a fittingly large scale, with the war producing a huge audience for this kind of entertainment. It saw not just the last of the hit shows, but with *Chu Chin Chow, The Better 'Ole* (1917) and *The Boy*, some of the biggest shows of all. The scale and nature of this impact is the subject of a later chapter, but it is appropriate at this point to consider musical comedy's staging of aristocracy in the war years because there were some significant divergences here from what had gone before. The war period saw a number of shows that had a specific focus on aristocracy – *Betty* (1915), *Tina* (1915) and *Theodore and Co.* (1916) being the most popular. Some, like *Tina*, a show that has an impoverished European monarchy being saved by American money, continued with the old signifying traditions; others broke rank in ways that were highly suggestive of a culture under strain. Here the idea of aristocracy gained a further lease of life, beyond assimilation and reconciliation. No longer a case of making space for tradition or defending it in the standard ways, musical comedy now began to depict an aristocracy more seriously concerned about saving its falling estate. Even more suggestively, the wartime aristocracy was constructed as being empowered enough to find its own way back to position and status.

Theodore and Co., for instance, the Gaiety blockbuster notable for being the first full-length Ivor Novello musical, maintained a declining aristocracy, but here the new generation of aristocrats, although spongers and faintly bogus, are also fun, eventually effective and, crucially, independent. Young aristocracy, in this as in other wartime shows, becomes sufficiently dynamic, inventive and connected to save *itself* from disgrace, with the result that, in the last moments of *Theodore and Co.*, a new family inheritance arrives to maintain the old line. Most significantly, the virtually standard narrative business that has aristocracy saved by exogamous marriage into the new dynamic social orders is dropped in some of the wartime shows. Instead of marrying a real showgirl, the aristocrat hero of *Theodore and Co.*, for instance, marries Pansy, who only pretends to be a nightclub singer. In reality, she is nothing less than true-blue aristocracy, herself the daughter of a Duke who 'looked on Noah as a parvenue'.[39] *Theodore and Co.* (1916) becomes, then, one of the very few musical comedies where aristocracy marries into aristocracy as dénouement.

That new narrative twist involved a kind of back-pedalling, a rectification that rescued aristocracy from its former reputation for decadence and dissipation and from the imperative to 'integrate' with modernity. Similar ideas were affirmed in other ways in the same show. A secondary plot line here has the Duke of Shetland imagining that he is about to have a secret liaison with 'Baby Grand', who he thinks is a music hall star. This would be an entirely standard development of musical comedy, but in *Theodore and Co.* it is not allowed. In a further highly charged case of mistaken identity, this singer, the same Pansy, is revealed to be the Duke's own daughter. In this way aristocracy is prevented from straying, not just badly but perversely so. It is also forced into the correct paternal role of protecting family honour.

Theodore and Co., did more than redeem aristocracy. For all its modern framework, implied in the risqué or, as the Lord Chamberlain's Office put it, 'vaguely dashing', dialogue and song lyrics, this show placed a dynamic traditional aristocracy at the centre of things.[40] *Betty* was rather more conventional in some respects, but it similarly developed new ways of centring aristocracy. An appropriation of the Cinderella story which ran for a year in the West End and almost 400 performances, *Betty* responded even more emphatically to what appeared to be a new public taste for old order. This show, slightly earlier than *Theodore and Co.*, was fixed very precisely at the apparent end of aristocracy and it is this final demise that gives the plot its urgent dynamic. Its male lead is Gerrard, the son of the Duke of Crowborough – 'the last of the direct line' and 'just as well' in his opinion.[41] His father insists that he must marry and return to the country to take up the traditional role of landed aristocracy. But Gerrard finds this 'talk of duty to one station's' so 'old-fashioned'. He refuses not just marriage, but the recognition of any local or national responsibility:

> What do I owe my ancestors? It's true the first Crowborough was a hero – a grateful nation gave him a fortune – but the next Duke gambled it away. Since then we've all been gamblers and spendthrifts – including myself. That's why I'm glad I'm the last of my line.[42]

In this way the show imagines, in quite strong and serious terms, a nation without its traditional leadership and implies even greater insecurities – the end of race, for example – to the extent that Gerrard is strongly identified with England itself in this play and the English estate.

The answer to this near-apocalyptic drift is at first sight a traditional one. Betty is the Cinderella figure, the family maid, who Gerrard, in a fit of drunkenness and spite, agrees to marry. But instead of living happily ever after, Gerrard packs off his new wife to the country and states his intention of wasting the rest of his time in town as a dissipated, and eventually, broke aristocrat. Whilst Betty spends his inheritance and educates herself in aristocratic style, Gerrard becomes increasingly bitter. However, Betty is no usurping gold-digger. Her transformation into a 'real' lady is effected only because she believes it will make her desirable to Gerrard. The ploy fails and in the final scene Betty changes herself back into a maid. With this extraordinary restoration of the social status quo, Gerrard himself is finally able to declare his love for Betty. Now that order has returned to the world, he can go back to his country estates and take his position at the centre of society and culture.

Betty operated as a curious metonym, apparently holding out the offer of a return to normalized traditional social relations, if only aristocracy could find a way of behaving itself. This return included imaging a resumption of both class relations and traditional gender roles, for Betty the character was not exactly representative of the Gaiety girl energy so closely aligned with modernity in the earlier shows. Rather, she suggested a more old-fashioned and, again, traditional feminine identity. Like other shows of the wartime years, *Betty* was illustrative of a popular culture that was rallying round traditional leadership and authority, a return to the security of orthodoxy that reflected a more general retrenchment from modernity and innovation at a time of great national crisis. *The Better 'Ole*, the show about how 'old Bill' and his mates did for the Hun, is sometimes regarded as the classic wartime show, but a show like *Betty*, although it makes no direct reference to war, was every bit as suggestive in articulating how the war had changed things and, in particular, how concerns about leadership and authority were being experienced.

This revivification of aristocracy was not restricted to stage life. Aristocrats in reality embraced the war as the great turning point, for it did much more than simply shift the Government's priorities away from democratization and the modernization of administration. The old magnates regarded the war as a crisis that would require their special talents for command, authority, service and perhaps even chivalry. Here, it was thought, was a golden opportunity to regain some of the civil status that had been so substantially eroded over the previous generation. A play like *Betty* undoubtedly addressed this return and illustrated how this escapist culture was at the same time so intimately engaged with contemporaneity, although it should be emphasized that closeness did not always mean having a finger on the pulse. Indeed, it can be argued that musical comedy's wartime response to aristocracy may have signified one sense in which the culture was beginning to misjudge things, because it very quickly became apparent that war would *not* revive the traditional authority and reputation of British aristocracy. On the contrary, the wartime death toll among young male aristocrats, which was disproportionately high, probably accelerated the process of aristocratic collapse, as did the later exposures of incompetent leadership. In its exaggerated form, the officers killed in the 'Great War' became at best a mythological 'lost generation', fictionalized by a number of influential writers of the period, including Siegfried Sassoon and Robert Graves. At worst, old aristocrats were, in the late 1920s, to became the donkeys responsible for leading lions to an early and, as far as many were concerned, unnecessary death. The cultural treatment of the returning aristocrat as a crippled, emasculated and dependent figure (Clifford Chatterley in Lawrence's *Lady Chatterley's Lover* and Basil in his 'The Ladybird', for instance) was unequivocal. From the vantage point of the1920s, it was clear that the decline and fall of traditional aristocracy in Britain had become a reality. It may be, then, that a show like *Betty*, for all its popularity and the immediacy of its response to the national crisis, was one of the early signs of a musical comedy that was misjudging events, and, perhaps, losing its grip on the modern and the modern dynamic.

5
Interventions in the Politics of Gender and Sexuality

The biggest stars of musical comedy were women, whether as leads or in terms of the famous troupes – the Gaiety girls, the Gibson girls, the Bath Buns, the Sandow girls, and so on, who often proved key to box office success. Ada Reeve was one of many who acknowledged the astonishing popularity of these groups, describing in her memoirs how 'the Gaiety girls of those days really were more important than the principals in the show, and were quite as well known to the public. Their photographs could be seen everywhere'.[1] Often described as a 'worshipping' culture, musical comedy put women, configured as 'girls', on a pedestal and invited the adoring gaze. It was a celebration of feminine performance in more ways than one, establishing what it understood to be the new qualities of the female actor – a 'bewitching' personality, 'dainty' singing, 'piquant' acting and an 'exquisite sense of humour' – and mapping these against what it took to be the essential feminine characteristics – 'grace', 'charm' and 'fascination'.[2] It was this customized notion of female beauty and glamour that provided the essential spectacle of musical comedy, a spectacle taken by the historian of the Gaiety, Macqueen-Pope, to represent nothing less than essential femininity, a cultured articulation of 'womanhood incarnate' (Illustration 8).[3]

It is important to recognize that this was a cleaned-up, modernized version of display, a formulation established against theatrical styles and genres that continued to provoke outrage in the moral majority. In this sense musical comedy again worked to position itself outside traditions that were more exclusive and, from many contemporary perspectives, thoroughly immoral. As a respectable institution, it was imperative for musical comedy to break the connections that had become established between music theatre and the unsavoury.[4] Fully sensitive to the commercial value of the erotic, musical comedy was, at the same time,

Illustration 8 'Womanhood incarnate' (*Our Miss Gibbs*)

mindful of the importance of its status as harmless entertainment. Thus it maintained the eroticized stage, but in very careful ways. Erotic *mise-en-scène*, characterized by 'diaphanous fabrics', did not have a place in musical comedy. Exotic ballet steps also disappeared. Certain kinds of male impersonation, popular in burlesque and music hall, were similarly ousted, particularly where these involved revealing costume. The point about replacing 'fleshings' with high-class fashion dress was precisely that it measured the crucial distance between musical comedy and what was constructed as a seedy world of vulgar voyeurism, for pink-coloured tights carried an evident signification. They were 'most

invested with indexical significance of skin, eroticism, and sexual stim-
ulation' and it was for this reason that they disappeared from the West
End musical comedy stage.[5]

At the same time as it worked for respectability, musical comedy
developed and sustained the illusion of its status as a deeply feminine
culture. This undoubtedly involved constituting gender difference 'as a
relationship between a male spectator and a desirable female image', but
it would be quite inadequate to see the gendering of musical comedy
solely in such ways.[6] This was a mainstream culture, geared to the conservative centre and promoted in terms of the well-appointed urban and
suburban 'everyone', the general enthusiast who could be expected to
take an interest in such matters as Lily Elsie's 'return to *The Count of
Luxembourg* after the honeymoon holiday has run its course'.[7] Far from
operating in a near underworld, as some have implied, musical comedy
was a decisively public institution.[8] It was quite astute in some respects,
but it was at the same time self-consciously innocent and thoroughly
legitimate. Where it appealed specifically to men, it addressed not sala-
cious instinct, but 'the ordinary Englishman' who might need advice on
where to take 'his wife or family to dinner before the play.'[9] For the most
part, however – and this is central to any understanding of musical comedy – the implied audience of musical comedy was not exclusively male
at all. As Erica Rappaport has shown, 'theatrical managers, writers and
retailers', in a specific commercial strategy, imagined a female as well as
a male spectator, and made a product that they assumed, correctly,
would be attractive to both. In Rappaport's account, the 'attractive
young actress', so much at the heart of musical comedy, was the key box
office draw and for obvious reasons. 'This figure,' she writes,

> was so common on the turn-of-the-century stage because theater own-
> ers wanted to appeal to a mixed-sex, mass audience. Entrepreneurs
> attracted heterosocial audiences by constructing narratives that
> emphasized heterosexual pleasure and gender difference. They envi-
> sioned audiences as looking at different aspects of the same produc-
> tion. They believed the male audiences desired youthful female bodies
> and female audiences coveted the clothing covering these bodies.[10]

(See Illustration 9.)

But musical comedy's gendering of the stage was far more than a
simple matter of putting women on show in order to appeal to the sexual
and consumer desires that were assumed to be motivating audiences.
There was a very specific and quite complex formulation of femininity

Illustration 9 The spectacle of the feminine (*Our Miss Gibbs*)

at the centre of the musical comedy narrative that was specifically aligned with the modern world. Indeed, musical comedy formulated a modernity feminized as 'the shop girl', 'the girl on the film' and 'the girl from up there'. This construction of a crucial identification between femininity and the modern estate made the musical comedy stage one of the growing number of public cultural spaces, along with the modern high street and, again, the department store, that helped define the modern world – or at least a highly circumscribed version of it – as a woman's world.

The seriousness of this latter function could hardly be explicitly articulated, given the imperative of maintaining the association between musical comedy and gaiety, but it was essentially an attempt to fix and secure an idealized notion of femininity at a time of great cultural change and insecurity. As many cultural historians have shown, the *fin de siècle* was crucially a period of changing gender roles and shifting sexual identities. In the public perception, at least at some social levels, what were once thought of as the unchangeable conditions of normal life were becoming matters of social and cultural construction as 'men became women. Women became men. Gender and country were put into doubt. The single life was found to harbour two sexes and two nations.'[11] Against this background, where 'New Women',

'Odd Women' and 'Queer Men' became the symptomatic configurations, there was clearly an important political signification to musical comedy's deep insistence on maintaining the essentials of the 'natural' order, albeit with some important readjustments. The issues of gender and sexuality, then, become key for understanding musical comedy's general cultural articulation and the specifics of its often contradictory responses to change and stability, innovation and tradition, conservatism and radicalism. On the one hand, it is a modern culture that wants to embrace, or at least assimilate, what it perceives as the new conditions of the twentieth century. Thus it finds a central place for modern women. As a mainstream culture, however, and one largely constructed by men, it wants to maintain the status quo against what is implicitly seen as the excesses of an 'uncontrollable' and 'chaotic' modernity. As a popular culture it is crucial that it appears up-to-date and open to changing public perceptions of morality. At the same time, as a mainstream culture it manages decorum on behalf of the state and the Lord Chamberlain's Office. In these ways and more, the issues of gender and sexuality are suggestive of some of the defining contradictions of musical comedy and go to the heart of its character as popular culture.

The magic power of his rod – licence and the musical comedy stage

> Behold! Behold!
> Dancers ripened by the sun,
> Quick with passion, vigour, fun
> Slender virgins everyone
> Others weighing half a ton.[12]

These lyrics come from scene 4 of *Chu Chin Chow*, which is set in a slave market. For all the moral outrage caused by W. T. Stead's exposés of child prostitution and 'white slavery' in the late 1880s, and other major sex scandals of the *fin de siècle*, there were no censorship difficulties here. The National Vigilance Association may have battled against the 'coarse suggestiveness' of musical theatre generally and what was seen as the 'compulsory sexualization of women in thrall to male viciousness', but this was hardly the view of 'the public'.[13] The eroticization of slavery, at least in the *Chu Chin Chow* context, met with no recorded resistance whether from the audience or the Lord Chamberlain's Office. It can be imagined that the staging of the slave market would have been understood as part of the standard comic Oriental stylization and the fat joke, also part of musical comedy Orientalism, would have been thought of as a further lightening of things. The stage direction for the scene that had these actresses '*uncovering their nakedness*' did, however, cause some concern, prompting the Lord Chamberlain's Office to seek elucidation.[14] Oscar Asche, the writer and producer of this hugely successful wartime show, had good contacts in the Lord Chamberlain's Office and was able to demonstrate that any disrobing would be largely gestural and entirely strategic. After a brief exchange, it went ahead unaltered. With a West End run of 2,235 performances *Chu Chin Chow* went on to become the most popular musical comedy ever, reaching new levels of commercialism in terms of how it was publicized and merchandised.[15]

The scene and the anecdote are suggestive of some of the ways in which musical comedy was both gendered and sexualized as a culture. It was, to a considerable extent, written and produced by men and men operated the censorship mechanisms that governed it. Gladys B. Unger, the librettist responsible for the English adaptation of *The Marriage Market* (1913), *Toto* (1916) and co-author of *Betty*, was one of the few woman writing West End musical comedy during this period, and there were a handful of women producers, Ada Reeve, May Yohe, Kitty Loftus and Lily Brayton – mostly former actresses who had moved across to production but usually for a short period of time. There were exceptions in other theatres, high-profile women established in management – Marie Wilton, for instance, who took over the Prince of Wales and refurbished it in a 'feminine style' – and there were instances of women positioning themselves strategically behind the scenes. After her husband's death, Adelaide Stoll, it is said, ran the Liverpool music hall, although her son, Oswald, appeared as the public face of authority. Similarly, Mary Moore, 'a prominent suffragist', was the 'business brains' behind the management of Wyndham's, 'both before and after her marriage' to Charles Wyndham.[16] Musical comedy, however, seems to have involved relatively few such exceptions. Women performed in musical comedy; but they did not compose, write or produce it, at least on the professional West End stage (see appendices 1–3).[17] For all this masculine predominance, however, musical comedy was not presented as a men-only culture. On the contrary, it was a genre that implied a mixed and mainstream auditorium. Where musical comedy was mildly risqué and faintly erotic, it had to be so in ways consistent with the rescue mission that would distance the 'new' theatre from any seedy associations with failing burlesque and reposition it as a modern mainstream culture.

Musical comedy was supposed to be youthful and exhilarating, but its *joie de vivre* had to be kept within the bounds of public acceptability as generally understood by middle-class society and implemented by theatre censorship.

The codes governing these standards were ostensibly strict, especially with regard to the maintenance of 'decency' and the avoidance of any possible offence to 'religious reverence'.[18] Any overt political intervention would also be closely scrutinized, particularly where reference was made to living persons, and censors were obliged to remove material that might 'impair relations with any Foreign Power'. Plays could not contain 'offensive personalities' or be calculated to 'conduce to crime or vice'.[19] These regulations were applied to all forms of theatre, but probably not with equal force. There were, for example, special concerns with regards to 'serious' drama and conflicts between the censor and the writers of 'social' plays flourished during the Edwardian period. A series of high-profile dramas, including Granville Barker's *Waste*, Edward Garnett's *The Breaking Point* and Shaw's *Blanco Posnet*, were refused licences at this time. The subsequent debate led to the appointment of a Joint Select Committee of the Lords and Commons to review the whole issue of theatre censorship in 1909, and a confirmation of most of the existing protocols.

Musical comedy functioned in this framework, but it did not excite the interest of the Lord Chamberlain's Office and the wider political environment in the way that 'serious' theatre did. The main concern of the Joint Select Committee of 1909 was the 'drama of ideas' and what appeared to be the lax licensing of music halls. No specific reference was made to musical comedy in the Committee's report, an omission which suggested that, by this date, the establishment had satisfied itself with regard to what was the most popular form of Edwardian theatre. Certainly, this is the implication from the licences issued by the Lord Chamberlain's Office. After the initial concerns, reflected in doubts about *A Gaiety Girl*, these now indicated a high level of recognition and acceptance, with officers typically making reference to the standard, predictable nature of the texts they were examining. By the wartime period there can be no doubt about the safety and propriety of musical comedy as far as the censor was concerned. *Tina* was described as having 'not much point in either plot or characterization; but both are wholly devoid of offence'.[20] Likewise *Theodore and Co.*: 'I find no harm in the dialogue or songs, though the former may be vaguely dashing at times, and nothing suggestive seems to be intended by the business of the play.'[21] *Betty* was considered to be 'quite harmless in its sketches of fast society' and *The Better 'Ole*, a show dealing with potentially controversial territory, was considered to be 'sound and truthful throughout'.[22]

Responses such as these said as much about the acceptance of musical comedy as about any intrinsic levels of 'offence'. Musical comedy was considered to be safe in part by virtue of being musical comedy. *Theodore and Co.*, for example, which included the plot line of a woman attempting to sell sexual favours in exchange for a position for her husband, was far more racy than Eden Philpott's *The Secret Woman* in some respects, yet it was the latter, a serious, social drama, that was refused a licence. As a musical comedy *Theodore and Co.* was perceived to be, by definition, light, insignificant and without any didactic purpose. The so-called 'drama of ideas', however, raised expectations of a wholly different kind, which was presumably why it fell subject to a different degree of tolerance and sensitivity.

In this way musical comedy, although it remained respectable and entirely within the law, enjoyed a relative degree of licence. The case of innuendo, for instance, a staple of the musical comedy, is illustrative here. The genre made 'extensive use of "knowingness", the technique of hints and silences that left the audience to fill the gaps'.[23] Most of this was trite and predictable, as in the song which opens *The Girl from Kays* to explain what 'a girl has to do for it' (i.e. to get a husband), but some not entirely so. The following from a song in *A Greek Slave*, ostensibly concerning the magic powers of a soothsayer, may not be consistent with everyday notions of mainstream culture's tolerance to the sexual imagination in the late Victorian and Edwardian period. The example, incidentally, comes from a show which at least one reviewer considered to be 'high art':[24]

> If we doubt the magic power of his rod
> Or the bona fide wonders of its prod
> He has other rods in pickle
> Which he thinks are sure to tickle
> In a manner that's particularly odd,
> Oh it's odd![25]

Other kinds of sexual innuendo and imagery were smuggled in via the theatrical conventions of cross-dressing where transvestite roles were conventionally given songs around ideas of sexual ambiguity – 'If I Were a Girl' in *The Silver Slipper*, for example, or 'When I Was a Girl' in *A Country Girl*, both sung by men. Many plot lines involved men dressing and behaving as women, and vice versa, and these were exploited for both humour and erotic suggestion, although of a kind that would have been sanitized by comparison to some music hall versions of cross-dressing.[26] In *San Toy*, for instance, the female character San Toy initially appears as a boy. In this guise she has something approaching a love scene with her female friend Poppy, whom she embraces not just from the disguised position of a precocious 'boy', but also as an adult woman. The subsequent and 'legitimate' Bobbie/San Toy love affair is likewise full of homoerotic suggestions, because it involves two characters both ostensibly men (or, to be more precise, one a man and the other a boy). This kind of gender ambiguity, where San Toy is boy/girl and son/daughter, was always resolved by musical comedy in conventional ways. There were no serious threats to what Jeffrey Weeks has called 'the sacramental family' in this theatre.[27] In the end, the sexual world of musical comedy was formally normalized: gender had 'to be one or the other – not both'.[28] But along the way of the inevitable return to conventional heterosexual relations, musical comedy did license adventurous confusion. The opening of *The School Girl* is again suggestive. The show begins with the girls of a convent school wanting to stage a play. The Reverend Mother aims to banish men from the production, but her charges explain how they themselves can take the male roles:

> *Lillian*: I'm sure you won't object, ma mère, when you see me make love to Cicely: I'll do it so nicely. I'll say to her (*putting her arm around Cicely's waist*), 'My darling! I've thought of nothing else since first I looked into your beautiful eyes!' And then I kiss her. So! (*All the girls pantomime appreciation and sigh*).
> *Mother*: I cannot allow this. The idea of this play of yours is too ridiculous.
> *Lillian*: But it won't be ma mère, when I'm dressed! When I've put on a moustache and taken off my skirt –
> *Mother*: Taken off –[29]

One point about this exchange is the recognition that it gives to both traditions of licence in some kinds of theatrical performance and the essential safety of those traditions. The scene points to all kinds of ambiguities and sexual possibilities and yet remains purposefully innocent, a piece of stage business doubly confined to the realms of the comedic stage inasmuch as it visualizes lovemaking between women in a play within a play. In this way the scene images something fundamental about musical comedy, a form that retained its reputation for the risqué while remaining at the mainstream centre of things. It was a very long way from being a celebration of sexual diversity, but it did not seem frightened of its own sexual shadow either. In some ways it confirmed the most important characteristic of gender roles in the 1900s, 'which was not simply that they had changed in a particular way but that by comparison with the early and mid-Victorian era, the very nature of these roles were increasingly contested and uncertain'.[30] At the same time, musical comedy pandered to sexual fantasies that at the time would have been ascribed primarily to men, although whether it really was seriously connected to a fringe and seedy 'sub-rosa world of pornography, prostitution and assignation that reached right up to the stage door' must be doubtful. Peter Bailey, perhaps mistaking the reputation that musical comedy had among moral crusade groups for the reality,[31] greatly overstates the point when he imagines a musical theatre where the likes of Ellaline Terris or Marie Tempest turned in performances that had the capacity to 'signify ... the fullest discharge of sexual desire in male terms of sexual intercourse and orgasm, the lot'.[32] There was suggestion and innuendo. The staging of 'joke' lovemaking scenes between women was fairly common and the exoticizing of the racial 'other' routine. Likewise, slave scenes, or at least scenes showing women in eroticized servitude, were standard. *A Greek Slave* opens with slave girls singing, *The Cingalee* with plantation workers picking tea, *The Geisha* with eager to please geishas, and so on. The sexual implications of this kind of scenario, quite apart from being subject to strong external controls, were moderated, however, by excessively beautifying production values – yet another function of spectacle in this culture. Musical comedy, then, involved a loosening of values and behaviour, but it also constituted something of a benchmarking exercise. Far from constituting a celebration of Dionysian energy, it remained highly controlled. Indeed, it was on the musical comedy stage that professional standards were set for progressive and respectable theatrical fun at the turn of the century and beyond.

Merry, jolly, natural girls – new girl versus New Woman

Defining the scope of the respectably sexualized stage implicated musical comedy in the representation of gender identities in obvious ways, not least through its exploitation of the male gaze. These shows clearly did make a very strong appeal to the voyeuristic, but that was only one of many pitches and not all were so confirming of traditional gender positions. It would be inadequate to understand the Gaiety girl image, for example, solely as part of a sexualized appeal to men. As suggested above, the Gaiety girl was much more than just a showgirl. Emerging as a dazzling version of the soubrette, this figure quickly became a cultural icon, constructed as a sign of the times.[33] She functioned both as a thorough subversion of Victorian stereotypes of the music theatre actress and as New Woman identity, albeit of a very particular kind, aligned with 'new times' thinking in quite specific ways. This is not to deny that musical comedy's stock in trade was sexual or that 'the rhetoric of the musical comedy woman as girl' traded on the idea of controlled availability, the 'naughty, but nice' syndrome, or, 'in another formulaic phrase, "not too good and not too bad" ' notion.[34] But musical comedy was also much concerned with the accommodation and assimilation of newer perspectives and these sometimes constituted significant challenges to both conventional and radical gender roles as they were commonly formulated. Masculinist posturing was often held up to ridicule, for example, as in the following song where Lieutenant Fairfax, a would-be hero, who plays no constructive part in resolving the complicated plot of *The Geisha*, attempts to flex his muscles. Here a woman does need rescuing. She is saved, however, not by the gung-ho singer of this song, but by the geisha girl of the show's title, who has a much more subtle approach to things. The song, then, becomes ironic, a comic exposure of worn-out ideas about gender relations:

> While Nature with manhood endows us
> And beauty our pulses can fire
> There's never a sight that will rouse us
> Like a woman in danger most dire.[35]

Most importantly, musical comedy organized a vibrant modernity around strong but traditionally feminized female roles. These flourished in the standard text of musical comedy where shop girls, typists, film actresses and, of course, Gaiety girls were largely in the position of running things, at least narratologically. Masculinity did not perform well in musical comedy. The surrounding men of these shows were often a 'debilitated lot – faceless manikins immobilized in their adoration of the girl'.[36] If the male romantic leads came off a little more dynamically, they were still, in almost all cases, invariably outpaced by the lively heroines, figures like Mary Gibbs in *Our Miss Gibbs*, Daisy Vane in *An Artist's Model*, Alma Somerset in *The Gaiety Girl*, Bessie Brent in *The Shop Girl*, Nan in *The Country Girl* and Winnie Harborough in *The Girl from Kays*. In this way musical comedy constructed a unique fantasy role model for the modern woman, a figure who might act the innocent and appear demure when it suited her, but was actually experienced and worldly. Easily able to stand up for herself and hugely efficient when it came to running rings around the local 'Johnnies', she was not a woman of 'advanced ideas' in the traditional sense, but was clever and sharp and wanted to do well for herself. She often thought strategically, as well as romantically, about her career and the all-important issue of marriage. Even those suitors dismissed could be useful on the grounds that they might later 'make an excellent defendant in a breach of promise case'.[37] To re-emphasize the point, this figure was routinely aligned with the idea of modernity itself. Associated with the technology, fashions and attitudes of the day, she was every bit, as Lady Virginia Forest predicted in *A Gaiety Girl*, the 'coming thing' and 'an end of century girl'. Licensed, up to a point, glamorous and bright, these were no doubt some of the reasons, beyond the extravagance of their costumes, why the Gaiety girl image appealed to women as well as to men.

This musical comedy variant of feminism was both light and lightweight, but it was not ideologically innocent. Indeed, it politicized a kind of innocence, primarily by positioning 'gaiety' against the more familiar versions of the New Woman identity.[38] The Gaiety girl persona and its counterpart in the world of retail, media, commerce, and so on, was a specific riposte not only to conservative class and gender conventions of the Victorian era, but also to the new identities being constructed by middle-class elites around issues of political, social and, more marginally still, sexual empowerment. The views of these elites were implicitly thrown over by a Gaiety girl image that was 'modern', but not obviously political or explicitly feminist and that eschewed 'rational dress' for the most wildly glamorous costumes possible. This vital appropriation of the modern woman image was accompanied by a more explicit rubbishing of views associated with the more familiar New Woman identities. For all its identification of a feminized modernity and its positive staging of women at work in modern environments, musical comedy diminished the idea of women's political emancipation and the opening of the professions to women:

> Some women now today
> Are doctors, they assure me
> In spite of that, I say
> Give me a man to cure me.[39]

Male leads complained about 'walking about and talking / To M.A. and L.L.B. girls', expressing their desires for more compliant females, their 'own darling tea girls' of Ceylon in the case of *The Cingalee*.[40] There was little or no investment in the representation of formally educated young women to challenge such views. *The Orchid* is set in a women's 'horticultural college' where students are 'given the knowledge ... that makes them the equal of men', but after this promising opening the plot returns to the more traditional business of seeking marriage partners.[41] *The Shop Girl*, for all the assertiveness of its female lead, takes issue with what it imagined as the strait-laced morality and sexual isolation of the New Woman:

> The woman commonly known as New
> Who's doing the Sarah Grundy,
> Will find that a woman's life looks blue
> With never a husband handy.[42]

Again, *The Silver Slipper* opens in what purports to be a 'school of astronomy', but the female students are keen to point out that while they might look 'advanced', this is no more than a pose. Their stockings are most definitely 'not blue', and their real instinct is for fun, not learning.[43] In all these ways the 'girl' of musical comedy was set against the New Woman of late Victorian and Edwardian culture, with the latter being typically constructed at the antithesis of the Gaiety girl as 'middle class and single on principle. She eschewed the fripperies of fashion in favour of more masculine dress and severe coiffure'.[44]

One of the few shows of the period that seemed to operate differently, involving a serious commitment to traditional forms of women's emancipation, was *Nelly Neil*. Here Nelly, a socialist, insists that 'life' is more important than the 'stage' and refuses to accept that politics should be a 'masculine employment'. She declares that 'Nothing in the world is strictly masculine' and thinks it 'too bad how we girls are expected to be nothing but girls. The world isn't fair!'[45] But this radicalism turns out to be something of a disguise. Towards the end of the show there is an astonishing 'confession' scene where it is made clear that for all her espousing of emancipatory ideologies Nelly is not that different from 'any other girl'. Indeed at the most fundamental level, a level well beyond the political, she is precisely 'just like every other girl':

> I long to be admired and I'm very fond of dress,
> I'm just like every other girl
> Perhaps you have suspected I'm a sort of suffragette,
> Because I want to set the people free,
> But really I'm like every other girl you've ever met,

> And in my heart I only want to be –
> Just something pretty, pretty.[46]

This painful letdown[47] constitutes a denial of the natural 'reality' of feminism and suffragettism, confirming the view of those like Otto Weininger who argued that feminists were gender freaks, 'intermediate types' or 'male women', who aspired to the acquisition of 'man's character, to attain his mental and moral freedom'.[48] *Nelly Neil* is the strongest indicator that the new girl of musical comedy was a diminutive version of New Woman identities, responding directly to feminist agendas and in ways that were highly suggestive of conservative insecurities. The new girl of musical comedy was, in some respects, an independent and striking figure, but she remained a 'girl' loved for her charm, beauty and 'gaiety', even where she was liberating the people as in *Nelly Neil*. The Gaiety girl image, then, was struck in relation to the New Woman, ambiguously positioned somewhere between the very wide space separating traditional paternalism from feminism. Indeed, this theatre was an attempt to define the 'authentic' characteristics of the feminine at a time of accelerated cultural change. Occupying the softer middle ground, musical comedy adopted an emphatic sensitivity to change, but at the same time, remained substantially congruent with what was generally understood to be the basics of 'tradition', above all insisting on the 'essential' femininity of a 'real' womanhood that was, indeed, beyond change. This positioning between 'extremes' was a strategy deployed repeatedly by musical comedy and 'gaiety' as part of the wider ambition to secure modernity as a familiar, safe, and joyful, condition.

Musical comedy and modernist machismo

However anodyne the Gaiety girl version of modernity may have been in many respects, it did constitute something of a challenge. It was designed to counter traditional conceptions of gender roles. Indeed, this positioning of 'gaiety' and the Gaiety girl at the centre of the culture was a key challenge of musical comedy to the receding Victorian world. At the same time, it responded to the radical and explicitly politicized edge of contemporary feminism, partly by deflating social purity perspectives. This was a normalizing culture, where the 'innocence' and 'good sense' of musical comedy functioned to expose the 'hysteria' of such figures as Beatrice Webb, who thought it necessary for women 'with strong natures' to sacrifice their sexuality to the social good in the new century, 'so that the special force of womanhood – motherly feeling – may be forced into public work'.[49] The Gaiety girl, happy at work and comfortable with men, was a 'common-sense' reply to the extreme, apocalyptic vision of a figure like the writer Frances Swiney, who maintained that 'sexual intercourse was inherently an abusive and dangerous act and that sperm was a virulent poison composed of alcohol, nicotine, and venereal germs'.[50]

As well as countering a range of New Woman positions, 'gaiety' and its feminized view of modernity also entailed turning musical comedy into a natural antagonist of degeneration accounts of the West that were differently gendered. Many of the most influential degeneration theorists imagined civilization's decline to be not the product of male baseness and sexual disease, as *fin de siècle* feminists had it, but precisely as a species of feminization. Across a range of cultural forms from the medical science text to philosophy writing, the forces of cultural anarchism and decay were very specifically represented as female, an association that produced some of the most spectacularly misogynistic effects of the period. From Nietzsche's epigrams ('woman would not have the genius for finery if she did not have an instinct for a *secondary* role') to Freud's astonishing new theories of the sexual aetiology of neuroses, women and feminization were held responsible for weakening the backbone of civilization:[51]

> [These women] set the pace…and the boys can't keep up with them …If women become more masculine, men must become more feminine…Is [this] going to make a better and more beautiful world, or is it a challenge against Nature itself, a sign of some decadence overtaking humanity because man, enfeebled and overwhelmed, is surrendering his natural rights and privileges? …Men are losing as women are gaining, and…the natural balance of the sexes and their biological relationship are being thwarted by the claims of women who are becoming unsexed, anarchical and rebellious against natural laws, while man, weakly acquiescing in his own destruction, is becoming emasculated, decadent and doomed.[52]

Musical comedy did not specifically attack such articulations, but its implicit dissent was everywhere and unavoidable. Given its overwhelming urge to celebrate, musical comedy could hardly be anything else but opposed to the apocalyptic historical imagination that stamped intellectual life so decisively at the *fin de siècle* and beyond. The image of civilization's collapse into an inchoate mess of womanly men and manly women clearly could not be shared by musical comedy. Musical comedy toyed with gender boundaries and visualized a mixed economy that included weak men and stronger women. But it did not, at least ostensibly, bother itself with fears for the 'swamping' of masculinity. For all its male constituency in terms of authorship and production, it remained an assimilative, reassuring culture in this respect, albeit with some darker and more concerned undertones hidden in the wings. It had no need to escape behind the frontline of gender war into secure masculinized zones, because it did not construct modernity in terms of gender war. Musical comedy largely ignored the parallel worlds where 'King Romance' and boys' own adventure prevailed and the retreat of the gentleman's club flourished.[53]

Nor did musical comedy share the equally combative positions of avant-garde modernism on this issue. The early 'modernist' van-guard carried gender insecurities into hugely influential art cultures. Characteristically demonizing women, Jews and, above all, 'mass-man' as being at the teleological end of civilization, early twentieth-century art cultures and, especially, literature took degenerative historiography to new extremes. The Nietzschean imagination filtered through the cul-tural avant-garde pictured contemporaneity as being made up of 'the dregs of Anglo-Saxon civilisation', 'softer' than anything 'on earth'.[54] Here women were anathematized by the likes of Ezra Pound as formless emptiness ('Your mind and you are our Sargasso Sea /... No! there is nothing! In the whole and all, / Nothing that's quite your own. / Yet this is you'). Women were held responsible for 'a botched civilization' itself imaged in gender terms as 'an old bitch gone in the teeth'.[55] Viewed with sexual disgust by T. S. Eliot, possibly the most prestigious 'modern' for a generation following the 1930s, women were also conflated with despised Jews and the hated 'masses'. Thus in 'Sweeney Amongst the Nightingales', 'Rachel, *née* Rabinovich / Tears at the grapes with her murderous paws'. Not surprisingly, such ways of looking at contem-poraneity stood at the very antithesis of a popular culture that crucially defined modernity in terms of its mesmerizing powers of prettification.

Again, to locate the 'high' and 'low' cultures of literary modernism and musical comedy in a common cultural environment in this way is not to suggest that the one necessarily took a deliberate stance against the other. Musical comedy did talk directly to the highly public culture of the suffragette. It did not, however, communicate much with the avant-garde of modernism, apart from the predictable mocking and a knowing sense of what the public *really* wanted from their art: 'old gents like Venuses rising from the waves, with more Venus than waves. Young ladies like the romantic troubadours and bedroom windows; then the commercial classes want pictures that tell a three volume novel at a glance.'[56] It would be entirely misleading to characterize musical comedy as a 'radical' response specifically designed to correct the gender 'conservatism' of high modernism in its 'men of 1914' guise.[57] At the same time, there can be no doubt that musical comedy was just as much out of synch with both the macho values of modernism and the adventure culture of *She*, *King Solomon's Mine*, *Treasure Island* and *The Powerhouse* as it was with the standard New Woman identities. Again, this confirms the sense of a culture occupying the wider middle ground as a conservative modernism that cultivated and maintained a relatively wide sense of social and cultural inclusivity.

The commodified gender image and the women of musical comedy

The feminization of musical comedy was more than a simple worshipping of the 'essential' woman. It was a cultural construction that articulated against a transforming modernity in complex ways. The very close association between the new and the feminine helped to register modernity as change, but it also reproduced the modern as a familiar, enchanting and, above all, safe place. In this respect the Gaiety girl image, and the inevitable marriage dénouement, operated a powerful and subtle ideology of assimilation and reconciliation. Here the modern world became identified as *the* contemporary reality, the world of fast-moving machines, strange new technologies, odd new behaviours and bizarre fashions, but still very much the known world where we love and have fun and the 'natural' order is maintained. 'Femininity' was essential to the maintenance of this 'balance'.

Although musical comedy did reserve a central place for the female identity, then, the identity it constructed was conservative in many ways, not least because what was once the new Gaiety girl soon became so 'standard' in its dimensions, so predictable. Indeed, its reproduction became mechanical in more than one sense. The musical comedy 'girl' resonated ideologically not only as a new stereotype for the modern world, steeped in consumption for instance, but also as a reproduced image that was being enforced in new ways and with a new efficiency. This image manufacture was achieved not only through textual registration and acting and production styles but also, indeed perhaps primarily, through promotion and the media status enjoyed and thoroughly exploited by musical comedy. The success of shows was, as we have seen, accompanied by a highly professional exposure of stars and their images. Contemporary stage magazines included articles written by and about performers and their lifestyles; newspaper coverage of opening nights and review culture – all promoted the idea of musical comedy as a glamorous visual experience. Here the invitation to observe the elegance, beauty and, above all, 'femininity' of the performers became compelling. However much the makers of musical comedy may have insisted on the skills and professionalism of actresses, reviewers produced highly gendered readings commending to their readers the spectacle of the female. Thus *The Times*, reviewing *The Gay Gordons*, commented on the 'tantalizing' aspects of the women clothed in Highland dress and praised the show for its staging of 'bevies of very beautiful ladies'.[58] This kind of response was entirely standard in reviews. In the same newspaper, in the same year, *Miss Hook of Holland* was described as a 'luscious display'. The 'scenery and effects were off the beaten tracks, and, like the accessory ladies, were unusually pretty'.[59] The feminine might have been central to the narrative dynamic and dramatic performance of musical comedy, but it was also constructed in highly commodifying ways as spectacle and, quite literally, part of the scenery, at least by its reviewers.

Advertising campaigns, programme designs, and so on worked similarly. These and the picture postcard culture referred to in earlier chapters worked together to produce a commercial exploitation of the feminine that with musical comedy reached modern proportions, perhaps for the first time (see Illustration 10). The images produced of stars like Edna May, Gertie Millar, the Dare sisters and Lily Elsie contained many of the essentials of what is now commonplace in the cultural reproduction of women. They were exotic and voyeuristic and produced stereotypes of 'English' beauty, schoolgirl temptation and gamine vitality. They routinely exploited fantasies of female innocence and submission. Some, although this was more rare, appealed to submissive instincts in men and imaged strong, powerful and masculinized women. Through magazine culture, journalism and the production of the twopenny and threepenny picture postcards, musical comedy became the first popular culture to market such images of women on a mass scale. It was in this respect the forerunner of the publicity machines later developed in cinema and television. To the extent that it produced, on an industrial scale, posed women at least partially for male gratification, it was in some sense a forerunner of the modern sex industry.[60]

Illustration 10 Twopenny postcards: the commercial exploitation of the feminine (Gabrielle Ray)

The commercial nature of musical comedy was clearly gendered in very specific ways, and the visual exploitation of the female image was certainly central to this process. The question of how actresses themselves may have experienced being part of this standardization and commercialization, however, is more problematic. As Tracy Davis and others have shown, the position of women in the Victorian and Edwardian theatre was characterized by complexity and ambiguity. On the one hand, the stage offered unique opportunities for women. In its West End context at least, the theatre could be an exciting world where women enjoyed 'an unequalled degree of personal and sexual freedom'. Here, for those talented and lucky enough to find mainstream employment, there were also considerable financial rewards to be had, 'better wages than any other legitimate occupation freely accessible to a woman', although, for most actresses, only while youth and good looks were retained. At the same time, even after the West End stage was cleaned up and commercialized, the reputation of actresses generally remained at best equivocal. The theatre did became 'a well established field of employment for women', but, however much it was developed at the cultural centre, it could never entirely shake off the associations with 'low life' and prostitution, especially at its edges.[61] From many perspectives, actresses, 'virtually by definition – lived and worked beyond the boundaries of propriety'.[62]

It is, in part, this traditional association between the stage and charges of immorality that has led to the assumption that, even in the highly organized and professionalized theatre of the early twentieth century, women must have been vulnerable, subject to a 'Pandora's box of pitfall and evils'.[63] Even where the evidence of actual harassment is, for good reason, simply not available, actresses have been understood as being constrained by strong authority and discipline, and perhaps even victimized and abused.[64] Taking a lead from Davis, who has focused more on the earlier nineteenth-century stage, Peter Bailey, for instance, has suggested that musical comedy was something of an enforcement that subjected its female performers to the firm hand of patriarchy. Thus his account imagines George Edwardes as a Svengali figure, 'variously … martinet, snooper and sugar daddy'.[65] If this Edwardes ever existed, however, he does not figure in any of the contemporary literature. Indeed, in the romanticizing reminiscence culture that built up round musical comedy, Edwardes is presented as a rather genial man. His construction of the Gaiety girl image is fully acknowledged, with Ellaline Terris, for example, writing of how he 'always glorified femininity. He put his girls into the most delightful dresses which filled them with feminine allure and tantalized the men. He could put a halo on a woman, surround her with an aura of charm. He glorified the "Girl" and put her in the title of his new form – Musical Comedy.'[66] But far from being understood as repressive and authoritarian, this commodification of the feminine is applauded here, for both its business acumen and good taste. In Terris's account, the musical comedy appropriation of the New Woman is welcomed not just commercially but also artistically – exploitative it might be in some ways, but Terris is hardly concerned about its conservative signification. Indeed, she sees it as a creative and beautifying construction that plays to natural human instincts. Of course, such responses, expressed in the highly public form of autobiographical writing, are to be expected – especially from a figure like Ellaline Terris, who made her fame and fortune from musical comedy and was part of the music theatre establishment. Those lower down the hierarchy and possessed of much less status and authority might well have seen things rather differently.

But there are further reasons for questioning the notion that generalizes the musical comedy actress into the victim role, positioned at the mercy of a patriarchal and thoroughly voyeuristic culture. In the first place, and despite the views of the contemporary critics, women were not merely pretty objects in these shows, but professional performers possessed of highly developed skills. Seymour Hicks is characteristic of the industry here when he legitimizes musical comedy as a progressive development of the Victorian stage, a maturation that produced better conditions for actresses in particular and new standards of performance. Keen to disassociate musical comedy from any suggestion of impropriety, he writes of his dislike of the term 'show girl' for musical comedy actresses and describes the technical skills of a hardworking 'set of ladies who in a properly conducted theatre ... are a very great attraction in the lighter forms of entertainment'. Not only 'beautiful ... they were clever at playing small parts – admirable in picking up extremely difficult stage business, and ... excellent dancers'.[67] Not withstanding the patronizing tone and obvious vested interest, Hicks is surely right to draw attention here to the professional pride of the musical comedy performer working in what was a legitimate theatre. Irrespective of their gender, these would have been highly trained personnel, rather than lifeless objects waiting to be manipulated at will by unscrupulous producers. They would also have been complicit in the development of their theatre skills, rather than simply moulded into submission.

Quite apart from undervaluing the skills, talents and ambitions of these performers, the image of the passive, posing 'Gaiety girl' also misses the senses in which women were constitutive of this culture in other ways. The women who performed the Gaiety girl role, and other roles of the musical comedy stage, clearly were contributing to a conservative intervention in many ways, but as professional theatre workers they can also be seen as operating at the cutting edge in terms of the challenges they made to conventional views about the female role in society and culture. Indeed, women performers have been understood as defying ideas of 'passive middle-class femininity' and as personifications of 'active self-sufficiency'.[68] To put it more simply still, and in rather different terms, there can be no doubt that figures like Ada Reeve and Connie Ediss, both famous for their cigar smoking, were more than a match for figures like Edwardes. Indeed, Ediss had three contracts with Edwardes during her career and broke them all. On the third occasion she became ill during the rehearsals of *Three Little Maids*. She returned to work only to discover that her co-principals had carved up her part leaving a role 'no longer worth ... playing.' Her job was now to play 'a stooge, feeding the lines from which the other two girls scored'.[69] A legal battle ensued, against Edwardes, which was eventually settled out of court. And it was not only the big stars that had the nerve to take on theatre management in these formal ways. In 1896 the Gaiety was 'sued by a female chorus singer for back pay of 35s a week'.[70]

Such women were not victims of musical theatre, but part of the culture and as such they fully exploited their potential, in all senses. This meant pandering to men's fantasies, but also involved realizing the commercial value of their public image, by, for example, product endorsement. Iris Hooey and Florence Smithson were among the many figures willing to attach their images to commercial wares. In their case it was Helena Rubenstein's 'Valaze Complexion specialities' that was commended to the public; Marie Tempest praised the virtues of 'Hall's Wine, The Guaranteed Tonic Restorative'.

It is hard to imagine figures such as these being blindly led. On the contrary, these were highly self-motivated career-builders whose progress through the modernizing world of Edwardian entertainment stood as an example in the industry to both their less successful contemporaries and to future performers, people like Jessie Matthews who, even as a young starlet, performing in the West End staging of the Rodgers and Hart musical *Evergreen* (1930), was clear that she would resist being manipulated by 'four old men', whatever their status:

> 'Dancing on the Ceiling' was the big song and dance number of the show, and the way those men mauled it about. 'She's too coy', [said Benn] Levy. 'She isn't coy enough', [said] Rodgers. 'Sweet and light, that's the theme', [said] Collins. And Cochran said, 'I don't like it'.
>
> I looked down at these four men so busy manipulating me. I felt like a puppet with tangled strings. Some demon took hold of me. What was I to them? Nothing but some image they had in their minds, an object, a bloody blueprint to scrawl their ideas on. I was sick and tired of letting four old men mess me about. What the hell did they know about love? How did they know how a girl in love really feels?[71]

6
The Decline of West End Musical Comedy, 1912–1939

According to some musical theatre historians, West End musical comedy was struggling even before the outbreak of the Great War. Ganzl, for example, identifies the early signs of collapse in a number of ways. He continues to describe the popularity of 'foreign' shows and 'foreign' composers – especially Franz Lehár, Oscar Strauss and Leo Fall – as evidence of a 'British' decline. It was the case that shows like *A Waltz Dream* (1908), *The Dollar Princess* (1909), *The Chocolate Soldier* (1910), *The Count of Luxembourg* (1911) and *Gipsy Love* (1912) were very successful, but again it is hard to see how this signified the collapse of West End musical theatre. Quite apart from the difficulties in distinguishing 'foreign' shows from their British counterparts, once they had been subjected to the West End musical comedy treatment, these 'Viennese' shows shared an environment with musicals that were entirely 'home-grown' – Monckton's *The Quaker Girl* with 536 performances at the Adelphi and the Rubens show *The Sunshine Girl* (1912), which had 336 performances at the Gaiety are notable in this respect. Moreover the war period itself saw a string of hugely successful West End musical comedies. Besides *Chu Chin Chow*, *Betty* had a West End run of 391 performances; *Theodore & Co*, played 503 performances; *The Maid of the Mountains*, 1,352; *The Better 'Ole*, 811; *The Boy*, 801; *A Southern Maid* (1917), 306; *Yes, Uncle* (1917), 626; and *Kissing Time*, 430 (see appendix 1). This wartime popularity hardly bears out the suggestion that musical comedy was in irretrievable decline before the outbreak of war; nor does it wholly support another familiar idea – that the pre-war period saw the fading of West End composers and writers of musical comedy.

There were *some* problems in this respect. Ivan Caryll, a key figure in the development of the 'British' musical, had gone to America – a journey that was not at all uncommon in the context of musical theatre.

He continued to write musicals, but now in an American idiom. At the same time, Leslie Stuart found himself in the bankruptcy courts and Sidney Jones had produced very little since the failure of *A Persian Princess*. But it can hardly be claimed that the musical comedy muse expired with the war. Monckton was still writing, as was Howard Talbot, and Paul Rubens was prolific until his early death in 1917. Moreover there were new writers appearing, Oscar Asche, for instance, and Ivor Novello.

Musical comedy continued to be written and composed, remaining an important part of West End theatre throughout the war. Despite Edwardes' death in 1915, the Gaiety persevered, managed first by the highly successful combination of George Grossmith and Edward Laurillard and, a few years later, albeit less successfully, by Alfred Butt. Musical comedy also continued to be produced at other prestigious West End venues, including Daly's, the Adelphi, His Majesty's, the Prince of Wales and the Winter Garden. The fact that music halls were now incorporating short musical comedies into their programmes, far from indicating a decline in musical comedy, implied the reverse. Music hall was here attempting to capitalize on musical comedy's continued success in the mainstream, although whether it could really compete against the authentic West End experience with these mini-shows, as Ganzl suggests, must be doubted.[1]

It is easy to see why the idea of musical comedy's decline has been associated with the pre-war years. Although musical comedy had periodic resurrections in the 1920s and 1930s, it never again reached the pre-eminence of its position in its late Victorian and Edwardian glory days (see appendix 3). In attempting to explain this decline, historians of musical theatre have naturally looked for 'origins' and these have been found in the pre-1914 period. The war itself, so frequently featuring as a watershed for all kinds of change, is understood as somehow inevitably continuing the decline of musical comedy and.'gaiety'. It also marks the death of the man so closely associated with musical comedy since its beginnings, George Edwardes. However, something more complicated than a simple decline in popularity seems to have characterized the later years of musical comedy. It did begin to lose some its former cultural purchase, and probably as early as 1912, but this did not mark the beginning of a linear decline into oblivion. More accurately, musical comedy receded and it did so in a rather slow and uneven fashion. There were those semi-recoveries in the 1920s and 1930s and, above all, a cultural retreat into the familiar during the actual war years so strong that it could easily be mistaken for a continuation of the tradition begun with so much success in the mid-1890s (see appendices 1 and 3).

Both the dating of and the reasons for the demise of musical comedy, then, are complex issues. Its fall was uneven rather than precipitous and not simply the sad outcome of a forced retreat from what is often constructed among musical theatre enthusiasts as 'innocence'. Musical comedy was the hard-headed application of commercial and industrial culture to entertainment; it never was 'innocent', although it did imagine an innocent and highly simplified world, as popular culture often does, and it is the case that its particular version of modernity did lose currency in the inter-war period. Nor was its decline entirely the simple change in fashion that it sometimes appears to be in theatre history. Far from reflecting random changes in taste, the demise of musical comedy was a cultural phenomenon that registered important wider shifts in the economic environment, in social and cultural values and in the technological forms and operating frameworks of popular culture. Eventually, musical comedy failed not because it was the victim of a whimsical change in fashion, but because it was so inextricably tied to a highly specific populist and racialized image of the modern. In the post-war period this simply could not be sustained. Against the background of world revolution and global economic depression, the British modern as celebrated by West End musical comedy became thoroughly redundant to a changing British middle class, even before the arrival of a buoyantly confident and technically expert American music theatre.

There was, in short, a whole range of factors impacting on musical comedy, all reducing the viability not just of musical comedy, but of live theatre generally. However, it should be emphasized that musical comedy was *especially* ill equipped to respond in any meaningful way to the new conditions of the 1920s and 1930s. This was, in part, a matter of the tried-and-tested narrative, a narrative so central that it contributed substantially to the essential nature of West End musical comedy. It is not difficult to imagine how every bit of that upbeat celebration of modernity, with its confident and naive assertion of faith in progress and social inclusion, particularly in its 'British' formulation, was, by the end of this period, not just under threat but decisively wrecked. At one time resonating with all the confidence of the *belle époque*, musical comedy must have sounded astonishingly dissonant and quite out of touch in the inter-war period, especially to the English middle class, whose sense of society as community was under considerable stress. Indeed, it was in many ways this class that felt itself to be most threatened, even endangered, by the new modernity of post-war Britain. However much middle-class incomes may have risen from the mid-1920s to the late 1930s, and they did by and large, the middle-class experience of this period was typified by a sense of insecurity and displacement. This was intimately connected to a national politics dominated by labourist and trade unionist issues, to an extent that radicalized the English middle class into a defence of the 'public' against what it saw as the assaults of the barbarian. The most dramatic expression of this was the routine participation in strike-breaking, a highly public manifestation of an anti-working-class sentiment that some historians position as the single most defining characteristic of middle-class sensibilities up to the 1950s.[2] Needless to say, such antipathies could hardly be squared with the one-world vision of musical comedy.

The fall of musical comedy was substantially connected to a culture that was insecure in many ways, and not just at the level of the intelligentsia. Crucially, its demise was about changes in the wider social and political world that could not be responded to if musical comedy was to maintain its identity. Without the specific version of fun, the particular brand of gaiety and the splendid invocation to 'join in', musical comedy simply could not be musical comedy. The problem, however, was that this styling could no longer serve as a meaningful metonym of the modern world. In the end, musical comedy died as a cultural form because in the post-war world it lost its grip over relevance, and it is difficult to see how things could have been otherwise.

Revue and the decline of musical comedy

The most important sign that musical comedy really was beginning to lose something of its contemporary significance was the rise of revue in the years just before the war. Revues began to appear on the London stage in big numbers between 1912 and 1913, starting with Albert de Courville's *Hullo, Ragtime* (1912). By 1915 a string of them were doing serious business in London: *Business as Usual* was playing at the Hippodrome; *The Passing Show of 1915* and *Bric-a-Brac* at the Palace; there were three shows at the Alhambra in that year – *5064 Gerrard*, *Push and Go* and *Joyland* – *More* played at the Ambassador and *Shell Out* at the Comedy. All these shows 'clocked up runs of over 300 performances'. Throughout the war and beyond, revue was 'riding high', surpassing musical comedy in popularity, even during the years when musical comedy was itself producing highly successful shows.[3] It was quite simply 'the era's most vital, innovative and influential form of musical theatre'.[4]

What was revue? In its original form, revue originated in Paris in the early nineteenth century as an annual show that used sketches, song and dance to review and satirize the events of the preceding year. Although it does not feature as 'legitimate' musical theatre in some accounts, including Ganzl's,[5] in its most complex form it did have 'a distinctive unity as a show'.[6] It was important in its own right and played a vital part in the development of musical theatre, in America and on the Continent, where it evolved into cabaret. In Britain it was probably introduced as early as 1825, by James Robinson Planché with a show entitled *Success; or a Hit if You Like It*.[7] It developed in Britain, if not as a staple, at least as a familiar form with George Grossmith Jr becoming the 'most diligent campaigner for and practitioner of this form'.[8] By the time it surfaced as a serious competitor to musical comedy, however, revue had developed through British and, especially, American traditions to become something rather different – nothing less, in fact, than the new musical theatre ascendancy of London.

West End musical comedy had been incestuously close to the American stage from its very early days when Seymour Hicks, or 'Stealmore Bricks' as New York dubbed him, was accused of being an inveterate 'borrower' of American material for West End shows. When George Cohan, the American musical comedy writer and producer, was asked to Americanize Hicks' *The Beauty of Bath* he replied that he had already written the play 'twice before myself'.[9] Revue, though, was different and more than simple exchange, or theft. Here were the definite beginnings of America's domination of the musical stage and of the fundamental association that was to establish the musical as a synonym for the idea of America itself.

One crucial intervention here is usually thought to be Ziegfeld's. From 1907 he began to create the sophisticated revues that were distinct from both American vaudeville and musical comedy. His shows retained the original satirical elements, but combined these with a fabulous chorus line and specifically written songs and music. Walsh and Platt have described the nature and significance of this kind of show:

> Although the allure of female flesh continued to be a major element, all aspects of the revue were now being specifically written and composed for it, acted by a single cast, played by a good orchestra and organized and directed by a single producer to create an integrated and distinctive musical show. In this form the revue became a major vehicle for the popular music and dance culture of America. It actively sought out new popular music and dance crazes providing a major commercial venue through which to test, advertise and spread them, and an artistic venue for composers, lyricists and writers to flourish.[10]

Although de Courville had tried to reproduce this grand scale in the West End – his *Razzle Dazzle* (1916) had a 300-strong chorus line, for instance – the London revues were not generally typical of Ziegfeld extravaganzas. After the success of Cochran's sparse show *Odds and Ends* (1914), London revues became less opulent and more 'intimate', typically with a cast of no more than fourteen. By comparison to West End musical comedy, these were small-scale affairs requiring considerably less capital outlay, which was part of their attraction and one reason why they spread so quickly round the country. Nor were revues necessarily American shows by composition. Indeed, although revue did produce new writers – Nat D. Ayer, for instance, Herman Darewski, Harry Grattan, Louis Hirsch and James Tate – it was often the work of the same writers and composers who had made musical comedy. Monckton, Rubens, Arthur Wimperis, Frederick Thompson, Howard Talbot, Ivor Novello and even Seymour Hicks – all tried their hand at revue. But alongside such continuities the London wartime revue was markedly influenced precisely by the new music and dance crazes of the American counterpart referred to above. It was here, for instance, that tango and ragtime became part of popular culture, and here also that the syncopated rhythms of a musical theatre version of jazz began to displace the more sedate dance and music styles of Edwardian musical comedy. This influence of style and musicality was the crucial American intervention and it connected with a new modern of revised class and gender identities.

It is necessary to register this cultural shift, but, equally, it is important to maintain some perspective on the nature, extent and meaning of the process. Some at the time saw it as a complete 'swamping' of British tradition. In the minds of the older musical comedy performers particularly, musical comedy was often imagined as a manifestation of true Englishness and the emergence of the new culture constructed in apocalyptic terms as an 'invasion', a thorough usurpation of 'real' musical theatre by 'the jazz trap-drummer'. In his autobiography *Gaieties and Gravities* (1931), the comedian George Graves, writing about musical theatre after 1918, racialized this dynamic very precisely. 'The London stage,' he wrote, 'was getting further and further away from the real national feeling.' The American influence was excoriated as a perverse combination of 'hot-jazz nigger crudities' or 'violent nigger jazz' and 'Jewish humour and sentiment'.[11] But Graves was quite wrong, of course, not only in his representation of the extent of displacement, but also in understanding the revue as a completely 'foreign' intervention. It may have been newly energized and appealing to a new generation middle class more relaxed in some ways about both its responsibility and respectability, but revue was hardly alien. For all its adoption of an American style, the London revue remained an Anglicized version in many key respects, and 'white' in all respects. It told stories about Britain in British idiom. Even the Americanization of its musical style was far from complete. One of the smash revues of the wartime years, *The Bing Boys are Here* (1917), for instance, was notable for the song, 'If You Were the Only Girl in the World', a long way from 'hot jazz' and much closer, in fact, to the musical styles of musical comedy. It is easy to exaggerate the extent to which revue represented an Americanization of the London stage. A show like *The Bing Boys*, set initially in the English market town of Binghampton and exploring the adventure of the Mayor's sons in the big city, clearly illustrated just how blurred the boundaries could be, even between revue and musical comedy. Most importantly, it also showed the continued capacity of the London musical stage for assimilation and appropriation. By the 1920s West End revue had come into its own. With the intimacy of Charlot's *London Revue* and the considerable talents of its stars – Gertrude Lawrence, Noel Coward, Jack Buchanan and Beatrice Lillie – the import–export tide was reversed. The West End had redefined revue and was making a success in America itself.

It is also important to realize that revue was no more homogeneous than musical comedy. There were differences in styles, quality, production size, and so on. Conventional revues sat side by side with those that were extreme and innovative. At this latter end of the market, revue was more than just clever sketches and new dance and music. Composers of London musical theatre latched on to revue precisely because it was an escape from musical comedy, an opportunity not just to try out new ideas, but also to establish distance from the outgoing culture. Thus in revues more radical than *The Bing Boys* self-conscious markers were laid down to separate the old from the new. The romantic songs so typical of 'straight' musical comedy now reappeared in comic mock versions:

> Wonderful words of slosh, dear
> I've got to sing to you
> Soft as my old galosh, dear,
> Wet with the evening dew!
> Mopping the maudlin tear, love
> Telling a tale of tosh!
> Gurgle and I shall hear, love,
> Beautiful, beery, bosh![12]

The makers of musical comedy were frequently referred to and even represented in revues as figures of a bygone age. There is an unflattering impersonation of Connie Ediss in *Kill That Fly* (1912) and Basil Hood appears in the extraordinary show *By Jingo if We Do* (1914) whinging that a chorus girl has ruined 'one of my best lines'. George Grossmith also figures here as a rural 'village Grossmith'.[13] Indeed, some shows were little more than modern burlesques of musical comedy. *The Girl from Dunnowhere* – the very title, of course, reflects the confidence of a new ascendancy – is a mock version of various musical comedy styles. This brilliant concoction takes the contemporary styling of a show like *A Gaiety Girl* and mixes it up with the stage exoticism and orientalism of something like *The Geisha* or *San Toy*. One scene takes place at Henley-on-Thames and includes the mandatory 'girls in bathing suits' routine; the next is set in 'Kiota' and has a mock version of the 'Chin Chin Chinaman' song from *The Geisha*. There are parodic versions of the traditional Gaiety girl chorus, here transformed into a group of 'lady police' and 'crackswomen' whose dance routine degenerates into something described in the stage directions as *'eccentric movement'*.[14] That scene, set on the Thames Embankment, is then transformed into the 'Island of Dunnowhere', which is inhabited by a character disguised as George Bernard Shaw. One of the final songs is a spoof of the *Floradora* hit 'In the Shade of the Palm':

> Princess of Dunnowhere, Pearl of the Sea,
> Humbly we make our obeisance to thee.
> Queen of the universe, we bow our knee,
> Who shall describe our devotion to thee.[15]

In these respects revue was not the destruction of a British musical theatre from the 'outside', but rather a new wave that frequently took iconoclastic positions from the inside and vis-à-vis what was now being perceived as the established, and tired, conventions of musical comedy. It was a new kind of entertainment that visualized, and celebrated, the passing of the old. Indeed, the revue of the war years took the fantasy worlds defined by musical comedy and seemed to turn them upside down. Operating a new sense of speed and urgency, it displaced the stately dynamics of the musical comedy plot with a wild energy. Far from creating a consistent fabric, whether in terms of narrative or style, the up-and-coming form aimed for bizarre shifts and dramatic transformations at every level. Melodrama could snap into showtime glitz at any minute; film was often interpolated into the performance implying not a reproduction of the modern, as in the old tradition, but a multi-media practice that emphasized difference rather than assimilation. The whole show, although written as a unified text with designed songs, dance routines and sketches, had far less interest in narrative coherency than musical comedy. It was not that revue was too unsophisticated to sustain traditional story, as is sometimes thought, but rather that it eschewed what it saw as the narrative simplicity and romanticism of the earlier form. Its humour was more abrasive, more risqué and less stylized than in musical comedy. There were fewer routines, of all sorts, although more parodies of routines. Indeed, parody and pastiche became hallmarks of revue. More than a simple displacement of one fashion for another, revue at its most challenging, then, was a complex expression of the new against the *passé*.

This dynamic, far from being alien or specifically American, was, and is, general to modern commercial culture. It expressed the characteristic imperative for innovation, or at least reinvention, and demonstrated how conceptions of cultural value could change almost overnight in the world of popular entertainment. But more than this, in the London manifestation, revue carried the idea not just that musical comedy was old hat, but that modernity itself, and the nation's relationship to it, had shifted in ways that the conventional musical stage simply could not accommodate. In its most disruptive, anarchic form, revue represented a kind of Walpurgis night version of modernity, where reality, far from being mediated, contained and generally made safe, as in the musical comedy tradition, was always in danger of running out of control.

By Jingo if We Do (1914)

By Jingo if We Do, performed in London in 1914, but off West End, illustrates the characteristics of revues which were often radical, although not usually in terms of conventional politics. Indeed, these shows, like musical comedy, were unashamedly patriotic, which sometimes meant that conservative positions were struck against labourist anti-war sentiment. *By Jingo*, for example, insists that the Kaiser is in cahoots with Keir Hardie and the show is punctuated by telegrams between the two, including one that announces that the German entry into London has been delayed, so the Kaiser's 'double turn with Keir Hardie at the Empire on the 24th, will have to be cancelled.[16] The very next telegram is stranger still. It is again from the Kaiser and reads: 'I and my brave troops are making awful examples of all babies found in arms. Kiss me Hardie!'[17] Neither the sophistication nor the radicalism of these shows, then, was political in the conventional sense, but essentially cultural and challenging in those terms. Crucially, it involved an extreme disruption not just of the now standard styles of musical theatre, but of the conceptions of modernity they embodied.

By Jingo, for instance, opens in all the bustle of a newspaper office. It echoes musical comedy here, in adopting a setting so obviously emblematic of the modern. But this is a much darker version of things. Far from being associated with vitality and modishness, the press here has an invasive and even malign influence. Permeating every aspect of 'domestic life, reading, feeding and breeding', it is constitutive of reality, rather than serving of its readership. The modern press no longer 'records' the news, but 'manufactures' it in the image of particular power groups. Thus this particular newspaper gives so much money to 'Party funds' that 'there is not one untitled member of the staff'.[18] The capacity of the modern media for reality formation is also suggested by the visit of a musical comedy actress, who, tellingly, needs the press to make her a 'real star'. This process involves 'Marjorie' being posed in a number of costumes against backdrops suggestive of the modern sophisticate. She is photographed wintering in Switzerland, playing tennis, fishing, golfing, and so on, and she sings a song suggestive of a new harder edge and a new degree of licence:

> If you've only got a dimple where it plays at hide and seek,
> You can do without a lot of lingerie.[19]

There is a more challenging sense of modernity in other respects. Musical comedy's embracing of a vital modern spirit is displaced by a satirical exposure of modernity as a panic culture, for instance. Far from constituting reality, this modern has a tenuous grip on things as the following song about war rumours shows:

> I hear the Norwegians have landed
> They tell me the Zulus are here
> I know that the Goeben has stranded
> I *saw* it from Whitstable pier!
> The Shah has been strangled in Sherbet
> A wolf has been shot in the Mall
> And the Kaiser disguised as a turbot
> Has swum up the Regent's canal.[20]

Here the show moves to the office next door, a bureau for domestic servants which two young, would-be maids for some reason mistake for

KING ALFRED'S COLLEGE
LIBRARY

a doctor's office. This 'interlude' is notable for both its innuendo and for a song that ridicules the suburban middle class. Again, the contrast with musical comedy is strong. This was a sharper, more satirical and altogether more knowing cultural form:

> If you want to see
> Life as it should be
> Try a London suburb and you will
> See what you learn.
> Take a third return
> Say to Peckham Rye or Streatham Hill,
> Fashions at its height
> Manners most polite
> Morals far superior to town.
> Nothing can surpass
> Britain's middle-class
> Smith or Jones or Robinson or Brown

> *Refrain:* Father likes to potter round the garden
> Mother likes to work around the house
> Pretty sister Kitty
> Is a typist in the City
> Mandie is a modest little mouse
> Sidney is a paragon of fashion
> Trixie is a terror of the town
> If you've ever been to Streatham,
> You are certain to have meet 'em
> Oh you couldn't miss the family of Brown.[21]

Up to this point there is some consistency to the show, consistency of place and of tenor inasmuch as *By Jingo* has found a number of targets to satirize: the press, musical comedy, the suburban middle classes, and so on. It also has a loose central plot, involving Lord Effingham, the owner of *The Daily Life*, his daughter Diana and Monty, the contender for her hand who is sent off to prove himself by finding a 'scoop'. But this framework is highly provisional and punctuated by extraordinary dislocating scenes that entirely break with the aesthetic to which musical theatre in most critical traditions is thought to aspire. Scene 2 provides the first real shock of this kind. It is a mime scene where Nell, a young woman forced onto the streets to feed her children (as the stage directions tell us), is shown standing outside a coffee stall trying to exchange sex for money. Her desperate out-of-work husband appears, realizes the situation and stabs her to death.

This astonishing interpolation of something between social realism and melodrama would have been unthinkable in musical comedy. It smashes the fantasy, the charm and the 'gaiety'. In musical comedy terms, this is not just a dramatic alteration of scene but, rather, a rude disturbance of the entire premise of a good-time song and dance show, not least because it is enacted in complete silence. This revue thus exploits musical comedy in its early scenes, and goes on to operate an entirely transgressive aesthetic that ignores the all-important boundaries usually set. One critical effect of this curious intervention is the exposure of the limits of traditional musical comedy, the revealing of a world outside its sugary charm and designated here as being dark, dangerous and, most importantly, 'real'. The further interpolations affirm such a reading with, if possible, even more startling dislocations of the traditional musical comedy world. Most notably in *By Jingo* there is the war scene, set in France, where the usually inept Monty intervenes to save two French women who are being threatened with rape by German soldiers. This scene, with its brutal overtones, is challenging by any standards. Placed in the context of the usually 'gay' musical theatre, its effect is doubly alarming and wildly disorienting.

Finally, *By Jingo* returns to England to finish with a play within a play set in the traditional musical comedy territory of the aristocrat's estate, here imaged as Effingham Towers. It is in this scene that the mockery of musical comedy takes most explicit shape, because Monty's show is, of course, a merciless parody of musical comedy, complete with the satirical versions of musical comedy romanticism described above and more joke versions of the cheap and cheerful versification deployed by musical comedy lyricists:

> We sing hurrah! We shout hooray!
> Because it rhymes with May today
> And when we've said hurrah! hooray!
> We sometimes add a tra la-la!
> And finish our delightful lay
> With hip-hurrah! and hip hooray![22]

These, then, were satirical shows, with musical comedy frequently finding itself the butt of the joke. The romantic plot of musical comedy, like the lyrics of its songs, became a further obvious target for sharp ridicule. When Myrtle and Bobbie are too poor to marry in Monty's revue version of musical comedy, Bobbie expresses the wish that his 'rich uncle from Arizona would turn up!' Instantaneously 'Scalplock Jake' is made manifest: 'Forgive my rough Western manners, my boy. Put it there!'[23] But there was more to them than satire of this knock-about kind. At their most extreme they pointed to something more serious about the inadequacies of musical comedy. They marked a final and perhaps much needed divorce from *la belle époque* and its seepage into the Edwardian Age. A revue like *By Jingo* could no longer continue with the embrace of glamorous modernity. It turned sharply against the *joie de vivre* of musical comedy, on the 'innocence' that had once constituted an important cultural strategy but had now served its time. For all its fun and humour, this revue insisted on squaring up to a world 'out there', a modernity that, far from being 'gay', was violent and unpredictable.

One would stress again that not all revue was like *By Jingo* in this respect, but at the same time it should be noted that somewhere this dramatic shift had taken place and the implication was clear enough. While the popular 'entertainment' of musical comedy with its increasing technical capabilities and management sophistication had grown up in some ways, it had also lost touch, not with reality as such – for it has always been escapist – but with a new audience that apparently expected something more of its escapism. It would have to grow up in new ways, if it wanted to continue to be taken seriously as popular culture.[24]

Musical comedy in the war years

It is difficult to know how the early audiences of revue may have differed from the audience of musical comedy and, indeed, whether the social composition of West End theatre audiences was generally altering during the wartime period. Certainly, there is evidence to suggest that contemporaries thought the latter was occurring and this has been passed down to theatre historians. Maggie Gale, for instance, points out that West End theatres closed during the first weeks of the war and claims that when they reopened things had changed to cater for a new audience. She quotes Pick, who refers to soldiers on leave seeking escapism, and assumes that these would have been working-class men, adding that 'similarly women moving into the public field of work might seek an evening's entertainment in the West End'.[25] Whether the generally middle-class and petty bourgeois make-up of traditional West audiences would have changed so quickly, however, must be doubtful. It seems more likely that, rather than 'take in a West End show', working-class soldiers on leave would have been inclined to return to their families and local forms of entertainment. Undoubtedly, the presence of uniforms created a sense of change, but the idea that the traditional social make-up of West End theatre audiences shifted radically overnight may have been nothing more than a reflection of middle-class antagonism to 'the workers', producing a sense of 'invasion' and a concern about 'signs of ill-breeding' in the West End and in the auditoriums.[26]

It is possible, however, that the revue audience would have been distinguished by age, finding a younger audience, at least initially, with a sense of its own sophistication. There would have been those stalwarts of an earlier generation, one imagines, who found in revue not a clever new entertainment, but a sad and puerile version of the 'real thing'. The continued popularity of musical comedy in the war years would suggest as much and perhaps more. With the embargo on all things 'German', Continental, especially 'Viennese', shows became entirely unstageable and remained so until Friml's versions of 'Vienna woods' in the mid-1920s, a renewal of tradition exploited with so much success by Ivor Novello in the 1930s. The war years, then, saw a new demand for the standard 'British' musical comedy, for a musical theatre that was comfortable and bright and most importantly a temporary escape from the war. It was for these reasons that shows like *Chu Chin Chow*, *The Maid of the Mountains*, *The Boy* and *The Better 'Ole* became the classic leave shows, rather than something like the strange and often alarming *By Jingo*. Far from addressing the violently changed conditions of the modern world, these shows specialized in escapist fantasy. *Chu Chin Chow* proved, in London as on Broadway, 'irresistible' precisely because of 'the contrast between the dark chilliness outside and the glow and gorgeousness inside the theatre'.[27] Similarly, *Baby Bunting* (1919) was praised because it offered what was wanted in these times 'a good sound tonic'.[28]

The fantasy and escapism of these wartime shows, however, was not quite the same thing as it had been in the early days. It responded to different and more urgent imperatives and, if we take the culture as a whole, was more pronounced than it ever had been. Indeed, it is not too much to say that escape became the virtual *raison d'être* of wartime musical comedy. This shift was not, as might be thought, just a matter of perspective. Of course, the musical comedy that had once staged the excitement and challenge of the *fin de siècle* was now being performed against a world crisis the scale of which had not been seen in modern times. In that context, it would have *seemed* more retreatist and fantastic without even trying. But the fact is that wartime musical producers *did* try. They specifically aimed to produce shows that were uncontroversial and 'took people out of themselves'. The earlier shows worked differently. For all their investment in fantasy, at the same time they struggled for contemporaneity. They looked for the current thing, the connection with some modern 'issue', or image, that would prove popular, be it socialism, department stores, the girl on the film, the aeroplane, religious nonconformity, 'Japan', or whatever. Wartime shows, for very good reasons, did not operate in this way. The most pressing contemporary reality had become such that it could hardly be staged at all according to the standard musical comedy formula. *The Better 'Ole*, it is true, did manage to find a commercially successful way of making war itself escapist, but that was a risky strategy and, indeed, *The Better 'Ole* proved quite exceptional in this respect. For the most part shows avoided direct articulation with war. They were designed to overload on escapism and those that did often became hits.

These wartime successes were essentially of three kinds. First, there was the exotic orientalist show like *Chu Chin Chow*, which was a cross between pantomime and musical comedy. Second, there were the productions that enabled Robert Evett to rescue Daly's from the financial difficulties that had become exposed after George Edwardes' death. *The Maid of the Mountains* and *A Southern Maid* were spectaculars, both starring José Collins, the American performer who became fêted on the West End stage in these years. These veered towards very light opera interspersed with a good sprinkling of comedy. Like *Chu Chin Chow* they were set in romantic faraway places and in their romanticized treatment of banditry visualized a world of high derring-do and moral certitude. Finally, and perhaps most popular of all as a genre, or sub-genre, there were the musical farces, shows like *The Boy, Kissing Time, Theodore and Co., Who's Hooper* (1919) and *Yes Uncle*. These really took off in wartime Britain.

Even by musical comedy standards, such shows were light and produced to respond to a perceived need for the safe, the secure and the escapist. Evett's organized 'disembowelling' of Frederick Lonsdale's libretto for *The Maid of the Mountains* is suggestive here.[29] Evett and his team (Oscar Asche, Howard Talbot, Harry Graham and the composer Harold Fraser-Simpson) took what was quite a dramatic book and rendered it as a more comfortable mixture of romance and comedy. An ambiguous ending, which leaves the gypsy heroine, Teresa, stranded on stage while her bandit lover flees to the arms of the governor's daughter, was completely changed in favour of the traditional happy resolution and comic scenes and songs were interpolated, especially into what was potentially a quite dark second act. As far as the farces were concerned, these required no editing. They were simple 'hustling fun', as the Lord Chamberlain's Office had it.[30] *The Boy*, for instance, concerned a society woman, Millicent, who, in order to protect stories of her own about her age, had apparently brought up her son to believe that he was five years younger than he actually was. His 'fourteenth' birthday party, then, takes place in his nineteenth year. The consequent confusions, many of them resulting from what seems to be the wildly precocious maturity of 'the boy', form the substance, such as it is, of what follows. Similarly, *Kissing Time* was 'a good, lively, tuneful musical farce' with 'an endearingly silly story'.[31]

It is usually thought that these farces continued the traditions of West End and Gaiety musical comedy, but that is not entirely the case.[32] Recognizably musical comedy of the old school, they were, at the same time, quite distinct as wartime shows. They had less of the music hall comedic influence and relied much more on the slick performance of comic situation. They showed more of the American and revue musical influences. The chorus elements were styled differently and often with less formality. Above all, however, they deployed a very different narratology. Their contemporaneity was everywhere apparent, in dress and speech idiom, for instance, but there was little or no engagement with the *idea* of contemporaneity. In the earlier shows modernity was a condition to be articulated. It was also ambiguously related to tradition and convention. So it was that musical comedy acted as kind of mediator for modernity. The modern in these later shows, however, was quite distinctly staged as the taken for granted. Modernity was no longer the challenging new, but rather the now entirely familiar. No longer a self-conscious condition, modernity had become not much more than the surroundings against which mistaken identities and compromising situations could be played out in the tried-and-tested ways. In this sense there can be no doubt that while musical comedy remained a popular culture in the wartime period, it lost a good deal of its purchase as a culture of the moment, just as revue was claiming. Indeed, one of its crucial selling points now was not that it was new and innovative but, on the contrary, that it had become entirely familiar and predictable. At the time these qualities had a particular premium but that, of course, would not last. With the war over, musical comedy was badly placed to meet new challenges. It had, for good reason, tamed itself beyond controversy, which is one reason why it was so spectacularly ill equipped to respond with anything new in the 1920s. It was against this background that the American musical theatre was to make its first really unanswerable bid for hegemony over the musical theatre stage.

West End musical theatre between the wars

Musical comedy did not vanish overnight. Indeed, the London West End continued to produce significant numbers of shows in the 1920s and 1930s, some 55 divided roughly equally between the two decades (see appendix 3). Among all this continued activity there were some theatres that had strong seasons of musical comedy. The Winter Garden, for example, had hits through the 1920s, with shows like *A Night Out* (1920), *The Cabaret Girl* (1922) and *Primrose* (1928); likewise the Adelphi and the Hippodrome. *That's a Good Girl* (1928), *Yes, Madam* (1934) and *Please Teacher* (1935), all at the latter, had runs of over 300 performances. One of the biggest successes of the 1920s, a cross-dressing version of Cinderella entitled *Mr Cinders* (1928), had a run of 529. Daly's, on the other hand, put on few musical comedies in this period and had few successes, apart from *This'll Make you Whistle* (1936) which achieved a run of 190. Similarly the Gaiety had a difficult time, although there were periods here that saw musical comedy resurfacing to make an impact, notably in the mid- to late 1930s when Firth Shephard took over the theatre's management and instigated the building of a new company. This level of organization and continuity, missing since the days of Grossmith and Laurillard, paid off. The new company, built around Leslie Henson, Fred Emney, Louise Browne and Richard Hearne, proved highly effective and the shows, many of them written by Guy Bolton, Frederick Thompson and Douglas Furber, pulled in audiences. *Seeing Stars* (1935) managed 236 performances; *Swing Along* (1936), 311; *Going Greek* (1938), 306; and the last show to play at the Gaiety, *Running Riot* (1938), 207. Above all there was one huge smash in the period and that was *Me and my Girl* (1937) with its hit title tune and what became the ubiquitous song of British dance halls everywhere, 'The Lambeth Walk'. This 'Cockney' show played 1,646 times at the Victoria Palace.

But this patchy performance was a long way from the Edwardian heydays when musical comedy had dominated the West End stage and beyond, and it was clear that the long-term trend for the musical comedy, at least in its 'British' variety, was now down. Of the 55 West End musical comedies produced in these two decades, 17 played fewer than 100 performances and some considerably less. Oscar Asche's production of *The Good Old Days* (1925) collapsed after just 37 performances and *Nicolette* (1925) at the Duke of York lasted for just twelve. These were not simply idiosyncratic disasters but, rather, the worst examples of what was a general decline in the popularity and, most importantly, the prestige of West End musical comedy.

This is quite often understood in terms of a wider phenomenon, a decline in musical theatre, and, indeed, theatre *per se* and usually explained by the emergence of radio and film as major media of popular culture. Sheridan Morley writes of these as 'the two greatest threats to live theatre', pointing out that they emerged in the early 1930s almost simultaneously.[33] As McKibbin shows, 'going to the pictures' quickly became 'not simply the most important leisure activity of the English, at least outside the home, it was more important to them than to any other nationality'. Throughout the 1930s, between 18 and 19 million people attended the cinema in Britain every week and the numbers rose throughout the 1940s. By the end of that decade, British cinema attendance made up a staggering '10 per cent of *total* world attendance'.[34] Similarly, listening to the radio displaced live entertainment, becoming the essential British relaxation activity and here the figures are also impressive. 'Between 1922 and 1939 the number of radio licences per 100 households increased from 1 per cent to 71 per cent – from a total of 36,000 to 8.9 million' – the crucial point about the radio, of course, being that it kept people at home and out of the West End.[35]

But, again, it should be emphasized that it was West End musical comedy in particular that became *passé*. All theatre may have faced a relative struggle, certainly after the early 1930s, but musical comedy struggled more than most. By comparison to revue, for instance, which continued to do well throughout the 1920s, musical comedy looked especially weak. This was partly a matter of economics – it helped, particularly in these years, that revue did not require the huge investment of a fully-fledged musical comedy extravaganza. But it is easy to overestimate the impact of economic conditions on theatre history. Certainly this was a time of falling box office receipts and there were theatre closures throughout the period, including the Gaiety itself, which closed in 1938. However, while it would have had an impact on all disposable incomes, economic depression hit hardest those most vulnerable. Regular or even occasional theatregoers hardly figured predominantly here. Immediately after the war, middle-class families would have 'suffered an appreciable loss of real incomes and the social disappointment which comes with frustrated expectations', but, as Ross McKibbin has shown, this was a relatively short-lived reality, for the middle class at least. 'By 1923 ... these losses had for most been more than made up.'[36] As many historians have pointed out, there were sectors of the British economy that were actually developing in the 1920s and early 1930s. There was no simple correlation, then, between the post-war economy and theatre receipts, for musical comedy or otherwise, certainly over the longer term.

Other factors were involved in muscial comedy's particular difficulties in the 1920s and 1930s, and again the comparison with revue and the American musical helps to clarify the issue. With its eagerness to incorporate American musicality and chic, revue was, above all, a culture able to maintain a modern styling. Musical comedy in its West End version was failing in this respect and not only by comparison to English versions of the Americanized revue. There was also the authentic article to face, the American musical itself, in its most confident, thoroughly nativized form. Far from stagnating, this was the period when American musical theatre positively flourished. It took London by storm and, represented most famously by Fred and Adele Astaire, established new standards of professionalism and technical expertise. In a relatively short space of time America established complete authority in the field. By the end of the 1920s its stars and shows featured as the new icons of style and set the dimensions for 1920s panache. Even the briefest listing of America's hits on the West End stage in the 1920s indicates the nature of America's rise in this respect. The 'musical farce' *Stop Flirting*, featuring the first appearance of the Astaires, came to the West End in 1923. Gershwin's *Lady, be Good* appeared in 1926 and *Funny Face* in 1928. These were the shows, along with *No, No Nanette* and *Rose Marie*, both in London in 1925, that helped to secure the crucial identification between 'America' and the 'musical', which was maintained for the next fifty years. The appearance of *Show Boat* in 1928, with Paul Robeson, was a further landmark, and perhaps the most substantial one yet in the development of what was to become the 'American musical'. Both in musicological terms and by virtue of the range and depth of its signification, *Show Boat* was seen by many not just as a new musical, but a new *kind* of stage musical with a hugely increased capacity for expression. For all the talent of the rising generation of British performers – many of whom, like Lillie, Coward, Buchanan and Lawrence, had emerged from revue – this American invasion was difficult if not impossible to withstand. There were individual successes, Coward's *Bitter Sweet* in 1928 for instance, but if these bucked the trend they were hardly enough to displace America's rising status. 'In the face of such breathtaking competition,' as Morley puts it, 'what else could the British musical look in 1928 but insipid?'[37]

Again, all musical theatre felt the impact of the American musical, but musical comedy felt it most, for a number of reasons. Quite apart from being outclassed in terms of singing and dancing, the status of the American musical meant that West End musical comedy could no longer make the crucial connections with modernity. Far from speaking for contemporaneity as it once had, the typical narrative and standard style of West End musical comedy now seemed to belong to a fast-disappearing age. And the new configuration was no simple matter of changing fashions. It undoubtedly reflected a much wider dynamic – essentially, a changed world order with America positioned not just as the leading economic power, but also as the new home of modernity and innovation. The energy at the heart of the American musical was very much a reflection of America's new status in the world, and precisely an echo of the vitality once possessed by the West End musical comedy at an earlier stage. By 1930, that species of musical comedy, which had once spoken for its age, now seemed tame and old-fashioned. For all this displacement, however, the culture that had once articulated England's condition with such confidence and style did not become, as one might have expected, entirely irrelevant. It had one last dynamic incarnation in the nostalgia of the 1930s as represented by the retro shows of Ivor Novello and, especially, Noel Coward. Here it was both reconstructed as an historical culture and reinvented as a focal point for 'lost England'.

Musical comedy as nostalgia – new wave West End musical theatre in the 1930s

> Blues, Twentieth Century Blues are getting me down.
> Who's escaped those weary Twentieth Century Blues?
> Why, if there's a God in the sky, why should he grin?
> High above this dreary Twentieth Century din.
> In this strange illusion,
> Chaos and confusion,
> People seem to lose their way.
> What is there to strive for,
> Love or keep alive for?
>
> (Noel Coward, *Cavalcade*, 1931)

Noel Coward did not write in the 'straight' musical comedy tradition at all, but he did write musical comedy pastiche. *Cavalcade* (1931), apart from many references to musical comedy, contains a musical comedy scene and *Operette* (1938) is a full-blown version of a musical comedy show and of the lives of musical comedy artists. Here Coward produces a musical comedy imitation, with standard plots, exploding cars, romantic love songs, cheap one-liners and '*a mood of gay and tender sentiment*'.[38] This show is juxtaposed against the private lives of the performers to produce the 'play within a play' structure commonly used in the 1930s. It should be emphasized, however, that *Operette* was not the real thing. As a 1930s reconstruction of a past culture it was a reminder that Coward represented the very dynamics producing the decline of 'native' musical comedy. He was a prolific writer and accomplished performer of revue, the displacing form of the 1920s. As Morley points out, he was also 'one of the first of the 20s generation to recognize the virtues of the Broadway stage, its pace and its urgency and its attack'.[39] He was one of the innovators of a style of comedy, often described as 'urbane', that operated at the antithesis of the 'variety' styles of humour characteristic of the Edwardian musical. In all these ways, Coward's work, and the Coward persona, were entirely suggestive of musical comedy's decline, its collapse into a singalong parody of the earlier engagement and vitality. While the 'real' 1930s musical comedy staggered along with uninspiring productions and tired plots, Coward stood for contemporary chic and, tellingly, a characteristic tiredness and even indifference towards modernity.[40] Again, the contrast with traditional musical comedy could hardly be greater. In contrast to the latter's rosy optimism, Coward invented a languid pose that reproduced modernist *angst* as sophisticated irony. In this way he performed the trick that enabled a style virtue to be created out of England's displacement as the foremost nation of modernity. No longer running to catch up with the Americans, the West End musical experienced a temporary resurgence as an arch culture quietly withdrawn from its present and distinctly nostalgic for its past.

This is not to say, however, that Coward's musical theatre was wholly iconoclastic; far from it. However much he may have registered his dissent from the degeneration of the musical comedy tradition, especially in his 1920s work, he had a real appreciation for what he understood to be the authentic thing: musical comedy in its late Victorian and Edwardian incarnation. For this 'real' culture, Coward had considerable affection. This is everywhere apparent in his pastiche versions. He also registered a deep sense of its cultural significance, insisting on its historical importance as a national culture, a culture that somehow named 'Britishness' at a particular historical period. In this way Coward had a particular importance in the history of musical comedy and for apparently contradictory reasons. As well as being suggestive of its decline, he was, in fact, the first and perhaps only significant cultural figure to reconstruct musical comedy as a 'national' culture of any importance.

Thus in *Cavalcade*, the new-style 'pageant' that attempted to capture British life over two generations from the gay and 'innocent' 1890s to what was presented as the decadent and directionless 1920s, musical comedy featured prominently as a signifier of popular British culture. Songs from *The Merry Widow* and *'Miss Gibbs'* (an allusion to *Our Miss Gibbs*) are sung in a restaurant scene set in 1909. A character, Marion, recalls being sick in a cab after 'the two hundredth performance of *Floradora*' and a musical comedy performer in the company reminisces about her performances in the late 1890s.[41] Here musical comedy becomes the means by which characters measure their lives and assert their cultural identity. Even more importantly, musical comedy is connected with the big historical events. In the armistice night scene of *Cavalcade* a bus carrying the huge posters advertising *Chu Chin Chow* takes centre stage. In one of the earlier scenes a musical comedy is actually reproduced in the form of the staging of 'Princess Mirabelle'. Described in the stage directions as '*a typical musical comedy of the period*', with '*the scene on the stage*' being '*excessively rural*', Coward's pastiche depicts a love scene between Princess Mirabelle, disguised as a farm girl, and a naval officer.[42] There is a comic interlude with a soubrette '*dressed as a dairy maid*' and a chorus routine.[43] The suggestion is that this show somehow captures Britain at the *fin de siècle*, a linkage strongly emphasized at the climax of this scene. Here the stage manager rushes on stage in a dramatic intervention and makes an extraordinary announcement: Mafeking has been relieved! With the subsequent outpouring of relief and national pride, musical comedy becomes identified not just as a characteristic culture of the age, but as nothing less than the embodiment of national identity at a particular time.

Cavalcade was double-edged terms of its presentation of musical comedy. In one sense it extended the cultural life of musical comedy by establishing it as a key cultural reference point and, even more so, by relating it so closely to national history on a grand scale. Musical comedy may have been light and ephemeral in some ways, but it was also deeply implicated here with a conception of the character of the nation. In another sense, however, *Cavalcade*, like *Operette*, represented a burying of musical comedy. At a time when a show like *Under Your Hat* (1938), a standard musical comedy, could achieve a 512 performance run at the Palace Theatre, Coward was insisting that 'real' musical comedy, the kind that had once had a vital cultural life of its own, was not just in reverse, but confined to the historical condition. In many ways this was a more fitting end to West End musical comedy than the attempts of managements to wring one last formulaic show out of the tradition, but Coward's nostalgic lament for and celebration of this culture was not to prevail for long. Perhaps partly because it had been so much reheated and served up as fresh, West End musical comedy became redundant and soon completely forgotten. Far from being mythologized in any grand sense, it was not long before musical comedy became mixed up with the generic old-fashioned quaintness that became 'England before the War' and entirely disconnected from the dynamic forces that had once secured its true origins in modernity.

Postscript – a note on the 'megamusical'

At the heyday of West End musical comedy, Britain could reasonably consider itself to be a premier world power. The essential argument of this study has been that, far from being marginal and obscure, musical comedy was a mainstream popular culture that both confirmed and was, in its way, constitutive of this position. By formulating itself as a conservative modernism and achieving huge success at home and abroad, it sustained the essential conflation between the nation and the modern condition, and did so through a rendition that reproduced modernity as gaiety. For all the darker elements that shaped the ambiguities and contradictions of musical comedy, its status was hugely dependent on its sense of fun. By the demise of musical comedy Britain's status in the world had changed decisively. National histories and theatre history run parallel here, reflecting each other in quite complex and instrumental ways. The rise of the American musical in the 1920s and thereafter is of crucial significance in this respect. The American musical did not simply out-produce British, and all other, musical theatre performance. It possessed a confidence that both reflected and, in an important sense, was constitutive of America's cultural grip on the idea of the modern. Like film, the musical became synonymous with the New World's economic and cultural predominance, a matter of technical capacity, but also a confident assertion of cultural identity that penetrated all aspects of production. Shows such as *Show Boat*, *Oklahoma*, *South Pacific* and *West Side Story* became established as among the most powerful metonyms for 'America'. Faced with this competition, the British tradition was represented by figures like Coward, Novello, Ellis, Wilson, Bricusse, Newley and Bart. These composed a whole variety of music theatre – in the form of operettas, comedies, romantic musicals, revues – but they remained marginal to the main tradition of musical theatre. In a way that was highly suggestive of the wider world history, British composers fell back on period-piece nostalgia (for example, Sandy Wilson's *The Boy Friend*, 1954), Dickensian familiarity (Lionel Bart's *Oliver*, 1963), or working-class salt of the earth (*Me and my Girl*, 1937). The serious technical resources and organizational capacities followed, as one would expect, what was now the only real living tradition of musical theatre – the American tradition. So it was that no theatrical organization was specifically set up in relation to musicals in Britain at this point to create an organized collectivity of producers, directors and performers as 'showbiz'. This latter came only as American musicals started to enter the West End after the Second World War to the point at which the West End, through London productions, developed both the companies and the performers to take on Broadway. This development led, in turn, to productions of American musicals and their performers being transferred in either direction.

With its quaint sense of humour, old-fashioned melodies and relatively uninspired dance routines, the British show now fully gave way to the magisterial style and blazing vitality of the new American products. Here the fully-fledged, thoroughly integrated, book musical became emblematic of a modern culture, apparently with demotic origins, that had reached full maturity and 'classic' dimensions. Thereafter, it was the American musical that set the standards, certainly until the 1980s. The history of British musical comedy, from its pre-1914 eminence to its eventual collapse, is a material and cultural product of this much wider social, political and economic sweep. It becomes implicated in the wider historiography where the twentieth century is understood in terms of great shifts in modernity's centre of gravity. Here Britain's (and Europe's) decline becomes America's rise.

But the musical did not remain in this classical (American) form, far from it. Eventually, in most traditions, the modern is understood as imploding under its own contradictions, giving way to, in some accounts, a postmodernity powered by globalizing economic and cultural forces. The signification of the latter development in terms of musical theatre would be the emergence of what has been referred to elsewhere as the transnational 'megamusical'. These share a number of essential criteria that set them apart from other music theatre productions including,

> first, markets characterized by rapid global expansion and marked internal growth since 1980 ... Second, megamusicals are produced and controlled by a select and specific group of highly capitalized globally competent ... players. Pioneer British megamusical producers Andrew Lloyd Webber and Cameron Macintosh, each heading what are now large global companies, have lately been joined by Disney. And the broader field of stage musical production is crowded with new

transnational players including Polygram, Viacom and M.C.A. [Finally, the] ... megamusical's third most distinctive characteristic is its cultivation of specific commercial, technical and aesthetic models of production. This has ensured the replication of any given show with unprecedented meticulousness across a greater number of international venues [to a degree uncommon in] the field of theatrical production even fifteen years ago.[44]

The result has been the globalized transnationalization of music theatre, the reproduction of the show on a uniform basis globally. That is to say, the musical has become subject to a

rationalizing, industrial logic, including a quality control model implemented and supervised outward from a given metropolitan centre [which is seen by many of those inside music theatre] to replicate technical and artistic production details with such rigour as to delimit the creative agency of performers to a significant degree. Hence the increasing use, by these ... insiders, of terms like 'cloning', 'franchising' and 'McTheatre' to describe the megamusical business.[45]

This is a development that clearly has some connections with the much earlier industrial culture of British musicals at the *fin de siècle*, although there are also important divergences. Most importantly for the purposes here, it involves British composers and impresarios and even British theatrical institutions, but it could not in any significant sense be 'nationalized' or 'racialized' as 'British'. Unlike the musical comedy of the earlier period, which specifically came out of, responded to and was constitutive of a national culture, the British dimension of the megamusical is non-functional. It may be the case that British producers, writers and directors have taken a lead in the making of such shows. But this is, of course, accidental and has little to do with the cultural registration of early musical comedy. It is, rather, a new development of a transnational culture industry where musicals have a global identity, one that, for all its apparent current strength, may not be entirely secure. The commitment to form over content and spectacle over text, to the creation of a global product for a global audience, opens up a field which can be treated in megamusical terms but also closes down any specific localized cultural character or identity to the musical. This undermines both its vernacularity and contemporaneity and thus its ability to engage with an existent social world. The link between the musical and popular culture increasingly reduces itself to the technological rather than the dramatic and carries the risk of producing an empty show about nothing achieved at huge economic cost. In this respect, it is interesting to note how many new megamusicals in recent years have been gigantic turkeys rather than geese laying golden eggs – *Moby Dick* (1992), for instance, *Martin Guerre* (1995), *Whistle Down the Wind* (1998), *Toulouse-Lautrec* (1999), *Notre Dame de Paris* (2000), *Napoleon* (2000), and so on. The virtual worlds thematically and theatrically created by megamusicals could become their downfall. Since they are addressed to a global audience of 'anybody', there is no 'somebody' to relate these worlds to. They can become virtual in the worst sense of being nobody's world. Thus the megamusical is stuck with a dilemma as a popular cultural form, because it has tended to abandon specific 'people' as its cultural referent. In this respect, the contemporary world of commerce and the market begins to threaten the popular vitality of the musical, whereas, with the musical in its heyday, in Britain at the *fin de siècle* as in America subsequently, commerce and the market provided a means to foster it.

Appendices

The idea of 'musical comedy' is quite problematic. As this study makes clear, the term does not describe a 'pure' form, far from it. Musical comedy was composite in its origins and has remained so. It characteristically borrowed from other kinds of musical theatre until a popular formula was arrived at. It is not surprising that there was very little consistency in contemporary use of the term. 'Classic' musical comedy shows were often billed quite otherwise. *The Runaway Girl*, for instance, was billed as a 'musical play', as was *The Arcadians, The Cingalee* and *A Country Girl. The Geisha* was 'a Japanese play'. To confuse matters more there was some appropriation of the term, particularly as musical comedy became increasingly popular. *M'lord Sir Smith*, for example, was billed as 'musical comedy', but was much closer to variety/burlesque, as would be expected from the involvement of Arthur Roberts, the comedic star of that show.

Appendices 1 and 2 list alphabetically most of the West End plays that made a reasonably strong commitment to 'musical comedy'. The fairly closely related 'musical variety' shows, like *The Lady Slavey* (1894) or *H.M.S. Irresponsible* (1900), are generally omitted. Similarly, the Slaughter/Hood shows that mixed burlesque and operetta, like *Her Royal Highness* (1898), are not included. Christmas shows, like the hugely popular *Bluebell in Faeryland* (1901), which had some strong musical comedy elements, are likewise excluded for the same reason, although *Chu Chin Chow*, a pantomime heavily influenced by musical comedy, remains on the list. Even with this degree of exclusivity, however, some controversy will inevitably remain. There will be disagreement, for example, over such issues as whether *In Town* really is a musical comedy or variety. This kind of debate is very much part of the territory.

There is one area, however, where the term 'musical comedy' is interpreted quite liberally here and this is at the operetta end. There will be many who would dispute that shows like *The Duchess of Dantzic*, or *The Merry Widow*, even in their West End forms, should be understood as musical comedy at all. One can only restate that in its heyday musical comedy was the most popular form of theatre, musical or otherwise, on the Edwardian West End stage. This meant that musical comedy assimilated all kinds of theatre and especially Continental 'operettas'. The tendency was to introduce musical comedy styles and routines as part of the Anglicizing process. It is for this reason that quite a few shows often thought of as 'operettas' or 'Viennese operettes' are included here, especially in Appendix 2, as musical comedies.

On the issue of authorship, it was not at all unusual for shows to be revised and/or put into 'second edition' and in both cases new songs or scenes could be interpolated. There was a certain degree of borrowing and much litigation over alleged theft of ideas, dialogue and music. Authorship, then, can also be difficult. The practice here has been to give only the 'main' composers/authors of the music and books and to list the main contributors of lyrics.

As far as constructing musical comedies on some basis of country of origin is concerned, as Chapter 3 has argued, such designations can be highly problematic. There have been debates, for instance, over whether Guy Bolton, born in England but of American parents, counts as English or American and over how to categorize a show where the music was written by Jerome Kern and the book by P. G. Wodehouse. It should be emphasized that the following appendices are not attempts to resolve such disputes but rather reflect a standard designation of musical theatre history. One would also want to point out that the favoured term for 'native' shows in this study remains 'West End' rather than British or English.

Appendix 3 lists shows produced between 1920 and 1939, not by name but by year. The aim here is to indicate something of the dynamics of the decline of musical comedy over this period.

These appendixes have been compiled from a number of sources, the most important of which are:

Rex Bunnet and Brian Rust, *London Musical Shows on Record, 1897–1976*.
Kurt Kanzl, *The British Musical Theatre*, vols 1 and 2.
J. P. Wearing, *The London Stage A Calendar of Plays and Players 1890–1899*, vols 1 and 2.
J. P. Wearing, *The London Stage A Calendar of Plays and Players 1900–1909*, vols 1 and 2.
J. P. Wearing, *The London Stage A Calendar of Plays and Players 1910–1919*, vols 1 and 2.
J. P. Wearing, *The London Stage A Calendar of Plays and Players 1920–1929*, vols 1 and 2.

Full bibliographical details for the above are given in the bibliography.

Appendix 1 Selected British musical comedies, 1892–1920 (London, West End)

Title/year (of London opening)	Composer	Playwright	Lyricist	Theatre/management/number of performances (→ = transferred to)	Original principals (selected)
After the Girl, 1914	Paul Rubens		Percy Greenbank and Paul Rubens	Gaiety/George Edwardes (105)	Lew Hearn and Isobel Elsom
The Antelope, 1908	Hugo Felix		Adrian Ross	Waldorf/Henry R. Smith (22)	José Collins and Joe Farren Soutar
Are you There?, 1913	Ruggiero Leoncavallo	Albert de Courville	Edgar Wallace	Prince of Wales/Albert de Courville (23)	Lawrence Grossmith and Shirley Kellog
An Artist's Model, 1895	Sidney Jones	Owen Hall	Harry Greenbank	Daly's/George Edwardes (392)	C. Hayden Coffin and Marie Tempest
Baby Bunting, 1919	Nat D. Ayer	Fred Thompson and Worton David	Clifford Grey	Shaftsbury/George Grossmith Jr (213)	Dorothy Brunton and Walter Catlett
The Balkan Princess, 1910	Paul Rubens	Frederick Lonsdale and Frank Curzon	Paul Rubens and Arthur Wimperis	Prince of Wales/Frank Curzon (176)	Isabel Jay and Bertram Wallis
The Beauty of Bath, 1906	Herbert E. Haines	Seymour Hicks and Cosmo Hamilton	Charles H. Taylor	Aldwych→Hicks/Charles Frohman (287)	Seymour Hicks and Ellaline Terriss
The Belle of Bond Street, 1914	Ivan Caryll and Cecil Cook		Owen Hall	Adelphi (40)	Martin Brown and Ina Claire
The Belle of Brittany, 1908	Howard Talbot	Leedham Bantock and P. J. Barrow	Percy Greenbank	Queen's/Tom B. Davis (147)	Maud Boyd and George Graves

Title, Year	Composer	Book	Lyrics	Theatre/Producer (runs)	Cast
The Belle of Cairo, 1896	F. Kinsey Peile	Cecil Raleigh and F. Kinsey Peile	F. Kinsey Peile	Court/Arthur Chudleigh and May Yohe (71)	May Yohe and Charles Wibrow
The Belle of Mayfair, 1906	Leslie Stuart	Basil Hood and Charles H. Brookfield		Vaudeville/A. and S. Gatti and Charles Frohman (416)	Courtice Pounds and Edna May
The Better 'Ole, 1917	Herman Darewski	Bruce Bairnsfather and Arthur Eliot	James Hurd	Oxford Theatre/ C. B. Cochran (811)	Arthur Bourchier and Madge Burdett
Betty, 1915	Paul Rubens	Frederick Lonsdale and Gladys Unger	Adrian Ross and Paul Rubens	Daly's/George Edwardes (391)	Winfred Barnes and Donald Calthrop
The Blue Moon, 1904	Howard Talbot and Paul Rubens	Harold Ellis	Paul Rubens and Percy Greenbank	Lyric/Robert Courtneidge (182)	Willie Edouin & Florence Smithson
The Boy, 1917	Lionel Monckton and Howard Talbot	Fred Thompson	Adrian Ross and Percy Greenbank	Adelphi/Alfred Butt (801)	Donald Calthrop and Maisie Gay
The Catch of the Season, 1904	Herbert E. Haines and Evelyn Baker	Seymour Hicks and Cosmo Hamilton	Charles H. Taylor	Vaudeville/A. and S. Gatti and Charles Frohman (621)	Seymour Hicks and Zena Dare
Cherry, 1920	Melville Gideon	Edward Knoblock		Apollo/ C. B. Cochran (76)	Marie Blanche and George Ricketts
A Chinese Honeymoon, 1901	Howard Talbot	George Dance		Strand/Frank Curzon (1075)	Picton Rozburgh and Louie Freear
Chu Chin Chow, 1916	Frederick Norton	Oscar Asche	Oscar Asche	His Majesty's/Oscar Asche and Lily Brayton (2235)	J. V. Bryant and Violet Essex

Appendix 1 (Contd.)

Title/year (of London opening)	Composer	Playwright	Lyricist	Theatre/management/number of performances (→ = transferred to)	Original principals (selected)
The Cingalee, 1904	Lionel Monckton	James T. Tanner	Adrian Ross and Percy Greenbank	Daly's/George Edwardes (365)	Rutland Barrington and Sybil Arundale
The Circus Girl, 1896	Ivan Caryll	James T. Tanner and W. Palings	Harry Greenbank and Adrian Ross	Gaiety/George Edwardes (494)	Seymour Hicks and Ellaline Terriss
A Country Girl, 1902	Lionel Monckton	James T. Tanner	Adrian Ross	Daly's/George Edwardes (729)	C. Hayden Coffin and Evie Greene
The Dairymaids, 1906	Paul Rubens and Frank E. Tours	Alexander M. Thompson and Robert Courtneidge	Paul Rubens and Arthur Wimperis	Apollo/Robert Courtneidge (239)	Phyllis Broughton and Carrie Moore
Dear Little Denmark, 1909	Paul Rubens	Paul Rubens		Prince of Wales/Frank Curzon (109)	Isabel Jay and Bertram Wallis
The Duchess of Dantzic, 1903	Ivan Caryll	Henry Hamilton		Lyric/George Edwardes (236)	Evie Greene and Denis O'Sullivan
The Earl and the Girl, 1903	Ivan Caryll	Seymour Hicks	Percy Greenbank	Adelphi→Lyric/William Greet (371)	Walter Passmore and Agnes Fraser
Flora, 1918	Herman Darewski and Melville Gideon	Harry Grattan	Davy Burnaby and James Heard	Prince of Wales/André Charlot (72)	Gertie Millar and Alfred Phillips
Floradora, 1899	Leslie Stuart	Owen Hall	E. Boyd Jones and Paul Rubens	Lyric/Tom B. Davis (455)	Melville Stewart and Ada Reeves

Show (year)	Music	Book	Lyrics	Theatre / Producer (performances)	Cast
The French Maid, 1896	Walter Slaughter		Basil Hood	Terry's→ Vaudeville/ W. H. Griffiths (480)	Kate Cutler and Richard Green
A Gaiety Girl, 1893	Sidney Jones	Owen Hall	Harry Greenbank	Prince of Wales→ Daly's/George Edwardes (413)	W. Louis Bradfield and Maud Hobson
The Gay Gordons, 1907	Guy Jones	Seymour Hicks	Arthur Wimperis	Aldwych/Charles Frohman (229)	Seymour Hicks and Zena Dare
The Gay Parisienne, 1896 (revised)	Ivan Caryll	George Dance		Duke of York/ Horace Sedger (369)	Ada Reeve and Hubert Willis
The Geisha, 1896	Sidney Jones	Owen Hall	Harry Greenbank	Daly's/George Edwardes (760)	Harry Monkhouse and Marie Tempest
The Gypsy Girl, 1905		Claude Arundale		Waldorf/Benbrick Blanchard (30)	Sybil Arundale and Leonard Russell
The Girl Behind the Counter, 1906	Howard Talbot	Leedham Bantock and Arthur Anderson	Arthur Anderson	Wyndham's/Frank Curzon (141)	C. Hayden Coffin and Isabel Jay
The Girl for the Boy, 1919	Howard Carr and Bernard Rolt	Austen Hurgon and George Arthurs	Percy Greenbank	Duke of York's (86)	Andrew Randall and Gina Palerme
The Girls of Gottenberg, 1907	Ivan Caryll and Lionel Monckton	George Grossmith Jr and L. E. Berman	Adrian Ross and Basil Hood	Gaiety/George Edwardes (303)	George Grossmith Jr and Gertie Millar
The Girl from Kay's, 1902	Ivan Caryll and Cecil Cook	Owen Hall	Adrian Ross and Claude Avelong	Apollo/George Edwardes (432)	Kate Cutler and W. Louis Bradfield

Appendix 1 (Contd.)

Title/year (of London opening)	Composer	Playwright	Lyricist	Theatre/management/number of performances (→ = transferred to)	Original principals (selected)
The Girl from Utah, 1913	Paul Rubens and Sidney Jones	James T. Tanner	Percy Greenbank, Adrian Ross and Paul Rubens	Adelphi/George Edwardes (195)	Alfred de Manby and Phyllis Dare
A Greek Slave, 1898	Sidney Jones	Owen Hall	Harry Greenbank and Adrian Ross	Daly's/George Edwardes (349)	Letty Lind and Marie Tempest
The Happy Day, 1916	Paul Rubens and Sidney Jones	Seymour Hicks	Adrian Ross and Paul Rubens	Daly's/Robert Evett (241)	José Collins and G. P. Huntley
Havana, 1908	Leslie Stuart	George Grossmith Jr and Graham Hill	Adrian Ross	Gaiety/George Edwardes (221)	Evie Greene and Leonard Mackay
The Honourable Phil, 1908	Harold Samuel	G. P. Huntley and Herbert Clayton	Harold Lawson	Hicks/Charles Frohman (71)	G. P. Huntley and Julia Sanderson
Houp-La!, 1916	Nat D. Ayer	Fred Thompson and Hugh E. Wright	Hugh E. Wright and Percy Greenbank	St Martin's/C. B. Cochran (108)	Gertie Millar and Nat D. Ayer

Show	Composer	Writer	Theatre/Producer	Cast
In Town, 1892	F. Osmond Carr	Adrian Ross and James Leader	Prince of Wales → Gaiety/George Edwardes (292)	Arthur Roberts, Florence St John
The Islander, 1910	Philip Michael Faraday	Major Frank Marshall	Apollo/Alexander Henderson (114)	Elsie Spain and Sam Walsh
The Kiss Call, 1919	Ivan Caryll	Fred Thompson Percy Greenbank and Adrian Ross	Gaiety/Alfred Butt (176)	Austin Melford and Evelyn Laye
Kissing Time, 1919	Ivan Caryll	Guy Bolton and P. G. Wodehouse	Winter Garden/George Grossmith Jr and Edward Laurillard (430)	Yvonne Arnaud and Stanley Holloway
Kitty Gray, 1900	Lionel Monckton, Howard Talbot, Victor Roger, and Augustus T. Barratt	J. Smyth Piggott	Apollo/George Edwardes and Charles Frohman (220)	Maurice Farkoa and Evie Greene
Lady Madcap, 1904	Paul Rubens	Paul Rubens and N. Newnham-Davies	Paul Rubens and Percy Greenbank	Prince of Wales/George Edwardes (354)	Maurice Farkoa and Eva Sandford
The Light Blues, 1916	Howard Talbot and Herman Finck	Mark Ambient and Jack Hulbert	Adrian Ross	Shaftsbury/Robert Courtneidge(20)	Albert Chevalier and Cicely Debenham
The Little Cherub, 1906 (revised as *The Girl on the Stage*-1906)	Ivan Caryll	Owen Hall	Adrian Ross	Prince of Wales/George Edwardes (114/29)	Evie Greene and Fred Kaye

Appendix 1 (Contd.)

Title/year (of London opening)	Composer	Playwright	Lyricist	Theatre/ management/ number of performances (→ = transferred to)	Original principals (selected)
Little Miss Nobody, 1898	Arthur E. Godfrey	Harry J. C. Graham		Lyric/Tom B. Davis (200)	Kate Cutler and Lionel Mackinder
The Love Birds, 1904	Raymond Roze	George Grossmith Jr		Savoy/Edward Laurillard (75)	Kate Cutler and Bertram Wallace
Maggie, 1919	Marcel Lattés	Fred Thompson and H. F. Maltby	Adrian Ross	Oxford Theatre/ C. B. Cochran (108)	Winifred Barnes and Peter Gawthorne
The Maid of the Mountains, 1917	Harold Fraser-Simson	Frederick Lonsdale	Harry Graham	Daly's/Robert Evett (1352)	José Collins and Lauri de Frece
The Medal and the Maid, 1903	Sydney Jones	Owen Hall	Charles H. Taylor	Lyric/Tom B Davis (98)	Ada Reeve and James E. Sullivan
The Messenger Boy, 1900	Lionel Monckton and Ivan Caryll	James T. Tanner and Alfred Murray	Adrian Ross and Percy Greenbank	Gaiety/George Edwardes (429)	E. J. Lonnon, Violet Lloyd and Teddy Payne
Miss Hook of Holland, 1907	Paul Rubens	P. Rubens and Austen Hurgon	Paul Rubens	Prince of Wales/ Frank Curzon (462)	G. P. Huntley and Isabel Jay
Miss Wingrove, 1905	Howard Talbot	W. H. Risque		Strand/Frank Curzon and Austen Hurgon (11)	Millie Legarde and Joe Farren Soutar

Monte Carlo, 1896	Howard Talbot		Harry Greenbank	Avenue/Henry Dana and H. J. Wilde (76)	Kate Cutler and Richard Green
The Mousmé (the Maids of Japan), 1911	Lionel Monckton and Howard Talbot	Alexander Thompson and Robert Courtneidge		Salisbury's under Robert Courtneidge (209)	Florence Smithson and Harry Welchman
Mr Manhattan, 1916	Howard Talbot	Fred Thompson and C. H. Bovill	Arthur Wimperis and Percy Greenbank	Prince of Wales/George Grossmith Jr and Edward Laurillard (228)	Raymond Hitchcock and Iris Hooey
Mr Popple of Ippleton, 1905	Paul Rubens	Paul Rubens		Apollo→Shaftsbury/Paul Rubens (173)	Olive Hood and G. P. Huntley
My Girl, 1896	F. Osmond Carr	James T. Tanner	Adrian Ross	Gaiety→Garrick/George Edwardes (183)	Kate Cutler and Connie Ediss
My Lady Frayle, 1916	Howard Talbot and Herman Finck	Arthur Wimperis and Max Pemberton	Arthur Wimperis	Shaftsbury/Robert Courtneidge (129)	Irene Brown and Courtice Pounds
My Mimosa Maid, 1908	Paul Rubens	Paul Rubens and Austen Hurgon		Prince of Wales/Frank Curzon (83)	Maurice Farkoa and Isabel Jay
Nelly Neil, 1907	Ivan Caryll	C. M. S. McLellan		Aldwych/Charles Frohman (107)	Joseph Coyne and Edna May
A Night Out, 1920	Willy Redstone	George Grossmith Jr and Arthur Miller	Clifford Grey	Winter Garden/George Grossmith Jr and Edward Laurillard (311)	Stanley Holloway and Phyllis Monkman

Appendix 1 (Contd.)

Title/year (of London opening)	Composer	Playwright	Lyricist	Theatre/management/number of performances (→ = transferred to)	Original principals (selected)
The Officer's Mess, 1905	Mark Strong		Cyril Hurst	West London Theatre→ Terry's (8)	Roland Bottomley and Grace Heywood
The Officer's Mess, 1918	Phillip Braham	Sydney Blow and Douglas Hoard		St Martin's → Prince's (200)	Doris Gorman and Murray Moore
Oh Julie!, 1920	H. Sullivan Brooke and Herman Darewski	Firth Shephard and Lee Banson	Harold Simpson	Shaftsbury→ Prince's/Ernest C. Rolls (143)	Ethel Levey and Fred A. Leslie
On the March, 1896	John Crook, Edward Solomon and Frederick Clay	William Yardley, B. C. Stephenson and Cecil Clay		Prince of Wales (77)	Thomas E. Murray and Alice Atherton
The Orchid, 1903	Ivan Caryll and Lionel Monckton	James T. Tanner	Adrian Ross and Percy Greenbank	Gaiety/George Edwardes (559)	George Grossmith Jr and Gertie Millar
Our Miss Gibbs, 1909	Ivan Caryll and Lionel Monckton	James T. Tanner	Adrian Ross and Percy Greenbank	Gaiety/George Edwardes (636)	George Grossmith Jr and Gertie Millar
Pamela, 1917	Arthur Wimperis and Frederick Norton			Palace/Alfred Butt (172)	Lily Elsie and Owen Nares
The Pearl Girl, 1913	Howard Talbot and Hugo Felix	Basil Hood		Shaftsbury/Robert Courtneidge (254)	Iris Hooey and Jack Welchman

Title, Year	Composer	Book	Lyrics	Theatre/Producer (performances)	Stars
Peggy, 1911	Leslie Stuart	George Grossmith Jr	C. H. Bovill	Gaiety/George Edwardes (270)	Phyllis Dare and George Grossmith
A Persian Princess, 1909	Sidney Jones	Leedham Bantock and P. J. Barrow	Percy Greenbank	Queens/Tom B. Davis (68)	George Graves and Ruth Vincent
Pretty Peggy, 1919	A. Emmett Adams	Arthur Rose and Charles Austin	Douglas Furber	Prince's/ C. B. Cochran (168)	Charles Austin and Lorna Pounds
The Quaker Girl, 1910	Lionel Monckton	James T. Turner	Adrian Ross and Percy Greenbank	Adelphi/George Edwardes (536)	C. Hayden Coffin and Gertie Millar
A Runaway Girl, 1898	Lionel Monckton and Ivan Caryll	Seymour Hicks and Harry Nicholls	Aubrey Hopwood and Harry Greenbank	Gaiety/George Edwardes (593)	Louis Bradfield and Ellaline Terris
San Toy, 1899	Sydney Jones	Edward A. Morton	Harry Greenbank and Adrian Ross	Daly's under George Edwardes (778)	C. Hayden Coffin and Marie Tempest
The Schoolgirl, 1903	Leslie Stuart	Henry Hamilton and P. Potter	Charles H. Taylor	Prince of Wales/ George Edwardes and Charles Frohman (333)	Edna May and G. P. Huntley
Sergeant Brue, 1904	Liza Lehmann	Owen Hall	J. Hickory Wood	Strand/Frank Curzon (280)	Willie Edouin and Zena Dare
The Shop Girl, 1894	Ivan Caryll	H. J. W. Dam		Gaiety/George Edwardes (546)	George Grossmith Jr and Ada Reeve
The Silver Slipper, 1901	Leslie Stuart	Owen Hall	W. H. Risque	Lyric/Tom B. Davis (197)	Connie Ediss, and Henri Leoni

Appendix 1 (Contd.)

Title/year (of London opening)	Composer	Playwright	Lyricist	Theatre/management/number of performances (→ = transferred to)	Original principals (selected)
A Southern Maid, 1917	Harold Fraser-Simson	Harry Graham and Dion Calthrop Clayton	Harry Miller	Daly's/Robert Evett (306)	José Collins and Mark Lester
The Spring Chicken, 1905	Ivan Caryll and Lionel Monckton	George Grossmith Jr		Gaiety/George Edwardes (401)	George Grossmith Jr and Gertie Millar
The Sunshine Girl, 1912	Paul Rubens	Paul Rubens and Cecil Raleigh	Paul Rubens and Arthur Wimperis	Gaiety/George Edwardes (336)	Phyllis Dare and George Grossmith Jr
Suzette, 1917	Max Darewski	Austin Hurgon and George Arthurs	George Arthurs	Globe/Alfred Butt (255)	Gaby Deslys and Harry Pilcer
The Talk of the Town, 1905	Herbert E. Haines	Seymour Hicks	Charles H. Taylor	Lyric/William Greet (100)	Agnes Fraser and Walter Passmore
Telling the Tale, 1918	Philip Braham	Sydney Blow and Douglas Hoare	Douglas Hoare	Ambassador/Gerald Kirby and John Wyndham (90)	James Crosbie and Ruth Siau
Theodore and Co, 1916	Ivor Novello and Jerome D. Kern	H. M. Harwood and George Grossmith Jr.	Adrian Ross and Clifford Grey	Gaiety/George Grossmith Jr and Edward Laurillard (503)	Fred Leslie and Madge Saunders

Title	Composer	Book	Lyrics	Theatre/Producer	Cast
Three Little Maids, 1902	Paul Rubens		Paul Rubens	Apollo→Prince of Wales/George Edwardes and Charles Frohman (348)	Edna May and Madge Crichton
Tina, 1915	Paul Rubens and Hadyn Wood	Paul Rubens and Harry Graham	Paul Rubens, Harry Graham and Percy Greenbank	Adelphi/Musical Plays Ltd (277)	Phyllis Dare and Godfrey Tearle
Tonight's the Night, 1915	Paul Rubens	F. Thompson	Paul Rubens and Percy Greenbank	Gaiety/George Grossmith Jr and Edward Laurillard (460)	Gladys Homfrey and Robert Nainby
The Toreador, 1901	Ivan Caryll and Lionel Monckton	James T. Tanner and Harry Nicholls	Adrian Ross and Percy Greenbank	Gaiety/George Edwardes (675)	Gertie Millar and George Grossmith Jr
Toto, 1916	Archibald Joyce and Merlin Morgan	Gladys Unger	Arthur Anderson	Duke of York (77)	Mabel Russell and Peter Gawthorne
Who's Hooper, 1919	Howard Talbot and Ivan Novello	Fred Thompson	Clifford Grey	Adelphi/Alfred Butt (349)	W. H. Berry and Kate Zoller
The Yasmak, 1897	Napoleon Lambelet	Seymour Hicks and Cecil Raleigh		Shaftsbury/A. H. Chamberlyn (121)	John Le Hay and Kitty Loftus
Yes Uncle, 1917	Nat D. Ayer	Austen Hurgon and George Arthurs	Clifford Grey	Prince of Wales→Prince's→Shaftsbury/George Grossmith Jr and Edward Laurillard (626)	Leslie Henson and Fred Leslie

Appendix 2   Selected 'Imported' musical comedy, 1898–1920 (London, West End)

Title/year (of London opening)	Composer/ English adaptation	Playwright/ English adaptation	Lyricist (English adaptation)	Theatre/ management/ number of performances (→transferred to)	Original principals (selected)
Afgar, 1919	Charles Cuvillier	Fred Thompson and Worton David		Pavilion/ C. B. Cochran (300)	Harry Welchman and Lupino Lane
An American Beauty, 1900	Gustave Kerker	C. M. S. McLellan		Shaftsbury/ George Musgrove (69)	Edna May and Nicholas Long
Arlette, 1917	Mme Jean Vieu, Guy Le Feuvre and Ivor Novello	Claude Ronald and L. Bouvet/Austen Hurgon		Shaftsbury/ George Grossmith Jr and Edward Laurillard (257)	Joe Coyne and Winifred Barnes
The Bell of Bohemia, 1901	Ludwig Englander	Harry B. Smith		Apollo/George Lederer (73)	Richard Carle and Marie George
The Belle of New York, 1898	Gustave Kerker	C. M. S. McLellan		Shaftsbury/ George Musgrove (693)	Dan Daly and Edna May
The Casino Girl, 1900	Ludwig Englander	Harry B. Smith		Shaftsbury/ George Lederer (193)	Mabelle Gillman and Richard Carle
The Chocolate Soldier, 1910	Oscar Strauss	R. Bernauer and L. Jacobson/Stanislaus Stange		Lyric/Fred C. Whitney (556)	Constance Drever and Roland Cunningham
The Cinema Star (Die Kino-Königin), 1914	Jean Gilbert	G. Okonowski/Harry J. C. Graham and J. Hulbert		Shaftsbury/ Robert Courtneidge (108)	Fay Compton and Harry Welchman

Title	Composer	Book	Lyrics	Theatre/Producer (performances)	Cast
The Count of Luxembourg, 1911	Franz Lehár	Alfred M. Willner and R. Bodanzky/ Basil Hood	Adrian Ross	Daly's/George Edwardes (339)	Lily Elsie and Willie Warde
Cupid and the Princess (L'Amour Mouille), 1899	Louis Varney	Jules Prével and Armand Liorat		Lyric/Tom Davis (42)	Kate Cutler and John Le Hay
The Dollar Princess (Die Dollarprinzessin), 1909	Leo Fall	Alfred M. Willner and F. Grunham/ Basil Hood	Adrian Ross	Daly's/George Edwardes (430)	Joe Coyne and Lily Elsie
The Gay Delphine, 1913 or Oh! Oh! Delphine (revised 1915)	G. Berr and Marcel Guillemand/ Ivan Caryll	C. M. S. McLellan		Shaftsbury/ Robert Courtneidge (173/165)	Courtice Pounds and Iris Hoey
The Girl from Up There (Die Geschiedene Frau), 1901	Gustave Kerker	C. M. S. McLellan		Duke of York's (101)	Edna May and J. Farren Soutar
The Girl in the Taxi (Dies Keusche Suzanne), 1912	Jean Gilbert	G. Okonowski/Frederick Fenn and Arthur Wimperis		Lyric/Michael Faraday (385)	Amy Augarde and Arthur Playfair
The Girl in the Train, 1910	Leo Fall	Victor Leon	Adrian Ross	Vaudeville/ George Edwardes (339)	Phyllis Dare, Fred Emney
The Girl on the Film (Filmzauber), 1913	W. Kollo, W. Bredschneider and A. Sirmay	R. Bernauer and R. Schanzer/ James T. Tanner	Adrian Ross	Gaiety/George Edwardes (232)	Robert Nainby and Connie Ediss

Appendix 2 (*Contd.*)

Title/year (of London opening)	Composer/ English adaptation	Playwright/ English adaptation	Lyricist (English adaptation)	Theatre/ management/ number of performances (→transferred to)	Original principals (selected)
The Girl who Didn't (Der Lachende Ehemann), 1913	Edmund Eysler	Julius Krammer and A. Grunwald/Arthur Wimperis		Lyric/Michael Faraday (68)	Lionel Mackinder and Amy Augarde
Gypsy Love (Ziegeuner Liebe), 1912	Franz Lehár	Alfred M. Willner and Robert Bodanzky/ Basil Hood	Adrian Ross	Daly's/George Edwardes (299)	Rosina Filippi and Gertie Millar
Going Up!, 1918	Louis Hirsch	Otto Harbach, James Montgomery		Gaiety/Alfred Butt (573)	Joe Coyne and Marjorie Gordon
High Jinks, 1916	Rudolph Friml	F. Lonsdale	Percy Greenbank and Clifford Grey	Adelphi (383)	Maisie Gay and Nellie Taylor
His Little Widows, 1919	William Schroeder	Rida Johnson Young and W. C. Duncan		Wyndham's/ Frank Curzon 172	Jack Morrison and Mabel Green
In Dahomey, 1903	Will Marion Cook	Jessie A. Shipp	Paul Dunbar and Alex Rodgers	Shaftsbury/Tom B. Davis (250)	George Walker and Bert Williams
The Lady Dandies (Les Merveilleuses), 1906	Hugo Felix	V. Sardou/ Basil Hood	Adrian Ross	Daly's/George Edwardes (197)	Evie Greene and Robert Evett

Show	Composer	Book	Lyrics	Theatre/Producer	Cast
The Little Dutch Girl (Das Hollandweibchen), 1920	Emmerich Kálmán	Harry J. C. Graham and Seymour Hicks		Lyric/Seymour Hicks and Joseph Sacks (215)	Maggie Teyte and 'A. C. Torr' (Fred Leslie)
The Little Michus (Les P'tites Michu), 1905	André Messager	Albert Vanloo and George Duval/Henry Hamilton	Paul Greenbank	Daly's/George Edwardes (401)	Willie Edouin and Mabel Green
Madame Sherry, 1903	Hugo Felix	M. Ordonneau/Charles Hands	Adrian Ross and Paul Rubens	Apollo/Tom Davis (102)	Louis Bradfield and Florence St John
Mam'selle Tra-La-La, 1914	Jean Gilbert	G. Okonowski and Leo Leipziger/Arthur Wimperis and Hartley Carrick		Lyric/Michael Faraday (107)	Violet Cameron and C. Renshaw
The Marriage Market (Leányvásár), 1913	Victor Jacobi	M. Brody and F. Martos/Gladys Unger	Arthur Anderson and Adrian Ross	Daly's under George Edwardes (423)	Gertie Millar and G. P. Huntley
The Merry Widow, 1907	Franz Lehár	Victor Léon and Leo Stein/Edward Morton	Adrian Ross	Daly's/George Edwardes (779)	Joseph Coyne and Lily Elsie
The Naughty Princess (La Rein's Amuse), 1920	Charles Cuvillier	André Barde/J. Hastings Turner	Adrian Ross	Adelphi/Robert Courtneidge (270)	George Grossmith Jr and Lily St John
Oh, Joy!, (in America as Oh Boy!), 1919	Jerome Kern	P. G. Wodehouse and Guy Bolton	Julian Frank and Clifford Grey	Kingsway→ Apollo/George Grossmith Jr and Edward Laurillard (167)	Beatrice Lillie and Tom Payne

Appendix 2 (Contd.)

Title/year (of London opening)	Composer/ English adaptation	Playwright/ English adaptation	Lyricist (English adaptation)	Theatre/ management/ number of performances (→transferred to)	Original principals (selected)
The Pink Lady, 1912	Ivan Caryll	G. Berr and M. Guillemand/ C. M. S. McLellan		Globe/Charles Frohman (124)	Fred Wright and Irene O'Donnell
The Prince of Pilsen, 1904	Gustave Luders	Frank Pixley		Shaftsbury/ A. H. Canby (160)	Camille Clifford and Harry Fairleigh
Princess Caprice (Der Liebe Augustin), 1912	Leo Fall	R. Bernauer and E. Welisch/ A. M. Thompson	A. Craven, H. Beswick and Percy Greenbank	Shaftsbury/ Robert Courtneidge (265)	George Graves and Cicely Courtneidge
Shanghai, 1918	Isadore Widmark	W. C. Duncan		Drury Lane/ Joseph Sacks (131)	Dennis Hoey and Joan Hay
(Her) Soldier Boy (Der Gute Kamerad), 1918	Emmerich Kálmán/ Sigmund Romberg and C Crawford	Adapted by Rida Johnson Young and Edgar Wallace	C. Crawford and Douglas Furber	Apollo/ George Grossmith Jr and Edward Laurillard (374)	Winifred Barnes and Maisie Gar
Véronique, 1904	André Messager	English version by Henry Hamilton	Lilian Eldee and Percy Greenbank	Apollo/ Tom B. Davis (495)	George Graves and Rosina Brandram

Very Good, Eddie, 1918	Jerome Kern	Guy Bolton and Phillip Barthlomae		Palace/ André Charlot	Nelson Keys and Madge Saunders
A Waltz Dream (*Ein Walzertraum*), 1908	Oscar Strauss	Felix Doerman, Leopold Jacobson	Adrian Ross	Hicks; revised at Daly's, (1911) (146)	Ethel Cadman and George Grossmith Jr
The Wild Geese (*Son Petit Frère*), 1920	Charles Cuvillier	Ronald Jeans		Comedy, under by André Charlot (112)	Jack Buchanan and Olive Groves

Appendix 3 Selected musical comedies, 1921–1939 (London, West End)

Title/year (of London opening)	Composer	Playwright	Lyricist	Theatre/management/number of performances	Original principals (selected)
The Cabaret Girl, 1922	Jerome Kern	George Grossmith Jr and P.G. Wodehouse	George Grossmith Jr and P.G. Wodehouse	Winter Garden under George Grossmith Jr and Edward Laurillard (361)	Peter Haddon and Vera Lennox
His Girl, 1922	Ernest Longstaffe and Max Darewski	Austen Hurgon and F. W. Thomas	Claude E. Burton	Gaiety/Austen Hurgon (81)	Walter Gay and Patricia Malone
The Island King, 1922	Harold Garstin	Peter Gawthorne	Peter Gawthorne	Adelphi/Charlton Mann (160)	Gladys Tudor and W. H. Berry
Jenny, 1922	Haidée de Rance	Harry Grattan	Harry Grattan and John Plunkett	Empire/J. L. Sacks (66)	Edith Day and Billy Leonard
The Beauty Prize, 1923	Jerome Kern	George Grossmith Jr and P. G. Wodehouse	George Grossmith Jr and P. G. Wodehouse	Winter Garden/George Grossmith Jr and J. A. E. Malone (214)	Dorothy Field and Jack Hobbs
Head Over Heels, 1923	Harold Fraser-Simpson	Seymour Hicks	Adrian Ross and Harold Graham	Adelphi/Musical Play Ltd. (113)	Arthur Pusey and Jennie Richards

Title, Year	Composer	Book	Lyrics	Theatre/Producer	Cast
Toni, 1923	Hugo Hirsch	Douglas Furber and Harry Graham	Douglas Furber	Shaftsbury/ George Grossmith Jr and J. A. E. Malone (239)	Jack Buchanan and Sylvia Leslie
Patricia, 1924	Geoffrey Gwyther	Denis Mackail, Arthur Stanley and Austin Melford		His Majesty's →Strand/ Plancraft Ltd (160)	Dorothy Dickson and Frank Barclay
Primrose, 1924	George Gershwin	George Grossmith Jr and George Bolton	Desmond Carter and Ira Gershwin	Winter Garden/ George Grossmith Jr and J. A. E. Malone (255)	Leslie Henson and Vera Lennox
Dear Little Billie, 1925	H. B. Hedley and Jack Strachey	Firth Shephard	Desmond Carter	Shaftsbury/ Laddie Cliff and Firth Shephard (86)	Douglas Pierce and Phyliss Monkman
Nicollete, 1925	Patrick Barrow	Norman Frost and Kingsley Lark	Patrick Barrow	Duke of York/ Thomas J. Courtly (12)	Phyllys Le Grand and Cecil Musk
Merely Molly, 1926	Herman Finck and Joseph Meyer	J. Hastings Turner	Harry Graham	Adelphi/Daniel Mayer (85)	Evelyn Laye and Max Wall
Turned Up, 1926	Joseph Tunbridge	Arthur Rigby	Stanley Lupino	New Oxford Theatre / C. B. Cochran (89)	Lupino Lane and Anita Elson
Sylvia, 1927	Adapted by Carroll Gibbons	James Dyrenforth		Vaudeville/ Archie de Bear (51)	May Whitty and Irish Hoey

Appendix 3 (Contd.)

Title/year (of London opening)	Composer	Playwright	Lyricist	Theatre/ management/ number of performances	Original principals (selected)
Up With the Lark, 1927	Phillip Braham	Douglas Furber and Hartley Carrick	Douglas Furber	Adelphi/Westlan Productions (92)	Adrienne Ash and Allen Kearns
The Yellow Mask, 1927	Vernon Duke	Edgar Wallace	Eric Little	His Majesty's → Palladium/Julian Wylie and Laddie Cliff (218)	Winnie Collins and Frank Adair
Mr Cinders, 1928	Vivian Ellis and Richard Myers	Clifford Grey and Greatrex Newman	Clifford Grey and Greatrex	Adelphi→ Hippodrome under J. C. Williamson (529)	Binnie Hale and Basil Howes
That's a Good Girl, 1928	Phil Charig and Joseph Meyer	Douglas Furber	Douglas Furber, Ira Gershwin and Desmond Carter	Hippodrome/ Jack Buchanan and United Producing Corporation (363)	Jack Buchanan and Kate Cutler
Follow a Star, 1930	Vivian Ellis	Douglas Furber and Dion Titheradge	Douglas Furber and Dion	Winter Garden/ Jack Hulbert and Pal Murray (118)	Maisie Gay and Claude Hulbert
Hold My Hand, 1931	Noel Gay	Stanley Lupino	Desmond Carter	Saville/Jack Carter (212)	Sonnie Hale and Jessie Matthews
Out of the Bottle, 1932	Vivian Ellis and Oscar Levant	Fred Thompson and Clifford Grey		London Hippodrome/ Julian Wylie (109)	Polly Walker and Clifford Mollison

Mr Whittington, 1933	John M. Green, Joseph Tunbridge and Jack Waller	Clifford Grey, Greatrex Newman and Douglas Furber	Edward Heyman	Hippodrome → Adelphi (298)	Jack Buchanan and Elsie Randolph
Nice Goings On, 1933	Arthur Schwartz	Douglas Furber	Douglas Furber and Frank Eyton	Strand/Forth Shephard and Leslie Henson (221)	Leslie Henson and Madeleine Gibson
Lucky Break, 1934	Harry Archer	Douglas Furber	Douglas Furber and Harlan Thompson	Strand/Leslie Henson and Firth Shephard (198)	Richard Hearne and Sydney Fairbrother
Yes Madam, 1934	Jack Waller and Joseph Tunbridge	R. P. Weston, Bert Lee and K. R. G. Browne	R. P. Weston and Bert Lee	London Hippodrome/ Jack Waller (302)	Binnie Hale and Arthur Bentley
Fritzi, 1935	Carl Tucker	Sydney Blow and Edward Royce	Arthur Stanley	Adelphi →Pavilion/ J. W. Pemberton (64)	Rosalinde Fuller and Gerald Rex
Gay Deceivers, 1935	Moise Simon and Martin Broones	Reginald Arkell		Gaiety→Coliseum/ Lee Ephraim (123)	Jeffrey Piddock and Enid Lowe
Love Laughs, 1935	Noel Gay	Clifford Grey and Greatrex Newman	Mabel Wayne, Neville Fleeson and Desmond Crater	London Hippodrome/ Laddie Cliff and Clifford Whitley (96)	Barbara Newberry and Sydney Keith

Appendix 3 (Contd.)

Title/year (of London opening)	Composer	Playwright	Lyricist	Theatre/management/number of performances	Original principals (selected)
Please Teacher, 1935	Jack Waller and Joseph Tunbridge	K. R. G. Browne, R. P. Weston and Bert Lee	R. P. Weston and Bert Lee	London Hippodrome/ Jack Waller (301)	Arthur Bentley and Winifred Izard
Seeing Stars, 1935	Martin Broones	Guy Bolton and Fred Thompson	Graham John	Gaiety/Firth Shephard (236)	Leslie Henson and Richard Hearne
Certainly Sir, 1936	Jack Waller and Joseph Tunbridge	R. P. Weston and Bert Lee	R. P. Weston and Bert Lee	London Hippodrome/ Jack Waller (20)	Carl Bernard and Renee Houston
Swing Along, 1936	Martin Broones	Guy Bolton, Fred Thompson and Douglas Furber	Graham John	Gaiety/Firth Shephard (311)	Louise Brown and Fred Emney
Crazy Days, 1937	Billy Mayerl	Stanley Lupino	Desmond Carter and Frank Eyton	Shaftsbury/ Laddie Cliff (78)	Gillie Flower and Arty Ash
Going Greek, 1937	Sam Lerner, Al Goodhart and Al Hoffman	Guy Bolton, Fred Thompson and Douglas Furber	Sam Lerner, Al Goodhart and Al Hoffman	Gaiety/Leslie Henson (303)	Fred Emney and Richard Hearne

Show	Music	Book	Lyrics	Theatre/Producer	Cast
Me and My Girl, 1937	Noel Gay	L. Arthur Rose and Douglas Furber		Victoria Palace/ Lupino Lane and Jack Eggar (1646)	Betty Frankiss and Frank E. Evans
Bobby get Your Gun, 1938	Jack Waller and Joseph Tunbridge	Guy Bolton, Fred Thompson and Bert Lee	Clifford Grey, Bert Lee and Desmond Carter	Adelphi/Jack Waller (92)	Bobby Howes and Bertha Belmore
Running Riot, 1938	Vivian Ellis	Douglas Furber	Vivian Ellis	Gaiety/Firth Shephard (207)	Louise Browne and Leslie Henson

Notes

The abbreviation 'LCP' in these endnotes – Lord Chamberlain's Plays – refers to plays held in the manuscript room of the British Library. Numbers following the title citation refer to act and page number. In some manuscripts acts are divided into scenes. In this case, act, scene and page number are divided here in the usual way.

Preface

1. *The Play Pictorial* (1913), vol. 22, no. 137, i–vi.
2. Raymond Williams, *Marxism and Literature* (Oxford: Oxford University Press, 1977), 5 and 145.

1   Themes and Approaches

1. Gerald Bordman, *American Musical Comedy from Adonis to Dreamgirls* (New York and Oxford: Oxford University Press, 1982), 159.
2. For a discussion of these historiographies and of the distinction between musicals and opera see Dave Walsh and Len Platt, *Musical Theatre and American Culture* (Westport: Praeger, 2003).
3. G. Block, *Enchanted Evenings: The Broadway Musical from 'Show Boat' to Sondheim* (New York: Oxford University Press, 1997), 202.
4. Rhonda K. Garelick, *Rising Star: Dandyism, Gender and Performance in the Fin de Siècle* (New Jersey: Princeton University Press, 1998), 5.
5. Jose Harris, *Private Lives, Public Spirit: A Social History of Britain 1870–1914* (Oxford: Oxford University Press, 1993), 33.
6. Erika Diana Rappaport, *Shopping for Pleasure: Women in the Making of London's West End* (Princeton and Oxford: Princeton University Press, 2000), 178–206. Rappaport shows how Gordon Selfridge and Richard Burbidge of Harrod's 'financed plays that championed their shops and their understanding of shopping' (179). See also Joel Kaplan and Sheila Stowell, *Theatre and Fashion: Oscar Wilde to the Suffragettes* (Cambridge: Cambridge University Press, 1994).
7. James T. Tanner, *Our Miss Gibbs* (MSS: LCP, 1909), 2.
8. See Michael Booth, 'The Metropolis on Stage' in H. J. Dyos and Michael Woolf (eds), *The Victorian City: Images and Realities,* vol. 1 (London: Routledge & Kegan Paul, 1976). According to Booth 'the most significant fact of English theatrical history in the second half of the nineteenth century is the slow but sure upper-middle-class takeover of both the theatre and the drama, and the steady rise of middle-class respectability that it is even now trying so hard to shake off' (224).
9. Peter Stallybrass and Allon White, *The Politics and Poetics of Transgression* (London: Routledge, 1980), 2–3.

10. See also the attendance of Alfonso and Ena, the King and Queen of Spain, at a performance of *The Beauty of Bath* in 1906. This latter is recorded in Ellaline Terriss, *Just a Little Bit of String* (London: Hutchinson, 1955), 195.

11. W. McQueen-Pope, *Gaiety: Theatre of Enchantment* (London: W. H. Allen, 1949), 358. McQueen-Pope's account of the theatre, for all its out-of-date style and some serious inaccuracies, remains the fullest account of its earlier years.

12. Alan Hyman, *The Gaiety Years* (London: Cassell & Collier Macmillan, 1975), 87.

13. Ellaline Terris, *Just a Little Bit of String* (London: Hutchinson, 1955), 205. For the Joyce reference see *Ulysses* (Harmondsworth: Penguin, 1986), 180. It is here that Father Conmee recalls Vaughan's 'droll eyes and cockney voice. – Pilate! Wy don't you old back that owlin mob'.

14. Peter Bailey, ' "Naughty but Nice": Musical Comedy and the Rhetoric of the Girl' in Michael R. Booth and Joel H. Kaplan (eds), *The Edwardian Theatre* (Cambridge: Cambridge University Press, 1996), 52.

15. Kurt Ganzl, *The British Musical Theatre 1865–1914* (Basingstoke: Macmillan, 1986), vol. 1, 492.

16. *The Stage*, 20 January 1888, 13.

17. Writing against what she calls 'the myth of rise of the Victorian actor', Tracy Davis has shown how the stigma attached to working on the stage remained embedded for a long time, particularly for women and especially outside of the professional West End theatre. See her *Actresses as Working Women: Their Social Identity in Victorian Culture* (London and New York: Routledge, 1991), xii and chapter three.

18. Hyman, *The Gaiety Years*, 90.

19. See for example J. S. Bratton's fascinating account of Emmaline Ethardo's act – an act that involved cross dressing, quick change and joint dislocation – as a carnivalesque 'manipulation of the masks of the stereotype'. 'Irrational Dress' in Viv Gardner and Susan Rutherford (eds), *The New Woman and Her Sisters: Feminism and Theatre, 1850–1914* (Hemel Hempstead: Harvester Wheatsheaf, 1992), 77–91.

20. See Ross McKibbin, *Classes and Cultures: England 1918–1951* (Oxford: Oxford University Press, 1998), 46.

21. Harris, *Private Lives, Public Spirit*, 10.

22. Quoted in Ganzl, *The British Musical Theatre*, vol. 1, 604. This kind of dismissal did not last long in the case of *The Era*. It quickly capitalized on the public's support of the 'new' theatre.

23. *The Times*, 26 November 1894, 4.

24. James Agate, *Immoment Toys – A Survey of Light Entertainment on the London Stage, 1920–1943* (London: Jonathan Cape, 1945), 70.

25. *The Era*, quoted in Sheridan Morley, *Spread a Little Happiness: The First Hundred Years of the British Musical* (London: Thames & Hudson, 1987), 19.

26. Friedrich Nietzsche, *Beyond Good and Evil: Prelude to a Philosophy of the Future* translated with commentary by Walter Kaufmann (New York: Vintage, 1966), xi.

27. Ernest A. Randal, the Lord Chamberlain's Office, in the license for *Chu Chin Chow* (MSS: LCP, 1914).

28. Terris, *A Little Bit of String*, 133. See also *Nelly Neil* (1907) where Mrs Neil, an ex-Gaiety girl herself, wonders what life will be like for her daughter when

KING ALFRED'S COLLEGE
LIBRARY

she goes on the stage, is 'photographed in a hammock for the postcards' and 'gets a toothwash named after her'. C. M. S. McLellan, *Nelly Neil* (MSS: LCP, 1908), 2: 7.

29. Hyman, *The Gaiety Years*, 81.

30. For some signs of an emerging interest in late Victorian and Edwardian musical comedy see 'Musical Comedy and the Rhetoric of the Girl' and James Ross Moore, 'Girl Crazy: Musicals and Revue between the Wars' in Clive Barker and Maggie B. Gale (eds), *British Theatre between the Wars 1918–1939* (Cambridge: Cambridge University Press, 2000). See also P. Bailey, *Theatre of Entertainment/Spaces of Modernity: Rethinking the British Popular Stage, 1890–1914* in *Nineteenth Century Theatre* (1998), vol. 26, 5–21.

31. John M. Mackenzie, *Imperialism and Popular Culture* (Manchester: Manchester University Press, 1986).

32. Of the 49 productions that exceeded 350 performances between 1900 and 1914, 22 were musical comedies and 4 were revues. In addition there were 11 comedies, 8 'plays', 2 musical entertainments, 1 melodrama and 1 farce.

33. J. S. Bratton, Richard Allen Cave, Brendan Gregory, Heide J. Holder and Michael Pickering, *Acts of Supremacy: The British Empire and the Stage, 1790–1930* (Manchester: Manchester University Press, 1991).

34. The radio revivals, like the BBC's revival of *The Geisha* in 1934 and 1938, are notable here.

35. The show was a combination of sentimental children's Christmas show and musical comedy. It was a big success for Seymour Hicks at the Vaudeville in December 1901 where it ran for 294 performances.

36. The manuscript department of the British library does, however, contain some scripts of music-hall sketches. See Lois Rutherford,' "Harmless Nonsense": the Comic Sketch and the Development of Music-Hall Entertainment' in J. S. Bratton, *Music Hall: Performance and Style* (Milton Keynes: Open University Press, 1986), 131–51.

37. J. C. Trewin, *The Edwardian Theatre* (Oxford: Blackwell, 1976), 161.

38. See below, 148–51.

39. Alan J. Lerner, *The Musical Theatre: A Celebration* (New York: De Capo, 1986).

40. For a more detailed account of the origins of the American musical see Walsh and Platt, *Musical Theatre and American Culture*, chapter 1.

41. This figure of 120 is far from representing the limit of musical comedy. There were, in addition, many American, French and German shows staged in London. There was also the large number of musical comedies performed in the provinces (and the wider London area) that never got to the West End. See appendices 1 and 2 below.

42. Julian Mates, *America's Musical Stage: Two Hundred Years of Musical Theatre* (Westport: Greenwood, 1985), 174.

43. Dates here refer to the American openings. For London openings see the first mention of each show in this text and the dates given in the appendices.

44. Gerald Bordman, *American Musical Theatre: A Chronicle*, 2nd edition (Oxford and New York: Oxford University Press, 1992), 77.

45. *American Musical Theatre*, 57.

46. *American Musical Theatre*, 58.

47. *American Musical Theatre*, 56.

48. 'Theatres of Entertainment', 17.

49. *American Musical Theatre*, 118 and 297. There is a similar marginalization in Andrew Lamb's more recent account, *Popular Musical Theatre* (New Haven and London: Yale University Press, 2000). British musical comedy has a chapter here (113–32) but remains entirely secondary to 'America Ascendant' and 'The Musical Comes of Age'.

50. See the opening sentence of Mates, *American Musical Stage*: 'The musical stage has become so much a part of everyday American life that we hardly notice its presence outside the theatre – at political conventions sporting events, industrial shows, circuses and parades' (3).

51. Walsh and Platt, *Musical Theatre and American Culture*.

52. See *Musical Theatre and American Culture*, chapter 4.

53. There is a growing literature on black face theatre and on the black musical. See the bibliography of this study for some examples.

54. Gareth Stedman Jones, *Languages of Class: Studies in English Working Class History 1832–1982* (Cambridge: Cambridge University Press, 1983), 204–7 and 223–35.

55. Ganzl, *The British Musical Theatre*, vol. 1, 859.

56. *The British Musical Theatre*, vol. 1, 1079.

57. C. Geertz, *Interpreting Cultures* (London: Hutchinson, 1975), 10.

58. For a deconstructive discussion of the term 'entertainment', see Richard Dyer, *Only Entertainment* (London and New York: 1992), 11–15.

59. For a discussion of utopianism in the musical see *Only Entertainment*, 11–34.

60. Mates, *America's Musical Stage*, 7.

61. Daniel Bell, *The Cultural Contradictions of Capitalism* (London: Heinemann, 1976), 105ff.

62. Rubens was also a composer and lyricist.

63. These phrases appear in Bakhtin's historiographical account of the novel, 'Epic and Novel: Toward a Methodology for the Study of the Novel' in *The Dialogic Imagination* edited by Michael Holquist, translated by Caryl Emerson and Michael Holquist (Austin: University of Texas Press, 1981), 4.

64. It is emphasized again in the next chapter that musical comedy was, in many respects, a conservative bourgeois culture. It cannot be read as a challenge from below with any consistency. It does, however, articulate the new against the old and in this sense seems suggestive of Bakhtin's 'novelistic spirit' identifying with contemporaneity against traditional, conserving, 'epic' forms. Some readers might find musical comedy's affection for 'gaiety' suggestive of some further elements in the Bakhtin analysis, of carnivalesque for instance. It would not be difficult to find examples of the 'dialogic imagination' in musical comedy. Such parallels are not developed in this study, however, primarily because whilst quite suggestive they are too general to be deployed with sufficient precision. I just make the point that Bakhtin's historiography has been found useful, partly for thinking about musical comedy's cultural position vis-à-vis other forms of musical theatre but, more importantly, because Bakhtin helps to assert the importance of the musical comedy script as a discourse of contemporaneity.

2 Our Sickly Age's End – Musical Comedy and Modernity

1. See Bailey, 'Musical Comedy and the Rhetoric of the Girl', Bailey, 'Theatres of Entertainments' and Rappaport, *Shopping for Pleasure*.
2. *Shopping for Pleasure*, 182.
3. *The Times*, 5 October 1908, 8.
4. William Archer, *Theatrical World of 1896* (London: Walter Scott), 298–305.
5. Terris, *Just a Little Bit of String*, 108–09. Like many writers on this subject, Terris sees musical comedy as emerging from a decline in the popularity of burlesque.
6. They became literally aristocratic after Hicks was knighted in 1935. For an account of their music hall experiences see Terris's account of playing 'the Empires' in *Just a Little Bit of String*, 209–10.
7. See George Graves, *Gaieties and Gravities* (London: Hutchinson, 1931), 81.
8. McQueen Pope, *Gaiety: Theatre of Enchantment*, 128. Hollingshead's Gaiety was innovative in many other ways. It was the first theatre to produce a Gilbert and Sullivan collaboration, *Thespis, or the Gods from Old* (1871); allegedly the first to introduce regular matinees; the first to bring the Comédie Français and Sarah Bernhardt to London; with its production of *The Pillars of Society* (1880), it was the first West End theatre to stage Ibsen. McQueen Pope also states that it was the first theatre to be equipped with electric light, but this is doubtful. The Savoy is more usually credited as being first in this respect.
9. See Bordman's account of the distinctions between operetta and musical comedy in *American Musical Comedy*, 4.
10. 'Theatres of Entertainment' has a discussion of the musical comedy audience. There are difficulties in reconstructing this audience, as Bailey points out: 'our understanding of the audiences of these new forms [of popular theatre] is meagre and misleading, both in their composition and, as we learned to enquire, in their reception and use of text' (14).
11. Harris, *Private Lives, Public Spirit*, 70.
12. *The Era*, September 1893, np. Burlesque was not, however, comic by definition. Burlesque melodramas, like *Frankenstein or the Vampire's Victim*, also played at the Gaiety although it was the comedies that tended to be most popular.
13. Morley, *Spread a Little Happiness*, 20.
14. Ganzl, *The British Musical Theatre*, vol. 1, 363.
15. Terris, *Just a Little Bit of String*, 123. Seymour Hicks pointed out that the Americans may not have warmed to the show because he had brought 'a great many of the lines in it' back from America in the first place. See Seymour Hicks, *Twenty-Four Years of an Actor's Life* (London: Alton Rivers, 1910), 190.
16. *Just a Little Bit of String*, 121.
17. *Man About Town* (1897) quoted in Ganzl, *The British Musical Theatre*, vol. 1, 632.
18. Edwardes was responsible for the building of Daly's. After leasing it to the American producer Augustin Daly, he took the theatre over himself in 1898.
19. *The Telegraph*, 24 April 1896, 9. See also *The Sketch* review, which found the stage picture 'charming'. This review goes on to explain how the image is

'calculated to send one off on a wild goose chase to Japan, or, failing this to revel in Japan as set forth at Daly's'. *The Sketch*, 29 April 1896, 42.

20. Ganzl, *The British Musical Theatre*, vol. 1, 1094.
21. Rappaport, *Shopping for Pleasure*, 179–80.
22. Ganzl, *The British Musical Theatre*, vol. 1, 1070.
23. Morley, *Spread a Little Happiness*, 32.
24. Quoted in Kurt Ganzl, *The British Musical Theatre*, vol. 2 (Basingstoke: Macmillan, 1986), 32–33.
25. *The Times*, 25 October 1908, 11.
26. *The Illustrated Sporting and Dramatic News*, November 1899, quoted in *Spread a Little Happiness*, 24.
27. *The Illustrated London News*, 2 September 1905, np.
28. Hyman, *The Gaiety Years*, 83.
29. Davis, *Actresses as Working Women*, 48.
30. Ganzl, *The British Musical Theatre*, vol. 1, 519–20.
31. See Marshall Berman, *All That is Solid Melts Into Air: The Experience of Modernity* (Verso: London, 1983).
32. Alan O' Shea, 'English Subjects of Modernity' in Mica Nava and Alan O' Shea (eds), *Modern Times: Reflections on a Century of English Modernity* (London: Routledge, 1996), 18.
33. 'The danger of attempting to characterize a general Western modernity as lived is that one ends up specifying no-one's experience concretely enough to be useful.' 'English Subjects of Modernity', 26.
34. The literature on modernism is genuinely huge although it is the high status modern, in literature, art, music, science and so on, that has received by far the most attention. Chapter 2 of David Harvey's, *The Condition of Postmodernity* (Oxford: Blackwell, 1990), entitled 'Modernity and Modernism', is a good introduction. On the 'popular' modern see Mike Featherstone, *Consumer Culture and Postmodernism* (London: Sage, 1991) chapter 1 and *Modern Times*.
35. James T. Tanner, *Our Miss Gibbs* (MSS: LCP, 1909), 1: 1.
36. At the same time this opening mocks the 'skills' of the new film artistes. See the song where the actors and actresses of the studio sing the following lines: 'It is fine / Quite Unique / Not a line / Need we speak.' James T. Tanner, *The Girl on the Film* (MSS: LCP, 1913), 1: 1.
37. Henry Hamilton and P. Potter, *The Schoolgirl* (MSS: LCP, 1903), 2: 2.
38. C. M. S. McLellen, *The Girl from Up There* (MSS: LCP, 1901), 1: 6.
39. McQueen Pope was probably alone in thinking that a very early burlesque, *The Great Metropolis* (1874) witnessed 'if not the actual birth of musical comedy, at least the birth of English revue'. *Gaiety: Theatre of Enchantment*, 154. The full title of this show, incidentally, was *The Great Metropolis; or the Wonderful Adventures of Daddy Daddles and his Son in their Journeying from Stoke-in-the-Mud to Venice (via London) with Diddler's Tourist's Tickets*.
40. Terris is virtually alone in thinking *In Town* closer to 'real' musical comedy than *A Gaiety Girl*. See *Just a Little Bit of String*, 110.
41. Rex Bunnett and Brian Rust, *London Musical Shows on Record, 1897–1976*, 1. McQueen Pope also sees *The Shop Girl* as the first West End musical comedy, largely because it opened at the Gaiety whereas *A Gaiety Girl* did not.

See *Gaiety*, 318 and 322. Seymour Hicks had the same idea. He thought *The Shop Girl* the first and 'the best of its kind'. See *Twenty-Four Years of an Actor's Life*, 184.

42. *The Times*, 15 October 1893, np.
43. *The Era*, October 1893, np.
44. Owen Hall, *A Gaiety Girl* (MSS: LCP, 1894), 1: 18.
45. *A Gaiety Girl*, 1: 25.
46. *A Gaiety Girl*, 1: 25.
47. *A Gaiety Girl*, 1: 25 and 2: 5.
48. *A Gaiety Girl*, 2: 6.
49. *A Gaiety Girl*, 2: 26.
50. *A Gaiety Girl*, 2: 39.
51. This was after the old Gaiety was knocked down as part of a road-widening scheme. See Max Beerbohm, *Around Theatres*, quoted in Hyman, *The Gaiety Years*, 131.
52. *The Times*, 26 November 1894, 4.
53. Paul Rubens and Austen Hurgen, *Miss Hook of Holland* (MSS: LCP, 1907), 2: 40.
54. *The Times*, 26 November 1894, 4.
55. G. P. Huntley and Herbert Clayton, *The Honourable Phil* (MSS: LCP, 1908), 14.
56. Mark Ambient and Alexander M. Thompson, *The Arcadians* (MSS: LCP, 1909), 1: 18.
57. *The Arcadians*, 1: 3–4.
58. *The Arcadians*, 1: 8, 11 and 21.
59. Ganzl, *The British Musical Theatre*, vol. 1: 1033.
60. Ambient and Thompson, *The Arcadians*, 3: 1.
61. For a brief account of the 'dark' vision of Baudrillard see Iain Chambers, 'Waiting on the end of the world' in David Morley and Kuan-Hsing Chen, *Stuart Hall: Critical Dialogues in Cultural Studies* (London: Routledge, 1996), 202–3.
62. Ambient and Thompson, *The Arcadians*, 3: 3 and 26.
63. *The Arcadians*, 2: 27 and 3: 15.
64. Reminiscences of the heyday of musical comedy are full of references to the extravagant lifestyles of the stars and producers, of sudden rises to fame and so on. See, for instance, George Grossmith, *Random Recollections of the Serious Business of Enjoyment* (London: Stanley Paul, 1913).
65. Following Martin Wiener's *English Culture and the Decline of the Industrial Spirit 1850–1950* (Cambridge: Cambridge University Press, 1951), a substantial literature has emerged that claims to identify anti-modernism as the predominant response of English culture to modernity. For an critical reading of this literature see Peter Mandler, 'Against "Englishness": English Culture and the Limits to Rural Nostalgia, 1850–1950', *Transactions of the Royal Historical Society*, vol. 7, 1997, 155–75.
66. Harris, *Public Sprit, Private Lives*, 36.
67. Linda Dowling, 'The Decadent and the New Woman', *Nineteenth-Century Fiction*, vol. 33 (1979), 440–1.
68. T. W. H. Crosland, *The Suburbans* (1904) quoted in Roy Porter, *A Social History of London* (London: Hamish Hamilton, 1994), 322.
69. Owen Hall, *An Artist's Model* (MSS: LCP, 1895), 20.

70. James T. Tanner, *My Girl* quoted in *The British Musical Theatre*, vol. 1, 594.
71. See Alison Light, *Forever England: Femininity, Literature and Conservatism between the Wars* (London and New York: Routledge, 1991), 14–19 and 61–112.
72. Kelly Hurley, *The Gothic Body: Sexuality, Materialism and Degeneration at the Fin de Siècle* (Cambridge: Cambridge University Press, 1998), 5.
73. Stuart Hall, 'Notes on Deconstructing "The Popular"' in Samuel Raphael, *People's History and Socialist Theory* (London: Routledge, 1981), 229.

3   Chin Chin Chinaman – Doing Other Cultures

1. The connections between long term modernizing dynamics and racism are well established. D. T. Goldberg, for example, has shown how 'racial thinking and racist articulation have become increasingly normalized and naturalized throughout modernity', that is from 'the sixteenth century in the historical formation of … the West … . The spirit of modernity', he writes, 'is to be found most centrally in its commitment to continuous progress: to material, moral, physical and political improvement and to the promotion and development of civilization and general standards for which the West took to be its own values universalized.' See D. T. Goldberg, *Racist Culture: Philosophy and Politics of Meaning* (Oxford: Blackwell, 1993), 1–3.
2. See Ganzl, *The British Musical Theatre*, vol. 1, 893–94.
3. *The Times*, 4 May 1905, quoted in Ganzl, *The British Musical Theatre*, vol. 1, 893.
4. See *The British Musical Theatre*, vol. 1, 894.
5. Rubens and Hurgen, *Miss Hook of Holland*, 1: 37.
6. George Grossmith Jnr and L. E. Berman, *The Girls of Gottenberg* (MSS: LCP, 1907), 1: 33.
7. *The Times*, 16 May 1907, 8.
8. Seymour Hicks, *The Gay Gordons* (MSS: LCP, 1907), 1: 1–4.
9. *The Gay Gordons*, 1: 15.
10. *Ibid.*
11. James T. Tanner and Alfred Murray, *The Messenger Boy* (MSS: LCP, 1900), 1. 2: 77.
12. Seymour Hicks and Harry Nicholls, *A Runaway Girl* (MSS: LCP, 1898), 1: 56.
13. The Boer War had demonstrated Britain's fundamental isolation. It was followed with Balfour attempting an alliance with Japan (1904); an entente with the French (1905), and planning to work jointly with Germany on the Berlin–Baghdad railway (this was later abandoned due to British public opinion). For an account of foreign policy under Balfour see Richard Shannon, *The Crisis of Imperialism 1865–1915* (London: Hart-Davis & MacGibbon, 1974), especially part iv.
14. Arthur Balfour quoted in *The Crisis in Imperialism*, 303.
15. J. S. Bratton *et al*, *Acts of Supremacy*, 3–4.
16. See D. Forbes-Winslow's account in *Daly's: The Biography of a Theatre* (London: W. H. Allen, 1944), 22.
17. *The People*, 26 April 1896, np.
18. *The Illustrated London News*, 2 May 1896, 572.

19. *The Telegraph*, 24 April 1896, np.
20. *Ibid.*
21. Ernest A. Randal, the Lord Chamberlain's Office, in the license for *Chu Chin Chow* (MSS: LCP, 1914).
22. For an account of the staging of the India Exhibition in London in 1895 and of Imre Kiralfy's production *India* (1895–96) see 'Staging British India' in *Acts of Supremacy*. Apparently one and a half million people saw this spectacular at the 6,000 seat Empress theatre in London.
23. Eric Hobsbawm, *The Age of Empire* (London: Weidenfeld & Nicolson, 1987), 70–71.
24. Tanner and Murray, *The Messenger Boy*, 9.
25. *The Messenger Boy*, 4.
26. *The Messenger Boy*, 132–34.
27. See for instance the character Li, in *San Toy* and Wun-Hi in *The Geisha*. According to J. S. Bratton, the Oriental stereotype is 'black, boastful, proud and vengeful'. See J. S. Bratton *et al*, *Acts of Supremacy*, 1.
28. J. T. Tanner, *The Cingalee* (MSS: LCP, 1904), 1: 38.
29. *The Cingalee*, 1: 36.
30. Edward A. Morton, *San Toy* (MSS: LCP, 1899), 2: 44.
31. Owen Hall, *The Geisha* (MSS: LCP, 1896), 1: 29.
32. Tanner, *The Cingalee*, 2: 16.
33. *The Cingalee*, 2: 22.
34. See *The Cingalee*, 1: 61.
35. *The Telegraph*, 24 April 1896, np.
36. *The Illustrated London News*, 2 May 1896, 572.
37. *The Sketch*, 29 April 1896, 42.
38. *The Telegraph*, 24 April 1896, np.
39. There was a historiographical debate in the 1980s on the popular currency of imperialism and nationalism. Many influential historians, A. J. P. Taylor for instance, argued that ordinary men and women were never much convinced by the jingoism of the popular press. This post 1945 generation of academics had some difficulty in reconciling their conception of the national identity with the crude nationalism that imperial Britain seemed to imply. For an account of this response, and why it can no longer be maintained, see Mackenzie, *Imperialism and Popular Culture*, 1–6.
40. Hobsbawm, *The Age of Empire*, 70.
41. Mackenzie, *Imperialism and Popular Culture*, 3.
42. *The Illustrated London News*, 2 September 1905, np.
43. See, for example, Juliette in *The Geisha*, a French woman who chases a rich Japanese noble. In *The Cingalee*, however, it is an English aristocrat, Lady Pat who goes off to Japan to look for 'some nice little almond-eyed Count' (1: 61).
44. J. S. Bratton *et al.*, *Acts of Supremacy*, 5.
45. Morton, *San Toy*, 1: 31.
46. Harold Ellis, *The Blue Moon* (MSS: LCP, 1904), 1: 30.
47. Paul Brown, ' "This Thing of Darkness I Acknowledge Mine": *The Tempest* and the Discourse of Colonialism' in Jonathan Dollimore and Alan Sinfield (eds), *Political Shakespeare: New Essays in Cultural Materialism* (Manchester and London: Manchester University Press, 1985), 58.
48. Morton, *San Toy*, 1: 48.

49. The phrase is from another colonial/postcolonial context, James Joyce writing about Ireland in *Dubliners*. See 'After the Race' in *Dubliners* (Harmondsworth: Penguin, 1976), 40.
50. Morton, *San Toy*, 1: 31.
51. Or 'eight annas as we say out here ... half white, half native' (Tanner, *The Cingalee*, 2: 3). Interestingly an orderly called Charlie in this show dissents from inter racial relationships. When asked whether his girl friend is an 'ayah', he replies, 'No, Sir. I believe in fair trade and preference for homemade stuff' (1: 5). Quite apart from being a perfect expression of how trade, empire and sexuality converged, this alludes to specific contemporary events. Charlie is demonstrating his further dissent from Joseph Chamberlain's campaign to establish preferential tariffs throughout the empire. This policy mounted a strong challenge to a nineteenth-century liberal identity crucially shaped by its commitment to free trade. Liberals that fell for Chamberlain's romance became known as 'limps' (liberal imperialists).
52. *The Cingalee*, 1: 29.
53. Ellis, *The Blue Moon*, 1: 14.
54. Interestingly the Nizam, the native nobleman who also competes for Chandra in *The Blue Moon*, is neither stupid nor evil, as is usually the case with the indigenous nobleman figure. He permits Chandra to marry the Englishman Jack Ormsby, because he realizes that she loves him. This piece of plotting also seems to imply a restoration of good relations with India and responds to concerns about social cohesion and the stability of colonial rule in that region.
55. Hall, *The Geisha*, 1: 9.
56. *The Geisha*, 1: 14.
57. *The Geisha*, 1: 4.
58. Morton, *San Toy*, 2: 50.
59. In Tanner's *The Cingalee* the tea girls lead an charmed life, pretending to work for the white plantation owners, but actually taking life at slow pace and enjoying flirting with the 'pupils' who are training to run tea plantations. The pupils themselves mix 'Anglo-Saxon energy' with a taste for 'ease' (1: 5).
60. J. S. Bratton *et al.*, *Acts of Supremacy*, 6. The reference here is to pastoral innocence in British melodrama, but the same principle applies to musical comedy.
61. See, for instance, the representation of Sir Peter Loftus in Tanner's *The Cingalee*. He is an archetypal imperial lecher who cannot keep his hands off the 'delightful' natives. He is mocked in the local newspaper that prints a cartoon of Sir Peter and a black baby. The caption reads 'The English Solomon Judge in Ceylon – the wise old father who knows the right child' (1: 14).
62. Ellis, *The Blue Moon*, 1: 1.
63. Morton's *San Toy* is worth mentioning here because it contains an implicit critique of the worldwide trading system. There are a few dark references to trading concessions granted to the British by the Japanese Emperor and to a mysterious 'syndicate' of European business interests. In a nice moment of postmodern economics, Lieutenant Tucker expresses the view that 'the whole blooming world will be run by a syndicate one of these days' (1: 44).

64. Granville Bantock and G. G. Aflalo, *Round the World with a Gaiety Girl* (London: John McQueen, 1896), 91.
65. Henry Pelling, *Origins of the Labour Party* (Oxford: Oxford University Press, 1965), 187–88. See also G. B. Shaw, *Fabianism and the Empire* (London: Grant Richards, 1900).
66. See Walsh and Platt, *Musical Theatre and American Culture*, chapter 2.
67. See Brian Cheyette, *Constructions of the 'Jew' in English Literature and Society: Racial Representations 1875–1945* (Cambridge: Cambridge University Press, 1993).
68. For an account of responses see J. Garrard, *The English and Immigration* (Oxford: Oxford University Press for the Institute of Race Relations, 1971).
69. Owen Hall, *The Girl from Kays* (MSS: LCP, 1902), 3: 23.
70. *The Girl from Kays*, 3: 24.
71. Oscar Wilde, *The Picture of Dorian Gray* (Harmondsworth: Penguin, 1972), 57.
72. H. W. Wells, *Tono-Bungay* (London: Odhams Press, 1957), 82.

4 Aristocracy and the Cultural Politics of Modernity

1. See above, 15.
2. David Cannadine, *The Decline and Fall of the British Aristocracy* (New Haven: Yale University Press, 1990), 125.
3. R. Lacey, *Aristocrats* (London: Hutchinson, 1984), 133.
4. Quoted in Cannadine, *The Decline and Fall of the British Aristocracy*, 45.
5. *The Decline and Fall of the British Aristocracy*, 11.
6. Estimating the extent to which the British aristocracy lost power and authority even in the Edwardian period has proved controversial. Thus David Cannadine's magisterial account of Edwardian decline in *The Decline and Fall of the British Aristocracy* has been subject to some challenges. See W. D. Rubenstein, 'Britain's Elites in the Inter-War period 1918–1939', *Contemporary British History*, vol. 12, 1998, 1–18.
7. Marie Corelli, *The Sorrows of Satan* (Oxford: Oxford University Press, 1972), 212–14.
8 Stanley J. Weyman, *Chippinge* (London: John Murray, 1932), 134.
9. Howard Talbot and Hugo Felix, *The Pearl Girl* (MSS: LCP, 1913), 1: 1.
10. Leedham Bantock and Arthur Anderson, *The Girl Behind the Counter* (MSS: LCP, 1906), 1: 55 and 2: 15 and 28.
11. *The Girl Behind the Counter*, 1: 52.
12. H. J. W. Dam, *The Shop Girl* (MSS: LCP, 1894), 2: 87.
13. Contemporaries often thought of twentieth-century England as a post-feudal culture, although feudalism had not existed in England for some 300 years. For a reading of this ellipsis see Len Platt, *Aristocracies of Fiction* (Westport: Greenwood, 2001), 20.
14. Owen Hall, *The Silver Slipper* (MSS: LCP, 1901), 2: 1 and 17.
15. *Ibid.*
16. Paul Rubens, *The Sunshine Girl* (MSS: LCP, 1912), 1: 19.
17. *The Sunshine Girl*, 1: 37.
18. *The Sunshine Girl*, 1: 40.
19. See Walsh and Platt, *Musical Theatre and American Culture*, chapter 1.

20. Rubens, *The Sunshine Girl*, 2: 1.
21. Hall, *The Girl from Kays*, 2: 23.
22. Hall, *The Gaiety Girl*, 1: 17
23. Authorization for *A Gaiety Girl*, for example, involved last minute alterations at the insistence of the Lord Chamberlain's Office. See Ganzl, *The British Musical Theatre*, 1: 477–80.
24. Wyndham Lewis, *Tarr* (New York: Jubilee, 1979), 125.
25. See Platt, *Aristocracies of Fiction*, chapters 1 and 2.
26. Owen Hall, *Floradora* (MSS: LCP, 1899), 2: 12.
27. Tanner, *Our Miss Gibbs*, 2: 4.
28. Hall, *An Artist's Model*, 1: 64.
29. It is worth pointing out that the fantasy had a real flair for spilling over into reality. Connie Gilchrist of the Gaiety married the Earl of Orkney; Rosie Boote married the Marquis of Headfort; Gertie Millar, who had a string of affairs including one with the Duke of Westminster, later married the Earl of Dudley; Denise Orme became the Baroness Churston; Sylvia Storey became the Countess Poulet; Olive May (whose real name was apparently Meatyard) married Lord Victor Paget; a later Gaiety girl, Irene Richards, married Lord Drumlanrig. According to Hyman there were a 'score' of other 'Gaiety girls' who followed this route into aristocracy. See Hyman, *The Gaiety Years*, 131.
30. Socialism seems to be understood here as being a utopian, back-to-the-land ideology. Either the show is genuinely confused on this score, or, more likely, this association is part of a wider diminution of socialism produced by *Nelly Neil*.
31. McLellan, *Nelly Neil*, 1: 5.
32. *Nelly Neil*, 2: 1.
33. *Nelly Neil*, 1: 14.
34. *Nelly Neil*, 1: 20.
35. *Nelly Neil*, 3: 47.
36. *The Stage*, 1907, np.
37. McLellan, *Nelly Neil*, 1: 25.
38. Tanner, *The Cingalee*, 1: 25.
39. H. M. Harwood and George Grossmith, *Theodore and Co.* (MSS: LCP, 1916), 1: 8.
40. G. S. Street, the Lord Chamberlain's Office, in the licence for *Theodore and Co.* (MSS: LCP, 1916).
41. Paul Rubens, *Betty* (MSS: LCP, 1914), 1: 22.
42. *Betty*, 1: 35.

5 Interventions in the Politics of Gender and Sexuality

1. Ada Reeves, *Take it for Fact (A Record of My Seventy-Five Years on the Stage)* (London: Heinemann, 1954), 80.
2. B. W. Findon, 'Mimes and Music' in *The Play Pictorial*, vol. xiv, no. 85, 230. These terms come from an account of Gertie Millar's performance as Mary Gibbs.
3. McQueen Pope, *Gaiety: Theatre of Enchantment*, 395.
4. For an account of these associations see Davis, *Actresses as Working Women*.

5. *Actresses as Working Women*, 134.
6. Rappaport, *Shopping for Pleasure*, 191. For a history of the feminine spectacle see Abigail Solomon-Godeau, 'The Other Side of Venus: The Visual Economy of Feminine Display' in *The Sex of Things: Gender and Consumption in Historical Perspective*, edited by Victoria de Grazia with Ellen Furlough (Berkeley: University of California Press, 1996).
7. *The Play Pictorial*, vol. xix, no. 113, 1.
8. See Bailey, 'Musical Comedy and the Rhetoric of the Girl', 48
9. Lt-Colonel Newnham Davis, 'Dinner Before the Play' in *The Play Pictorial*, vol. xiv, no. 85, iii.
10. Rappaport, *Pleasures of Shopping*, 192.
11. Karl Miller, *Doubles: Studies in Literary History* (London: Oxford University Press, 1987), 209.
12. Oscar Asche, *Chu Chin Chow* (MSS: LCP, 1917), 37.
13. K. D. S. in *Votes for Women*, 3 April 1914, quoted by Sheila Stowell, 'Suffrage Critics and Political Action: A Feminist Agenda' in *The Edwardian Theatre*, 171.
14. Ashe, *Chu Chin Chow*, 35.
15. Morley, *Spread a Little Happiness*, 31. Morley points out how '*Chu Chin Chow* was given a poster advertising campaign on buses and hoardings the like of which had never been seen in London' (31).
16. Gardner and Rutherford, *The New Woman and her Sisters*, 8 and 11.
17. See Tracy C. Davis, 'Edwardian Management and the Structure of Industrialism' in *The Edwardian Theatre*, 111–27. Here Davis argues that women were relatively numerous in theatre management but does not specifically have musical theatre in mind. In *Actresses as Working Women* she examines the question of 'whether women were able to acquire the reins of management, raise capital, and take charge of the means of production. The answer is a qualified no' (50).
18. Quite apart from being subject to general laws of indecency, blasphemy and libel, all legitimate theatres had to be licensed, as did each individual play. The 1909 committee recommended maintenance of this system on the grounds that performance added a new dimension to things. According to the Committee the 'agency of acting' might have an effect more 'powerful and deleterious' than other cultural forms. It went on to argue that 'scenes in a play might stimulate to vice without falling within the legal definition of indecency.' *Report from the Joint Select Committee of the Lords and the House of Commons on Stage Plays (Censorship)* (London: HMSO, 1909), viii.
19. *Select Committee on Stage Plays (Censorship)*, x.
20. Ernest A. Bendall, the Lord Chamberlain's Office, in the licence for *Tina* (MSS: LCP, 1915).
21. G. S. Street, the Lord Chamberlain's Office, in the licence for *Theodore and Co.* (MSS: LCP, 1916).
22. Ernest A. Bendall, the Lord Chamberlain's Office, in the licences for *Betty* (MSS: LCP, 1915) and *The Better 'Ole* (MSS. LCP, 1917).
23. Bailey, 'Musical Comedy and the Rhetoric of the Girl', 48.
24. *The Era*, 1901, quoted in *The British Musical Theatre*, vol. 1, 669.
25. Owen Hall, *A Greek Slave* (MSS: LCP, 1901), 6.

26. See 'Irrational Dress' in Gardner and Rutherford, *The New Woman and Her Sisters*, 77–91.
27. Jeffrey Weeks, *Sex, Politics and Society: The Regulation of Sexuality Since 1800* (London: Longman, 1989), chapter 3.
28. Morton, *San Toy*, 2: 27.
29. Hamilton and Potter, *The School Girl*, 1: 9.
30. Harris, *Public Lives, Private Spirit*, 31.
31. In 1909, for instance, a performance by Gaby Deslys in *A la Carte*, which involved her dancing down a flight of stairs, fully clothed, was declared 'grossly indecent' by the National Vigilance Association.
32. Bailey, 'Musical Comedy and the Rhetoric of the Girl', 48. Bailey has Lottie Collins's performance of 'Tararaboomdeay' standing in for this 'frenzied' culture, but her extraordinary rendition was not musical comedy. As Bailey himself points out, Collins's performed this routine at the Gaiety in 1892, before musical comedy took off, and her act was, to put it mildly, idiosyncratic.
33. T. W. Robertson describes the typical soubrette as 'a short, somewhat stout, white-toothed, sweet-breathed, snub nosed, black-eyed, broad-hipped Hebe who played ..."the Chambermaid." She possessed a good voice, could sing by ear, and had a saucy way of tossing her head that was half-boyish, half-hoydenish, and wholly captivating.' 'Theatrical Types. No. VII – Chambermaids, Soubrettes and Burlesque Actresses', *Illustrated Times*, 23 April 1864, 27.
34. Bailey, 'Musical Comedy and the Rhetoric of the Girl', 45.
35. Morton, *San Toy*, 1: 44.
36. Bailey, 'Musical Comedy and the Rhetoric of the Girl', 54.
37. Hall, The Girl from Kays, 2: 20.
38. See Bailey, 'Musical Comedy and the Rhetoric of the Girl' which also argues that the girl of musical comedy 'can be read as a male construction of femininity – reactionary men defining their own ideal of the New Woman' (55).
39. James T. Tanner, *A Country Girl* (MSS: LCP, 1902), 2: 25.
40. Tanner, *The Cingalee*, 2: 36.
41. James T. Tanner, *The Orchid* (MSS: LCP, 1903), 1: 1.
42. Dam, *The Shop Girl*, 88.
43. Hall, *The Silver Slipper*, 1: 3.
44. Gardner and Rutherford, *The New Woman and Her Sisters*, 4.
45. McLellan, *Nelly Neil*, 1: 32.
46. *Nelly Neil*, 2: 16.
47. More 'serious' drama contained similar hostilities to the New Woman. See Viv Gardner's comments on Pinero's *The Notorious Mrs Ebbsmith* in *The New Woman and Her Sisters*, 8–9.
48. Otto Weininger, *Sex and Character* (London: Heinemann, 1912), 72.
49. Beatrice Webb, *My Apprenticeship* (Harmondsworth: Penguin, 1971), 223.
50. Quoted in Sheila Jeffreys, *The Spinster and her Enemies: Feminism and Sexuality 1880–1930* (London: Pandora, 1985), 35.
51. Nietzsche, *Beyond Good and Evil*, 89.
52. Phillip Gibbs, *Since then* (London: Heinemann, 1930), 382.
53. See Elaine Showalter, *Sexual Anarchy: Gender and Culture at the Fin de Siècle* (London: Virago, 1992), especially chapter 5 and Bailey, 'Musical Comedy and the Rhetoric of the Girl'. The latter argues that the male roles of musical

comedy do respond to the 'sense of masculinity in crisis' (52). If it registers such a crisis, it does not seem to worry very much about the men who under perform.

54. Lewis, *Tarr*, 17.
55. The first of these quotes is from Pound's 'Portrait d'une Femme' (1919), the second from his *Hugh Selwyn Mauberley* (1920). For a discussion of modernism in high literary culture see Marianne Dekoven, 'Modernism and Gender' in Michael Levenson (ed.), *The Cambridge Companion to Modernism* (Cambridge: Cambridge University Press, 199).
56. Hall, *The Artist's Model*, 1: 17.
57. This was how Wyndham Lewis described the group comprising himself, Pound, Eliot and Joyce as the key figures in literary modernism.
58. *The Times*, 10 September 1907, 4.
59. *The Times*, 1 February 1907, 4.
60. For a discussion of the connections between pornography and the theatre in the Victorian period see Davis, *Actresses as Working Women*, especially chapters 4 and 5. Here Davis argues that in Victorian theatre 'there was widespread objectification of the female body, and comparisons with contemporaneous pornography reveal how this objectification corresponds to heterosexual male fantasies' (xv).
61. *Actresses as Working Women*, 17–19.
62. *Actresses as Working Women*, 3.
63. *Actresses as Working Women*, 15.
64. 'It is difficult to prove, on the basis of a handful of reports, that sexual harassment was prevalent among any group of performers or from who it came.' *Actresses as Working Women*, 93. See the full discussion of this issue in *Actresses as Working Women*, 86–97.
65. Bailey, 'Musical Comedy and the Rhetoric of the Girl', 39.
66. Terris, *A Little Bit of String*, 111.
67. Hicks, *Twenty years of an Actor's Life*, 231.
68. Davis, *Actresses as Working Women*, xiiv.
69. Reeves, *Take it for Fact*, 83.
70. 'A Chorus Lady's Claim [Morris v. Edwardes]', *Era*, 7 March 1896, quoted in *Actresses as Working Women*, 26.
71. Jessie Matthews, *Over My Shoulder: An Autobiography* (London: W. H. Allen, 1974), 111.

6   The Decline of West End Musical Comedy, 1912–1939

1. Ganzl, *The British Musical Theatre*, vol. 1: 1079.
2. Eric Hobsbawm, *Age of Extremes: The Short Twentieth Century 1914–1991* (London: Michael Joseph, 1994), 86 and 94.
3. Ganzl, *The British Musical Theatre*, vol. 2, 2.
4. Moore, 'Girl Crazy: musicals and revue between the wars', 88.
5. Ganzl does refer to revue in *The British Musical Theatre*, but it is excluded from the lists of shows that here constitute the history of musical theatre between 1865 and 1984.
6. See Walsh and Platt, *Musical Theatre and American Culture*, chapter 2.

7. Mates, *America's Musical Stage*, 146.
8. Moore, 'Girl Crazy: musicals and revue between the wars', 92.
9. Hicks, *Twenty-Four Years of an Actor's Life*, 191.
10. Walsh and Platt, *Musical Theatre and American Culture*, chapter 2.
11. George Graves, *Gaieties and Gravities* (London: Hutchinson, 1931), 99 and 152–53.
12. Arthur Wimperis, *By Jingo if We Do* (MSS: LCP: 1914), 92.
13. *By Jingo*, 89.
14. Alec Flood, *The Girl from Dunnowhere* (LCP: 1914), 8.
15. *The Girl from Dunnowhere*, 49. The *Floradora* chorus is as follows:

> O my Dolores,
> Queen of the Eastern Sea
> Far one of Eden
> Look to the West for me!
> My star will be shining, love,
> When you're in the moonlight calm,
> So be waiting for me by the Eastern sea,
> In the shade of the shelt'ring palm.

16. Wimperis, *By Jingo*, 10.
17. *By Jingo*, 10
18. *By Jingo*, 7.
19. *By Jingo*, 18.
20. *By Jingo*, 56.
21. *By Jingo*, 36.
22. *By Jingo*, 88.
23. *By Jingo*, 93.
24. Sheridan Morley sees revue differently. In *Spread a Little Happiness* he argues, somewhat lamely perhaps, that revue 'a lighting, quick-change medium in which songs and sketches could be flashed on and off the stage', was invented for 'the entertainment of West End audiences whose attention span was at all time low' (41).
25. Maggie B. Gale, *West End Women: Women and the London Stage 1918–1962* (Routledge: London and New York, 1996), 39.
26. See J. Pick, *West End Management and Snobbery* (London: Offord Publications, 1983), 110.
27. *The Era*, 1 September 1915, np.
28. *The Era*, 26 September 1919, np.
29. Ganzl, *The British Musical Theatre*, vol. 2, 56.
30. Ernest Randall, the Lord Chamberlain's office in the license of Guy Bolton and P. G. Wodehouse, *Kissing Time* (MSS: LCP, 1919).
31. Ganzl, *The British Musical Theatre*, vol. 2, 109.
32. See *The British Musical Theatre*, vol. 2, 109 where Ganzl writes that critical approval of *Kissing Time* welcomed back 'the great days of the Gaiety which Grossmith and his allies had succeeded in recreating'.
33. Morley, *Spread a Little Happiness*, 66.
34. McKibbon, *Classes and Cultures*, 419.
35. *Classes and Cultures*, 457.

36. *Classes and Cultures*, 53.
37. *Spread a Little Happiness*, 53.
38. Noel Coward, *Operette* (London: Heinemann, 1928), 5.
39. Morley, *Spread a Little Happiness*, 54.
40. See Moore's characterization of the English musical comedies of 20s and 30s produced by 'Bolton (and his clones)' who 'kept writing the same plot' while 'unimaginative management kept presenting it and British audiences kept accepting it' ('Girl Crazy: musicals and revue between the wars', 99).
41. Noel Coward, *Cavalcade* in *Play Parade* (New York: Doubleday & Doran, 1932), 153.
42. *Cavalcade*, 129.
43. *Cavalcade*, 132.
44. J. Burston, 'The Megamusical: New Forms and Relations in Global Production', unpublished PhD, University of London, 1998, 205–06.
45. *Ibid.*

Bibliography

Agate, James. *Immoment Toys – A Survey of Light Entertainment on the London Stage, 1920–1943*. London: Jonathan Cape, 1945.

Archer, William. *Theatrical World of 1896*. London: Walter Scott, 1896.

Bailey, Peter. ' "Naughty but Nice": Musical Comedy and the Rhetoric of the Girl', in Michael R. Booth and Joel H. Kaplan (eds), *The Edwardian Theatre*. Cambridge: Cambridge University Press, 1996.

Bailey, Peter. 'Theatre of Entertainment/Spaces of Modernity: Rethinking the British Popular Stage, 1890–1914'. *Nineteenth Century Theatre*. Vol. 26, 1998.

Bakhtin, M. *The Dialogic Imagination*. Edited by Michael Holquist, translated by Caryl Emerson and Michael Holquist. Austin, TX: University of Texas Press, 1981.

Banham, Michael (ed.). *The Cambridge Guide to World Theatre*. Cambridge: Cambridge University Press, 1988.

Bantock, Granville and G. Aflalo. *Round the World with a Gaiety Girl*. London: John McQueen, 1896.

Bell, Daniel. *The Cultural Contradictions of Capitalism*. London: Heinemann, 1976.

Berman, Marshall. *All That is Solid Melts Into Air: The Experience of Modernity*. London: Verso, 1983.

Block, G. *Enchanted Evenings: The Broadway Musical from 'Show Boat' to Sondheim*. New York: Oxford University Press, 1997.

Booth, Michael. 'The Metropolis on Stage', in H. J. Dyos and Michael Woolf (eds), *The Victorian City: Images and Realities*. Vol. 1. London, Routledge and Kegan Paul, 1976.

Bordman, Gerald. *American Musical Comedy from Adonis to Dreamgirls*. New York and Oxford: Oxford University Press, 1982.

Bordman, Gerald. *American Musical Theatre: A Chronicle*. Second edition. Oxford and New York: Oxford University Press, 1992.

Bratton, J. S., 'Irrational Dress', in Viv Gardner and Susan Rutherford (eds), *The New Woman and Her Sisters: Feminism and Theatre, 1850–1914*. Hemel Hempstead: Harvester Wheatsheaf, 1992.

Bratton, J. S., Richard Allen Cave, Brendan Gregory, Heide J. Holder and Michael Pickering. *Acts of Supremacy: The British Empire and the Stage, 1790–1930*. Manchester: Manchester University Press, 1991.

Bunnett, Rex and Brian Rust, *London Musical Shows on Record, 1897–1976*. Harrow: General Publication, 1977.

Burston, J. 'The Megamusical: New Forms and Relations in Global Production'. Unpublished PhD, University of London, 1998.

Cannadine, David. *The Decline and Fall of the British Aristocracy*. New Haven, CT: Yale University Press, 1990.

Chambers, Iain. 'Waiting on the End of the World', in David Morley, and Kuan-Hsing Chen (eds), *Stuart Hall: Critical Dialogues in Cultural Studies*. London: Routledge, 1996.

Cheyette, Bryan. *Constructions of the 'Jew' in English Literature and Society: Racial Representations 1875–1945*. Cambridge: Cambridge University Press, 1993.

Coward , Noel. *Operette*. London: Heinemann, 1928.

Coward, Noel. *Play Parade*. New York: Doubleday and Doran, 1932.

Davis, Tracy C. *Actresses as Working Women: Their Social Identity in Victorian Culture*. London and New York: Routledge, 1991.

Davis, Tracy C. 'Edwardian Management and the Structure of Industrialism', in Michael R. Booth and Joel H. Kaplan (eds), *The Edwardian Theatre*. Cambridge: Cambridge University Press, 1996.

de Grazia, Victoria with Ellen Furlough. *The Sex of Things: Gender and Consumption in Historical Perspective*. Berkeley: University of California Press, 1996.

Dowling, Linda. 'The Decadent and the New Woman'. *Nineteenth-Century Fiction*. No. 333, 1979.

Dyer, Richard. *Only Entertainment*. London and New York: Routledge, 1992.

Featherstone, Mike. *Consumer Culture and Postmodernism*. London: Sage, 1991.

Forbes-Winslow, D. *Daly's: The Biography of a Theatre*. London: W. H. Allen, 1944.

Gale, Maggie B. *West End Women: Women and the London Stage 1918–1962*. London and New York: Routledge, 1996.

Ganzl, Kurt. *The British Musical Theatre*. Vols 1 and 2. Basingstoke: Macmillan, 1986.

Gardner, Viv and Susan Rutherford (eds). *The New Woman and Her Sisters: Feminism and Theatre, 1850–1914*. Hemel Hempstead: Harvester Wheatsheaf, 1992.

Garelick, K. Rhonda. *Rising Star: Dandyism, Gender and Performance in the Fin de Siècle*. Princeton, NJ: Princeton University Press, 1998.

Garrard, J. *The English and Immigration*. Oxford: Oxford University Press for the Institute of Race Relations, 1971.

Geertz, Clifford. *Interpreting Cultures*. London: Hutchinson, 1975.

Gibbs, Phillip. *Since Then*. London: Heinemann, 1930.

Goldberg, D. T. *Racist Culture: Philosophy and Politics of Meaning*. Oxford: Blackwell, 1993.

Graves, George. *Gaieties and Gravities*. London: Hutchinson, 1931.

Grossmith Jr, George. *Random Recollections of the Serious Business of Enjoyment*. London: Stanley Paul, 1913.

Hall, Stuart. 'Notes on Deconstructing "The Popular"', in Raphael Samuel (ed.), *People's History and Socialist Theory*. London: Routledge, 1981.

Hamon, W. Jr. *Raising Cain: Blackface Performance from Jim Crow to Hip Hop*. Cambridge, MA: Harvard University Press, 2000.

Harris, Jose. *Private Lives, Public Spirit: A Social History of Britain 1870–1914*. Oxford: Oxford University Press, 1993.

Harvey, David. *The Condition of Postmodernity*. Oxford: Blackwell, 1990.

Hicks, Seymour. *Twenty-Four Years of an Actor's Life*. London: Alton Rivers, 1910.

Hobsbawm, Eric. *The Age of Empire*. London: Weidenfeld and Nicolson, 1987.

Hobsbawm, Eric. *Age of Extremes: The Short Twentieth Century 1914–1991*. London: Michael Joseph, 1994.

Hollingshead, J. *The Good Old Gaiety*. London: n.p., 1903.

Hurley, Kelly. *The Gothic Body: Sexuality, Materialism and Degeneration at the Fin de Siècle*. Cambridge: Cambridge University Press, 1998.

Hyman, Alan. *The Gaiety Years*. London: Cassell and Collier Macmillan, 1975.

Jeffreys, Sheila. *The Spinster and Her Enemies: Feminism and Sexuality 1880–1930*. London: Pandora, 1985.

Jupp, James. *The Gaiety Stage Door: 30 Years of Reminiscences of the Theatre*. London: Jonathan Cape, 1923.

Kaplan, Joel and Sheila Stowell. *Theatre and Fashion: Oscar Wilde to the Suffragettes*. Cambridge: Cambridge University Press, 1994.

Lacey, R. *Aristocrats*. London: Hutchinson, 1984.

Lamb, Andrew. *Popular Musical Theatre*. New Haven, CT and London: Yale University Press, 2000.

Lerner, Alan J. *The Musical Theatre: A Celebration*. New York: De Capo, 1986.

Levenson, Michael (ed.). *The Cambridge Companion to Modernism*. Cambridge: Cambridge University Press, 1999.

Light, Alison. *Forever England: Femininity, Literature and Conservatism between the Wars*. London and New York: Routledge, 1991.

Mackenzie, John M. *Imperialism and Popular Culture*. Manchester: Manchester University Press, 1986.

McKibbin, Ross. *Classes and Cultures: England 1918–1951*. Oxford: Oxford University Press, 1998.

McQueen-Pope, W. *Gaiety: Theatre of Enchantment*. London: W. H. Allen, 1949.

Mandler, Peter. 'Against "Englishness": English Culture and the Limits to Rural Nostalgia, 1850–1950'. *Transactions of the Royal Historical Society*. Vol. 7, 1997, pp. 155–75.

Mates, Julian. *America's Musical Stage: Two Hundred Years of Musical Theatre*. Westport, CT: Greenwood Press, 1985.

Matthews, Jessie. *Over My Shoulder: An Autobiography*. London: W. H. Allen, 1974.

Miller, Karl. *Doubles: Studies in Literary History*. London: Oxford University Press, 1987.

Moore, James Ross. 'Girl Crazy: Musicals and Revue between the Wars', in Clive Barker and Maggie B. Gale (eds), *British Theatre between the Wars 1918–1939*. Cambridge: Cambridge University Press, 2000.

Morley, Sheridan. *Spread a Little Happiness: The First Hundred Years of the British Musical*. London: Thames and Hudson, 1987.

Nietzsche, Friedrich. *Beyond Good and Evil: Prelude to a Philosophy of the Future*. Translated with commentary by Walter Kaufmann. New York: Vintage, 1966.

O' Shea, Alan. 'English Subjects of Modernity', in Mica Nava and Alan O' Shea (eds), *Modern Times: Reflections on a Century of English Modernity*. London: Routledge, 1996.

Parker, John (ed.). *The Green Room Book*. London: T. Sealey Clarke, 1909.

Pelling, Henry. *Origins of the Labour Party*. Oxford: Oxford University Press, 1965.

Pick, J. *West End Management and Snobbery*. London: Offord Publications, 1983.

Platt, Len. *Aristocracies of Fiction: The Idea of Aristocracy in Late Nineteenth and Early Twentieth-Literary Culture*. Westport, CT: Greenwood Press, 2001.

Porter, Roy. *A Social History of London*. London: Hamish Hamilton, 1994.

Rappaport, Erica D. *Shopping for Pleasure: Women in the Making of London's West End*. Princeton, NJ and Oxford: Princeton University Press, 2000.

Reeve, Ada. *Take it for Fact. A Record of My Seventy-Five Years on the Stage*. London: Heinemann, 1954.

Report from the Joint Select Committee of the Lords and the House of Commons on Stage Plays (Censorship). London: HMSO, 1909.

Rubenstein, W. D. 'Britain's Elites in the Inter-War Period 1918–1939'. *Contemporary British History.* Vol. 12, 1998, pp. 1–18.

Rutherford, Lois. ' "Harmless Nonsense": the Comic Sketch and the Development of Music-Hall Entertainment', in J. S. Bratton (ed.), *Music Hall: Performance and Style.* Milton Keynes: Open University Press, 1986.

Seaman, L. C. B. *Post-Victorian Britain 1902–1951.* London: Methuen, 1966.

Shannon, Richard. *The Crisis in Imperialism: 1865–1915.* London: Hart-Davis and MacGibbon, 1974.

Shaw, G. B. *Fabianism and the Empire.* London: Grant Richards, 1900.

Showalter, Elaine. *Sexual Anarchy: Gender and Culture at the Fin de Siècle.* London: Virago, 1992.

Stallybrass, Peter and Allon White. *The Politics and Poetics of Transgression.* London: Routledge, 1980.

Stedman Jones, Gareth. *Languages of Class: Studies in English Working Class History 1832–1982.* Cambridge: Cambridge University Press, 1983.

Terriss, Ellaline. *Just a Little Bit of String.* London: Hutchinson, 1955.

Trewin, J. C. *The Edwardian Theatre.* Oxford: Blackwell, 1976.

Walsh, Dave and Len Platt. *Musical Theatre and American Culture.* Westport, CT: Praeger, 2003.

Webb, Beatrice. *My Apprenticeship.* Harmondsworth: Penguin, 1971.

Wearing, J. P. *The London Stage A Calendar of Plays and Players 1890–1899.* Vols 1 and 2. London: Scarecrow, 1976.

Wearing, J. P. *The London Stage A Calendar of Plays and Players 1900–1909.* Vols 1 and 2. London: Scarecrow, 1980.

Wearing, J. P. *The London Stage A Calendar of Plays and Players 1910–1919.* Vols 1 and 2. London: Scarecrow, 1982.

Wearing, J. P. *The London Stage A Calendar of Plays and Players 1920–1929.* Vols 1 and 2. London: Scarecrow, 1984.

Weeks, Jeffrey. *Sex, Politics and Society: the Regulation of Sexuality since 1800.* London: Longman, 1989.

Lord Chamberlain's plays quoted in the text

Ambient, Mark and Alexander M. Thompson. *The Arcadians.* MSS: LCP, 1909.

Asche, Oscar. *Chu Chin Chow.* MSS: LCP, 1916.

Bantock, Leedham and Arthur Anderson. *The Girl Behind the Counter.* MSS: LCP, 1906.

Bolton, Guy and P. G. Wodehouse. *Kissing Time.* MSS: LCP, 1919.

Dam, H. J. M. *The Shop Girl.* MSS: LCP, 1894.

Ellis, Harold. *The Blue Moon.* MSS: LCP, 1904.

Flood, Alec. *The Girl from Dunnowhere.* MSS: LCP, 1914.

Grossmith Jnr, George and L. E. Berman. *The Girls of Gottenberg.* MSS: LCP, 1907.

Hamilton, Henry and P. Potter. *The Schoolgirl.* MSS: LCP, 1903.

Hall, Owen. *A Gaiety Girl.* MSS: LCP, 1893.

Hall, Owen. *An Artist's Model.* MSS: LCP, 1895.

Hall, Owen. *The Geisha.* MSS: LCP, 1896.

Hall, Owen. *Floradora.* MSS: LCP, 1899.

Hall, Owen. *The Silver Slipper.* MSS: LCP, 1901.

Hall, Owen. *A Greek Slave*. MSS: LCP, 1898.

Hall, Owen. *The Girl from Kays*. MSS: LCP, 1902.

Harwood, H. M. and George Grossmith. *Theodore and Co*. MSS: LCP, 1916.

Hicks, Seymour and Harry Nicholls. *A Runaway Girl*. MSS: LCP, 1898.

Hicks, Seymour. *The Gay Gordons*. MSS: LCP, 1907.

Huntley, G. P. and Herbert Clayton. *The Honourable Phil*. MSS: LCP, 1908.

McLellen, C. M. S. *The Girl from Up There*. MSS: LCP, 1901.

McLellan, C. M. S. *Nelly Neil*. MSS: LCP, 1907.

Morton, Edward A. *San Toy*. MSS: LCP, 1899.

Rubens, Paul and Austen Hurgen. *Miss Hook of Holland*. MSS: LCP, 1907.

Rubens, Paul. *The Sunshine Girl*. MSS: LCP, 1912.

Rubens, Paul. *Betty*. MSS: LCP, 1915.

Talbot, Howard and Hugo Felix. *The Pearl Girl*. MSS: LCP, 1913.

Tanner, James T. *My Girl*. MSS: LCP, 1896.

Tanner, James T. and Alfred Murray. *The Messenger Boy*. MSS: LCP, 1900.

Tanner, James T. *A Country Girl*. MSS: LCP, 1902.

Tanner, James T. *The Orchid*. MSS: LCP, 1903.

Tanner, James T. *The Cingalee*. MSS: LCP, 1904.

Tanner, James T. *Our Miss Gibbs*. MSS: LCP, 1909.

Tanner, James T. *The Girl on the Film*. MSS: LCP, 1913.

Wimperis, Arthur. *By Jingo if We Do*. MSS: LCP, 1914.

Index

KING ALFRED'S COLLEGE
LIBRARY